W9-CFQ-382

BOOKER T
MY RISE TO WRESTLING ROYALTY

BY WWE HALL OF FAMER
BOOKER T. HUFFMAN
WITH ANDREW WILLIAM WRIGHT

MEDALLION
P R E S S
Medallion Press, Inc.
Printed in USA

Published 2015 by Medallion Press, Inc.

The MEDALLION PRESS LOGO
is a registered trademark of Medallion Press, Inc.

This work reflects the author's present recollections of specific experiences over a period of years. Dialogue and events have been recreated and in some cases compressed to convey the substance of what was said or what occurred. Some identifying details have been changed to protect the privacy of individuals.

Typeset in Adobe Garamond Pro
Printed in the United States of America
ISBN 9781605427041

10 9 8 7 6 5 4 3 2 1
First Edition

For my parents, Booker T. and Rosa J. Huffman,
who live on forever in my heart and daily thoughts.

CONTENTS

FOREWORD

Over twenty years ago, two young men full of dreams sat in a dressing room of a rotten old building in a bad part of South Dallas in the Sportatorium, where Elvis once played. We were waiting for our chance to perform and make our names in professional wrestling. The odds of succeeding were small for either of us, let alone both. Over two decades later, we still sit and laugh in dressing rooms, but this time we're waiting to go out in front of as many as eighty thousand people. We are now the old guys, two former World Champions, and Booker T is a Hall of Famer and one of the greatest singles and tag team wrestlers of all time.

I never dreamed this friend I laughed with—and made so little money with—in Texas, Japan, and Korea would be the one I'd perform with on six different continents to sold-out arenas. Most importantly, we laugh and enjoy each other's company as if it were still decades ago, when the only things we worried about were whether the promoter would pay us and who would book us the next week.

Booker and I have faced each other in the ring hundreds of times. If you add in my commentary, I've been a part of over a thousand of Booker's matches. We never called a match in the back. We both just said, "See you out there." Our only preparations were small talk and trash talk. We wanted to feel the crowd. Booker loved it as much as anyone I have ever seen. He thrived on it. Watching him come alive in front of an audience is awesome to this day.

Booker T and I parted ways when he went to WCW and I went to the WWF. Booker went on to win ten Tag Team Championships with his brother, making them one of the greatest tag teams of all time. Booker later became the five-time WCW Champion. I watched with pride as my friend became one of the all-time greats. We reunited in the WWE, where Booker continued to win championships and we faced each other for almost all of them.

I can say that at times, being out there with Booker was like being in a street fight. He loved it *real*. As they say in wrestling, that man should have been a potato farmer. Booker made you bring it. I loved that about him, and I think that was part of the huge appeal he had with the audience.

Fans see through most anything. They're very smart. But when a competitor like Booker hits an arena, the fans also see they're watching a performer who loves this business as much as they do. When Booker comes out, the mood changes. It gives me goose bumps just writing this.

Since the day I met him, Booker T has carried himself like a gentleman and role model. His story is one of inspiration to me and anyone who knows him. He's a loving husband to a wonderful woman, "Queen" Sharmell, and he's a caring father. He appears for WWE and also runs his own wrestling promotion because he simply loves this business.

Booker and I still sit together every week, laughing and joking, our old dreams accomplished and new ones made. Both of us are halfway through the journey but looking forward to the next day and the crowd each night. Now we aren't in a hurry, though, but just enjoying life.

Performing in front of a crowd is addictive. There's no drug in the world that can give you that feeling. However, when I was away for a short time due to injury, the thing I missed most was not the crowd but my family backstage. I'm proud to say Booker is part of my close family—a great brother I love.

John Layfield
April 14, 2014

1

A VICIOUS OPPORTUNITY

It was the end of the world. Well, at least for some. After hearing the rumblings in the locker room and offices for the last few months, the rumors proved to be true. On March 23, 2001, our long-dreaded rival, Vince McMahon and the World Wrestling Federation (WWF), purchased the company I worked for, World Championship Wrestling (WCW). Three days later in Panama City, Florida, would be our last *Nitro* broadcast. I looked around and saw many guys hanging their heads in disbelief as if the sky were crashing through the ceiling. The sale of WCW meant a dead end for most of the roster and crew.

Here we go, I thought. *It's about to get really interesting.*

Surprisingly, my buddy, WCW World Heavyweight Champion Scott Steiner pulled me aside in a rare moment of uncertainty. "Hey, Book, do you think Vince will take us?"

Although panic had set in around me, I saw this as a new opportunity. I'd developed a skill set that could be applied anywhere in the world, from the WWF to companies in Japan or Mexico.

I laughed. "Man, who else do you think they're going to take?" And I meant it. In the last six months, Scotty and I had set WCW on fire with top-drawing main events.

Dave Penzer said, "I can't believe it. Aren't you upset, Booker? This is the end of WCW."

I did feel a little sentimental, but because of my tumultuous early life on the streets in Houston without parents to steer me, I had a different mind-set. Since those days, I'd learned to detach from a situation, no matter how chaotic, and maintain focus on what I needed to do to survive.

Besides, that night I was on a different plane entirely. Executive Vice President turned Creative Codirector Eric Bischoff had informed me that in the first match of the show, I'd be going over Steiner for the win. In what would become the exclamation point of my tenure in WCW, I would be unifying my United States title with the World Heavyweight Championship. I was awestruck by the decision that would allow me to be the last champ standing in WCW history.

After the show's final confrontation between Ric Flair and Sting, who'd enjoyed a storied rivalry since 1988, the fans somberly filed out. I sat by myself in the back with the two belts for a brief, bittersweet moment before two WWF officials asked me to hand them over. They were now company property. It was an odd feeling, almost like handing over your children to the enemy. I shook my head and watched the two strangers walk away with my WCW legacy dangling precariously from their clutches. Little did I know that in an unexpected twist of fate, I'd have them back in a few short months.

Sitting on the bench, an empty-handed champion, I contemplated everything about my time in WCW. At that point, my time with the company spanned a little over seven years since debuting with my brother Lash (Stevie Ray) in June of 1993, and it all seemed like a passing illusion.

It all started in 1989. For about four years, Lash and I had been tirelessly running the roads all across Texas, working for WWF veteran "Polish Power" Ivan Putski's Western Wrestling Alliance (WWA), Tugboat Taylor's Texas All Pro Wrestling, the independent scene, and then finally the Global Wrestling Federation, featured on ESPN. All that changed with one phone call from Sid Vicious, the Ruler of the World, who offered us an opportunity. He wanted us to go to Atlanta to try out for WCW.

As the trek from Texas to Georgia drew to a close, the sun was rising and the Huffman brothers could feel the magic at hand. It was make-or-break time. After hitting the Georgia state line, we were neck-deep in WCW country, and it felt like home.

During our brief conversation with Sid, there'd been no talk about money. We had a foot in the door, and that was all the chance we needed. I kept analyzing everything on the way. *Will we impress them enough? Will they let us stick around or take one look at us in the ring and tell us to get out?* I was ready to find out.

When we drove into Atlanta, it was comforting to know we had somewhere to stay: Sid's place. Sid was a well-established main eventer who'd had a huge run in WCW from 1989 through 1991, rubbing shoulders with some of their biggest stars, like the "Nature Boy" Ric Flair, "The Enforcer" Arn Anderson, and Big Van Vader, and in the WWF from 1991 through 1992, with guys like Hulk Hogan, The Ultimate Warrior, Randy Savage, and even The Undertaker. Now he was transitioning into a position with WCW as a booker who could produce homegrown talent. We were his first handpicked projects, and he wanted to personally oversee our entry and take care of us.

That early morning, we got out of the car and walked to an apartment door to be greeted by the man himself. The first thing I can tell you about Sid back then was that he was big— really big. Not only was he six feet nine, but he was even more freakishly muscular in person than he looked on TV.

He shook our hands. "How was the trip? You must be tired as hell. Come on in."

We grabbed our bags and followed Big Sid, which was what I always called him back then, into his fairly modest three-bedroom apartment, where we'd be staying for the duration of our tryout process.

Although he was a gracious host, Sid wasn't the most

social of guys. For him, this was business. If we were success-ful, we'd follow in his footsteps, and he'd do everything he could to make that happen.

Sid took us to Sting and Lex Luger's gym, Main Event Fitness, not far from his place. When we walked in, it was a virtual cavalcade of the top guys we saw on TV—"The Stein-er Brothers" Rick and Scott Steiner, "Mr. Wonderful" Paul Orndorff, "Ravishing" Rick Rude, and even "The Icon" Sting and "The Total Package" Lex Luger were there.

Sid walked around as if he owned the place, and he might as well have because when he started hitting the weights, every-one took notice. It was impossible not to. We soon found out Sid was just as loud and intense in the gym as he was in the ring and on the microphone.

Lash and I were in awe as he introduced us to everybody we passed. As we got our workout in, I couldn't help but no-tice what the other guys were up to. I saw guys like "Big Poppa Pump" Scott Steiner doing 315-pound behind-the-neck presses.

Lord Steven Regal, who later became William Regal in the WWF, stared at me. Regal was a talented wrestler who began his career at the age of fifteen, and he was clearly aware we were Sid's boys. In his eyes, we were probably being express driven into one of the coveted WCW spots—maybe his.

There was no mistaking it. I was no longer in the bush league. These boys were from the big stage I'd always dreamed of walking onto. I hoped I could earn their respect and a place among them in the ring.

Now that Lash and I had a place to stay and a gym to work out in, we needed only one more thing: our first contracts and creative direction. The show was about to begin—but not before a lesson in professional wrestling contract negotiations.

Sid drove us to the WCW headquarters stationed at Ted Turner's CNN Center on Marietta Street in the heart of Atlanta. Sid, Lash, and I were escorted into an office where we met Ole Anderson, the original Rock of professional wrestling and part of the legendary Minnesota Wrecking Crew with Gene Anderson and then later Arn Anderson.

Ole was retired and basically in charge of the entire company after "Cowboy" Bill Watts had been ousted from the position. Ole had a solid crusher of a handshake and got right down to business as Sid oversaw the process from the corner.

"Boys," he gruffed, "we're going to start you out with three-year contracts at seventy thousand dollars with the incentive to make as much as you can draw. Sky's the limit. If you do well, you'll climb the ladder. If you don't, you're going back to Texas the same way you got yourselves here."

Lash and I looked at each other. Seventy grand was more than both of us had seen combined till that day. We were used to ten-dollar nights.

The moment was frozen in time. Now we were sitting in an office with Sid and Ole Anderson, signing our first contracts to work with a major international company. Was this really happening in the same room where many of the greats—Harley Race, "The American Dream" Dusty Rhodes, and the "Nature Boy" Ric Flair—got their start?

When we left Ole's office, Sid clarified the contract terms. "You always take everything up front, guys. You'll get monthly raises, and before you know it, you'll be making ninety thousand, then a hundred thousand a year. It's all trial and error, as you'll see. You'll get paid what you're worth."

Big Sid was a brilliant mentor. He knew exactly what he wanted and how to obtain it. He was a huge draw in the ring, which was the way to gain an audience backstage with the ones in the business who mattered. We have him to thank for delivering everything he said he would. All we'd needed was a shot. In professional wrestling, that's more than you usually get. He even gave me my first pair of wrestling boots, the tall black type he's known for, which I still have today.

With the ink drying on the contracts in our hands, the next order of business was to sit down with creative and learn what they had for us. Sid walked us around and introduced us to the good ol' boys.

We met Dusty Rhodes, the figurehead of story lines, writing, and booking matches. Back then there were no actual creative writers as there would be in the near future. At that time the veterans of the game, the proven leaders in and out of the ring, were in charge, and there was none more established than Dusty.

Following his lead was an impressive team of guys, including the late Mike Graham, an anointed one in the business who came from the lineage of his father Eddie Graham, a longtime successful performer and promoter with Florida Championship Wrestling. Mike was a go-to guy for character development and instructions.

There was also Greg Gagne, a onetime top performer for the now-defunct American Wrestling Association (AWA), which had been one of the Big Three organizations along with the World Wrestling Federation (WWF) and the National Wrestling Alliance (NWA) and was owned and promoted by his father, Verne Gagne. Greg ensured the guys knew the direction of their performances.

Lash and I were fresh from Global in Dallas, where we'd enjoyed a loyal following as Booker T and Stevie Ray, The Ebony Experience. We'd had creative input there, but here at the table I recognized it was time to be a listener and nothing more. I knew nothing and was prepared for anything they had in store.

Well, at least I thought I was. We were in the presence of a well-established Southern good ol' boy mentality, and the train of thought for directing our careers was, well, interesting.

"We're going to change your names to Kane"—Mike pointed at Lash—"and Kole"—he indicated me—"better known as Chi-Town Heat, billed from Chicago. Your story is that you've just been released from prison. You'll wear chains and shackles and jumpsuits into the ring. We think it'll get everyone's attention."

That was an understatement. I couldn't help but wonder if they were ribbing me about my time in prison over a decade before, but then the stark reality sank in and an uneasy feeling washed over me. The whole idea was a big red flag. My instinct was to object, until I remembered the advice of my mother: *Junior, know when to speak up and when to shut up.*

Mike said, "We're going to pair you up with Robert Fuller, who'll be your manager-slash-master known as Colonel Parker, a former plantation owner."

I was waiting for them to ask us to shuck and jive.

As insane as it all seemed, the reality was that they thought this was a solid plan.

This was the kind of racial obstacle Ox Baker had warned me about back in the WWA. But he'd said, "When someone draws and makes money, all the bullshit goes away."

If I had to go around, under, or straight through these barriers, rest assured I was going straight through.

2

SHUT DOWN AS CHI-TOWN HEAT

As leery as I was about our first creative assignment as the chain-gang duo of Kane and Kole in Chi-Town Heat, there was no turning back. How could we give up now when we were finally being tapped to go to the professional limits? But our debut at WCW's Center Stage Theater in Atlanta, where all the TV tapings took place, was a disaster waiting to happen.

In the back while we put on our jumpsuits and ankle chains, I could feel the silence in the locker room. Guys like Regal, Tom Zenk, Brian Pillman, Big Josh, and Marcus Bagwell uncomfortably looked on. As bizarre as our characters may have seemed to them, they knew we were doing as we were told. I'm sure they were just glad they weren't the ones putting on that gear. There's no doubt they couldn't wait until we walked through the curtain so they could watch the creative bomb explode firsthand.

As we walked by the audience in our shackles, I was mostly oblivious to the bewildered stares, including those of several black attendees. A scattered few surely recognized us as The Ebony Experience because of the ESPN exposure we'd had over the previous eighteen months in Global. I can only imagine how much of a disappointment it was for our fans to see us in such a humiliating change of character. We'd gone from energetic heroes in Dallas and on national television to the equivalent of a couple of escaped slaves straight from the cotton fields. It didn't help to see slick Colonel Parker leading us to the ring, dressed like Kentucky Fried Chicken's Colonel Sanders, complete with an old-fashioned white suit and black ribbon tie.

Greg Gagne gave us instructions for our match with two nameless jobbers: "Go out there and beat the hell out of them."

We did exactly what Greg asked of us. We went out there and worked those guys as hard as we could. With every fist thrown, every slam, every stomp, Lash and I could feel the animosity of the crowd growing. In wrestling, when you're working as a heel, it's important to generate what's known as heat—the boos and jeers of the fans, who know you're the villain. They paid good money to let everyone know how much they wanted their heroes to put the villain flat on his back. However, there's good heat and there's bad heat. This was bad heat. They weren't against us because we were the heels. The crowd was against us because the characters were so offensive.

Although the match was quick, the fans made it feel like an eternity. When it was all over, I noticed wadded-up cups and popcorn boxes landing around my feet in the ring. I looked up and felt the reverb of boos and jeers as more trash came flying into the ring. The crowd hated us. And they hated our first match in WCW.

But that proved to be the least of our concerns.

The word on Chi-Town Heat got out almost instantly. We'd monumentally offended fans with our presentation. A unanimously negative ripple effect from the media stated WCW had completely failed.

It didn't take a rocket scientist to figure out where most of the fingers back at CNN Center would be pointing when we arrived: our faces.

We found ourselves again seated in front of Ole, with Sid in the corner.

"We're shutting this thing down immediately," Ole said.

I gulped.

"That match won't air on TV. I'm getting destroyed from all directions and, to be frank, the feeling is the two of you should be released and sent back home."

A touch of panic set in.

Ole continued. "But I already know from Sid that you guys can work, and Gagne told me you showed something out there despite the unfortunate situation. We'll come up with a new plan."

Next thing I knew, we were sitting with Dusty and the boys of the creative round table again. To his credit, Dusty opened the floor to Lash and me. "What do you guys think? Do you have any ideas of how we can make you two successful?"

As a matter of fact, we did. Ever since we were kids, we loved the campy Blaxploitation films of the seventies like *Shaft* and *Super Fly.*

"Dusty, what do you think of Harlem Heat? Instead of a couple of chained-down slaves, we come out as a couple of badasses from Harlem?"

It barely escaped my mouth before he pointed at us and said, "That's it! Harlem Heat. I love it. The badasses from 110th Street!"

Lash and I laughed, and I said my favorite line from *Shaft*: "Can you dig it, sucka?" Little did I know those five words would stick with me for the rest of my life.

Dusty clapped, and everyone was in agreement. These were our new personas. We also pushed for them to let us use our Ebony Experience names of Booker T and Stevie Ray, but it was still a frustrating no. Although we were less than enthused about our character names, especially since Lash and I kept forgetting which of us was Kane and which was Kole, at least Dusty said we could repackage our image.

I was already imagining what our new characters would look like. I took some trips to local shops, and it didn't take long for something to grab my attention. There were these black shirts with orange-and-red flames all over the long sleeves and wrapping around the chest to the back. Funny enough, these shirts were for the country duo Brooks &

Dunn. What says Harlem thug more than a tailored country band's shirt?

From there it was simple. I improvised flaming do-rags from the cut-off sleeves, and we wore the rest of the fiery shirts almost completely unbuttoned and tied into a knot at the waist. The rest of our gear was basic enough to complement the Heat motif. We wore red trunks over long black tights, which I airbrushed with flames up the sides. We put on tall black boots, and I even found two cheap pairs of black sunglasses to top the whole thing off. The look cost us less than sixty bucks each. Eventually, after seeing the NFL players wearing them, we added nasal strips to finish the look.

Dusty also let us pick our Harlem Heat entrance theme from a catalog of rights-free music in the WCW library. We sat there and listened to generic track after track. Finally one of the last few available caught my attention. It came on really dramatic and had this series of bouncing notes that went higher and higher before a kind of whistle melody came in toward the end. We agreed it was perfect and went with it. Never in a million years would I have thought I'd be using it for the rest of my career.

Now it was time to focus on conditioning. Lash and I worked out regularly, as we always had. I was around six feet two and 230 pounds, and Lash was a true monster at six feet five and about 285 pounds. We weren't obsessive gym rats, but we were consistent, ate well, and weren't big partiers.

BOOKER T. HUFFMAN

Creatively, physically, and mentally we were poised to approach WCW from a whole new angle.

As a result of our controversial debut, Ole decided to keep us off TV and let the public clamor die down until Chi-Town Heat was all but forgotten. He thought a few weeks of house shows on the road would be a good way to reintroduce Harlem Heat one town at a time. It would also allow Lash and me to perfect our presentation.

Regardless of how hungry we were to get back on the WCW small screen with the rest of the boys, Lash and I agreed this was the best approach. We hit the road in June of 1993 for a quick loop of every small town and major market of WCW in about twenty-one days. With Lash behind the wheel, we found ourselves everywhere from Montgomery to Chattanooga and then in several towns through Georgia before heading deep into Florida.

One of the places we stopped was White, Georgia. The town with a population of almost seven hundred was, in fact, almost entirely white. Before the show, we went to grab a burger at a diner straight out of the late fifties, like Arnold's in *Happy Days*.

I wasn't too sensitive about being a young black man in the South, but when Lash and I walked in, it was as if Fonzi himself snapped his fingers and knocked the needle off the record.

Everybody stopped what they were doing and stared at us.

It was eerie and dead silent. I'm pretty sure they were thinking, *What are these boys doing in here? There are places for them elsewhere.*

As we looked around the diner, our sense of unease began to rise. Feeling out of place but overwhelmingly hungry, we looked at each other, ordered our burgers, and said in unison, "We'll take it to go."

During that first circuit of road dates, I received my first and only ribbing, a rite of passage for any new guy. I can't even remember which town we were in, but I recall being so hungry it was almost making me sick with a migraine. I had to get something to eat. Those were the days when all expenses came out of our own pockets, which was always painful for the wallet.

We had a tag match with 2 Cold Scorpio and Marcus Alexander Bagwell coming up quick, so I found this kid, gave him a twenty, and asked him to run to the concession stand for me for a couple of hot dogs and a Coke.

Lash and I were in the back with Scorpio, going over our match for a while, when I started thinking, *Where's this kid?* My migraine was becoming unbearable, and there was no way I was going to be able to perform at my best without getting some food in me.

Desperate to find him, I walked into the hallway and saw him standing out there, with no food in sight. "Where are my hot dogs?"

"I brought them to the locker room with your change and set them down just a few minutes ago. I'll show you where." He walked me to the locker room and pointed toward an empty bench. "A bunch of guys were there, and they told me to leave everything and they'd make sure you got it."

Then it hit me. *These fools stole my food* and *my money?*

Nothing like that had ever happened to me, so I made it loud and clear to everyone in the locker room that someone was going to get whupped if I didn't get my stuff back immediately.

Just then, Chris Benoit's entrance music began to play throughout the arena. As he walked past me to go through the curtain for his match, I could've sworn I saw mustard on his face.

"Hey, man, did you eat my hot dogs?"

He looked at me quizzically, gave a curt no, and breezed past.

"You guys don't know me," I yelled. "I'm going to show everyone here you don't mess with my stuff. As soon as that hot dog–stealing Benoit gets back here, I'm gonna punch him right in his Oscar Mayer mouth!"

Maxx Payne said, "Calm down. It's just a couple of hot dogs, bro. Relax."

I started pacing, ready to pounce on Benoit as soon as he stepped foot through the curtain. Just as I turned the corner to that same empty bench, I saw the hot dogs, Coke, and my change sitting there!

I picked up the change but didn't even eat the hot dogs. I was so mad, I'd even forgotten about my headache.

Those bastards got me and got me good, but I was in no mood to laugh about it yet.

The next night when I got to the locker room, an entire pack of Oscar Mayer wieners and a bag of buns were sitting on a bench waiting for me. At that point, I did laugh.

I never found out who did it, and Benoit had no clue how close he was to feeling my wrath for no reason.

Back in those days, whether we worked in front of five hundred or five thousand people, Lash and I brought out Harlem Heat every night like we owned the place. We were new to WCW but not to tag team wrestling. We'd cut our teeth at the Sportatorium in Dallas for over eighteen months, and we knew we could hit the ground running with any team anyplace, anytime.

As The Ebony Experience in Global, we were already prepared with four big fistfuls of specialized tandem moves. We had a rhythm inspired by Bruce Lee and all the other kung fu movies we'd obsessed over. As kids, we'd practiced in the living room and outside with our friends, and we had our act memorized. We knew how to incorporate our real-life brotherhood into a mesmerizing and amusing act. Not only were we entertaining. We were good. That was why Sid had called us in the first place; he'd worked with us in the ring before.

A couple of months before we'd made the drive to Atlanta, Sid saw us on ESPN and decided to come to the Sportatorium and check us out. He brought along a friend, Johnny Rotten, and approached us in the back. "I've heard about you two. The Experience? I want to see what you've got." Then he proceeded to lace up those big boots, put on the black leather vest, and make his way to the ring for a tag match against Lash and me.

When Sid's music hit, the crowd went berserk. Here came the maniacal Superstar everyone knew from TV, and he was here to see what The Ebony Experience was made of. He stepped over the top rope, and he and his buddy Johnny put on a show with us that was as intense as anything I'd ever experienced in a ring.

Lash and I pulled out all the stops and sold Sid's moves, and the big man did the same for us. Our chemistry was electric, and he even let us go over for the win in our home domain. The people in the Sportatorium, rooting for the hometown boys and on their feet the whole time, left that night with more than their money's worth. It was the kind of action that makes the business as great as it can be.

When Sid came up to us in the back, he had that huge smile. "I'm impressed. You two have what it takes to go to the big show. Let me see what I can do. Great job tonight."

We shook hands, and off he went into the night. Lash and I couldn't believe it. We'd just put on a show with one of the biggest, most powerful names in professional wrestling.

I *wanted* what Sid had. I knew that night we made the wheels in Sid's mind start smoking.

And that was the very reason we got Sid's personal invitation on the phone and why we were given a reprieve after our dismal debut: Sid believed in us. Had we been unleashed straight from the gate as Harlem Heat instead of sandbagged with the Chi-Town Heat debacle, we would've been a few weeks ahead of the game, but now was our chance to rebuild the momentum.

We were in an entirely different, broader world than what we'd been accustomed to. This was the very beginning of a true education.

We were extremely fortunate to have the assistance of not only Big Sid but also some of the road agents, who gave us the highest degree of advice. One of those agents was Grizzly Smith, a former great in professional wrestling and the father of WWE Hall of Famer Jake "The Snake" Roberts. As soon as we'd arrive at any venue for a house show, we'd go right to Grizzly, and we'd heed his every word as if it were scripture. He was a selfless and wise mentor who wanted to see us grow beyond everyone's expectations.

Grizzly put us in matches with other young guys like 2 Cold Scorpio, Van Hammer, Brad Armstrong, Bagwell, and

Maxx Payne, who had varying levels of experience and interesting repertoires of moves.

Of the grouping, Scorpio was the most dynamic, and I wanted to learn from him. At 229 pounds and five feet eleven, he was versatile and experimental with his moves, especially from the top. He'd pull off a full backward flip from the top into a leg drop across a guy's neck and nail it every time. I'd been working on a move for a while that was the same thing only a forward flip into the leg drop, but I wasn't ready to bring it out yet. I've never committed to anything new in the ring until I could do it ten times out of ten. Scorpio was a great guy and my age, so we naturally gravitated toward each other and became true friends in the business, a rarity indeed.

On the other end of the spectrum was Van Hammer. Hammer was two years younger than me and kind of looked like a smaller version of Sid. Billed at six feet six, he was pretty muscled and had long curly blond hair, but he was green as hell in the ring. Getting in there with Hammer was never a cakewalk because he was awkward to lead around. You also couldn't be sure if he remembered key aspects of the match or how hard he was going to lay in some potatoes to the face out of sheer inexperience and adrenaline. But he would make it through all right and was easy enough to get along with.

Performing with such a diverse talent pool proved to be a huge asset to me and Lash as we worked hard to develop trusted reputations with WCW.

Just when we felt some burnout at the end of a tour, Lash and I found ourselves immediately assigned to yet another loop. We'd be off to Grand Rapids or St. Louis and then down through almost every theater and civic center you could fathom in every no-name town in Indiana, Ohio, Kentucky, and West Virginia.

The travel was brutal, nonstop, and exactly what we'd signed up for. We were wide-eyed kids having fun doing something we never imagined in a million years we'd get to do. It was extraordinary. This was our ticket. *The* ticket. If we could handle these basic, extremely short road trips as mere grunts, we could learn to make it one day as main eventers with big-show commitments.

It was an eye-opening experience to now lose 85 percent of our matches, but it was just part of the game as rookies. We were paying our dues, and it was our job to put on the best show possible, win or lose.

Every match was a chance to strengthen our character skills and athleticism. The fans would continue to come if we captured their imaginations. We'd show those hardworking people something different, something memorable, and they'd buy tickets, concessions, and merchandise for themselves and their families and maybe even their friends, making us a draw for the company. That's all that mattered.

The crowd was the instant barometer of our success. I

never lost sight of that or my identity as I worked to do better every night out there.

The whole time Lash and I were off the tapings, we never knew how long the break was going to last. Finally, during the final days of June, Sid decided he was joining us on the road in Six-Man Tag Team Matches.

"Get ready, guys. We're about to put you back on TV," he said, "so I'm getting in there with you to mix it up and give you the rub."

That's when we knew we were being jettisoned into the spotlight sooner than we expected. Sid was climbing in to establish us with the WCW crowd as new forces to be reckoned with.

It was awesome being in there with him on our side against Scorpio, Hammer, and Bagwell. Harlem Heat and Sid were a unique experience for all the people who'd never seen us before, and we put on a dynamic show. Sid was never selfish, always tagging us in for a double-team on Hammer and letting us shine for the crowd as though we belonged. His psychological interactions with the people through a simple hand gesture or facial expression drove them into hyperspace with the same magnitude as when he'd demolish Bagwell with his trademark powerbomb for the finish. The man had giant presence.

Finally, the days ticked down and we were ready to return to the tapings.

By this time, Eric Bischoff, who'd originally been an on-camera microphone man with the company, was executive producer. Eric had a vision in 1993 to escalate WCW to a playing field level with the uncontested powerhouse of the WWF, and one of his first big maneuvers was to sign a deal with Disney-MGM Studios in Orlando. For Eric, moving the tapings from Atlanta to Walt Disney World, even making WCW a free attraction for theme park visitors, meant a monumental upsizing to company exposure.

There was a long period of transition when WCW was taping the TV shows from both Center Stage Theater in Atlanta and Disney-MGM Studios in Orlando. It didn't make much of a difference to me, except that Florida weather definitely had its appeal. I'd always hated being in Northern cities on the road during the winter. When those cold months eventually came rolling back in, it would be perfect to have Orlando on the schedule for a few consecutive days to recharge in the vibrant sun.

The inaugural tapings were held in Orlando on July 7, and we picked up a win in another Six-Man Tag Team Match with Sid against Scorpio, Hammer, and Bagwell as well as in a standard match against two jobbers named Scott Allen and Alex Gibson on July 9.

Harlem Heat was held off from the broadcasts for a few more weeks, but we knew our day was coming. Those tapings

BOOKER T. HUFFMAN

started as a breakfast session at eight in the morning, and we'd film several shows per day into the early afternoon. Back then, neither WCW nor the WWF had live programming. Everything you saw on TV was taped weeks or months in advance.

That first day at the Disney tapings, Eric tried one of his new production concepts. For something a little different, he had the ring slowly revolve clockwise on a platform. I never really noticed it while in the ring, but from outside, it was a little odd to see it rotating 360 degrees while guys were performing. It was phased out not long after as Eric continued to look for ways to capture the audience.

For the rest of July, Lash and I looped up and down the South as Harlem Heat. We enjoyed the sights, the weather, and the work. As we traveled, we discussed living arrangements. We were still staying with Sid and thought it was time to find our own places before we wore out our welcome. Lash opted to stay back in Houston, but I decided I'd move to an apartment in Atlanta to be close to all the WCW action.

I was leaving home behind—where as a teenager I'd struggled after my mom passed away, where as a young man I'd made stupid choices that put me in prison, and where people had given me a chance in a career that had put me back on my feet. It was time to run through the door of opportunity—but I'd never forget my roots.

3

HARLEM HEAT IGNITES

As I made plans to move, my thoughts were on my son, Brandon, who would be ten that December of 1993. His mother had left when he was an infant, and since my wrestling career had me on the road all the time, Brandon lived with my sister Carolyn. Just as I'd relied on my siblings while we were growing up without our parents, now I relied on them for help with my boy. Carolyn had welcomed Brandon into the safe haven of her home. She had a son Brandon's age, and they were like brothers. I was grateful he had a positive female role model in his life. And as much as I wanted him with me, I simply couldn't pull him away from everything he knew, especially when I'd be traveling full-time with WCW.

Still, I worried about him. Since he'd been a toddler, he'd struggled in a way I hadn't understood. He didn't do well in school, and I regularly had conferences with his teachers. We developed game plans and provided the best tutoring available, but it wasn't working.

I couldn't help but wonder if Brandon was destined to walk the path I had. His parents were virtually gone, and he was struggling at school. His journey in my footsteps was already in motion.

I didn't know what to do. The one thing I thankfully could do was provide for him. Taking care of all his material needs until his adulthood—from clothes to his first car and, someday, even college—motivated me to take a chance at this career. Atlanta and the WCW promised me an opportunity to make things better for Brandon, so I set out with that vision in mind.

On the road, things were about to speed up for Lash and me. Just as Sid had suspected, we rose from the ashes of the Chi-Town Heat disaster as Harlem Heat. Not only did he still support us, but he had big plans for us. Being repackaged as Harlem Heat allowed us to explore who we really were: two hungry guys from the streets of Houston who knew how to take care of business in and out of the ring.

After toiling in untelevised WCW shows since the middle of June, we had our first televised taping on August 1 for *WCW WorldWide* on TBS in Orlando.

We were more than ready to take on opponents Dave Hart and Mike Thor. We walked toward the ring and, as Lash always had since day one back at Global, we yelled at the camera and pushed the people's hands out of our way. We loved mixing it up with the fans as we charged down the aisle. Decked out in our custom Brooks & Dunn outfits and with our theme music blasting, we exuded more magnitude than the sound of the crowd.

On the playback later, I got a huge kick when commentator Tony Schiavone gave us our first on-air introduction: "We're getting ready to see two big and bad men in WCW—newcomers Harlem Heat!"

Jesse "The Body" Ventura quipped, "And those ain't two happy campers, Tony!"

We attacked Hart and Thor ferociously with a pounding The Road Warriors would've been proud of, and I even tossed Hart out of the ring while Lash kept clubbing Thor. Early in the performance, Lash smashed Thor in the gut, stunning him while I ran off the ropes and did something even Ventura couldn't believe.

"Whoa! Look at that move! A spinning crescent kick!"

I went for the cover, but in a display of arrogance, I pulled him up at the two count. I was playing the perfect heel.

At one point, I tossed Thor to the canvas and, wanting to add some intensity to my performance, raised my arms, looked at the crowd, and screamed, "Aaaaaaahhhhhhhh!"

Over the years, fans have heard me do that during matches to get a reaction. It started in 1985, when I saw Stallone do it in *Rambo: First Blood Part II*.

We ended the match with a move we called the Harlem Heat Bomb. Lash picked up Hart for a huge powerbomb while I climbed to the top turnbuckle. Just as Lash went for the release, I jumped off with a big elbow to the chest.

The badasses from 110th Street had just knocked out their first suckas on TV. Now people everywhere—from the stadium to backstage, homes, and the office—took notice. Business was about to pick up for Harlem Heat.

After getting that first WCW TV win under our belts, we were immediately thrown into the main mix. We returned to Atlanta for a few days to do a month's worth of taping. Along with Sid, Lash and I battled the company's top performers in Six-Man Tag Team Matches with Scorpio, Bagwell, and none other than Ron Simmons, one of my main influences in the business and the first black WCW World Heavyweight Champion. We usually took those wins with Sid powerbombing Bagwell.

During this time, I was also sent out as a singles performer for a few matches to warm up the crowd. I wasn't a stranger to singles matches, and I gave it my all.

One time after a singles match, I walked back through the curtain and Dusty was standing there. "T-Book, my man." He always called me that. "I've been watching you wrestle out there and practically stealing the show. You're never going on first again. You'll see, brother. You're on a different level than an audience warm-up."

The next day, August 10, Scorpio, Bagwell, Lash, and I began a quick tour of Indiana. We hit Bloomfield, Martinsville, and Linton, where we performed in front of small crowds and lost by DQ every night.

Eight days later was the big event, Clash of the Champions XXIV at the Ocean Center in Daytona Beach, Florida. Lash and I knew being a part of WCW's flagship free TV show of the year meant more exposure and a potential spot on the main roster.

We were even going to be part of Ric Flair's interview show, *A Flair for the Gold*, alongside Sid in opposition of Sting, "The British Bulldog" Davey Boy Smith, and The Nature Boy himself. Of all the fanfare surrounding these events, what would be remembered most was not Harlem Heat but one man and his shocking live debut.

Flair, the mediator on the set, held a microphone while Sting and Bulldog came out talking about some mystery partner they acquired as an equalizer against the three of us: "The Shockmaster" Fred Ottman. Fred had formerly performed under the names of Tugboat and Typhoon in the WWF, and it was clear that WCW wanted to build him up as a different character altogether. Unfortunately, Fred's Shockmaster persona was this incongruous outfit composed of what looked like a satin coat and jeans along with a real Star Wars Stormtrooper helmet painted blue with sparkles. It was ridiculous but, well, Lash and I had been in chains and jumpsuits not long before.

Upon Sting's introduction, Fred was supposed to bust through the wall in an intimidating display of strength, striking fear in our hearts. In reaction, we were all to step back in amazement at the awesome power of The Shockmaster.

It didn't happen that way at all.

Apparently someone on the production team left a wooden beam on the floor or something, and Fred couldn't see through the helmet visor. So in one of the most infamous debut scenes in professional wrestling history, Sting announced, "Our partner is going to *shock* the world because he is none other than *The Shockmaster.*"

On cue, Fred crashed through the Sheetrock, tripped, and fell onto the floor as his helmet popped off—all on live TV! He scrambled to put his helmet back on, but it was far too late. There was just no salvaging any part of it. Everyone onstage completely broke character as we turned away, trying to hide our laughter.

Though he'd fallen flat on his face, Fred still had a few lines he was supposed to deliver. Actually, all his dialogue was just Ole Anderson in the back on a microphone reading the script with his voice distorted.

The live audience was dead silent, and so were the commentators. I can only imagine the viewers at home wondering what had just happened.

Flair said, "Oh my gosh," as he stared at the floor in disbelief.

I tried not to laugh. "Man, who is this guy?"

Bulldog was right next to me. "He fell on his arse. Flat on his arse!"

I looked over at Sid. Every vein in his neck was pulsing as he watched Fred attempt to play it off, struggling to put the Stormtrooper helmet back on. I thought Big Sid might go over and put *him* back through the wall.

I never knew how anyone looked at that helmet and thought it was a good idea. There was no way in a million years Fred would've been able to wrestle or even speak with it on.

As funny as the scene was, I felt bad for Fred, though, and it made me think of Lash and me entering the scene as Chi-Town Heat.

Thankfully, the disaster didn't spell the end of The Shockmaster. Like us, he was an investment WCW wasn't prepared to release its grip on. Fred just took some time off and resurfaced to wrestle without the mask as if the whole debacle had never happened.

And in the many years since, Fred has completely embraced the whole thing and even does convention appearances with the original helmet. He's a huge hit.

Through the end of that summer, the momentum Sid gave Harlem Heat continued. Then we were told we'd be in the main event of Fall Brawl 1993. It was going to be our first PPV, and it happened to be taking place in our hometown of

Houston at Astro Arena.

I thought, *Houston! The family will see us in the big time!*

But my excitement was abruptly halted when Sid said what the main event was. "Boys, are you familiar with the War Games?"

We knew exactly what he was talking about.

The War Games was the brainchild of Dusty Rhodes, who came up with the idea of having two rings side by side, completely enclosed by a huge steel cage that surrounds the ring aprons. The match is between two teams of four to five wrestlers. The War Games begin with only one wrestler from each team inside the cage. After a certain amount of time, a coin is flipped to determine which team is allowed to have another member enter the ring first. After that, each team alternates until all wrestlers are finally in the war zone. Once both teams have all their men inside, the War Games becomes known as the Match Beyond, where the only way to win is to submit your opponent or have him surrender. It's a brutal match with bodies everywhere, and the risk of injury is incredibly high.

When Sid told us we'd be a part of the action, I guess I must have cringed.

"Aw, don't worry about it. I've been in it. It's kind of fun."

It was going to be Sting, Bulldog, Dustin Rhodes, and The Shockmaster, who'd since been repackaged in an electrician look with a hard hat and flannel shirt with jeans, which suited him much better. They took on our team of Sid, Big Van Vader, Lash, and me. I'd never been in a Steel Cage Match in my life. I'd seen the ones with The Four Horsemen, Nikita Koloff, Dusty, and The Road Warriors from The Great American Bash 1987, and it looked like the apocalypse landed directly inside that double-ringed cage with a fenced-in rooftop.

As our team walked out first, the crowd went insane. Fireworks exploded as the double cage slowly lowered over the two rings. Even I was in awe. Having never seen it go down live before, I knew WCW was pulling off something amazing.

Once both teams arrived, Dustin would go in first. First up from our side would be Big Van Vader, an ominous sight for anyone lumbering toward him. At six feet five, the 450-pound Vader would trade blows with Dustin for what seemed an eternity. When the coin toss landed in our favor, Lash was the next to go in, so he and Vader took the two-on-one advantage and started laying in to Dustin like a ton of bricks. I was next to last, and The Shockmaster followed, officially beginning The Match Beyond. The live Houston viewers were on their feet from beginning to end, and it sounded like the Roman Colosseum must have. From there, nothing was planned. A spontaneous, cage-contained riot of eight guys broke out, and everyone swung over everyone else in a crippling melee.

I bumped around that contraption as I'd never done

before. Being in that event made me realize pressure I didn't know was possible. It was my job to make Sting and Bulldog and all the other boys look good, and they did the same for me. That's what the whole game's about.

Sting and Dustin took care of me and worked like pros while Vader went ballistic in what looked like a barely contained rage. He was beating people up and pouncing like a bear. The last thing any of the opposition wanted was to get caught in a corner by Vader, because he could legitimately crush anyone like a car compactor.

In the end, I submitted to a giant bear hug from The Shockmaster seventeen minutes in. Despite the scripted loss, I felt Harlem Heat had won. We'd proven once again we belonged on the big stage and could perform with the very best in WCW in the most unorthodox and mentally challenging tasks the company had to offer.

When it was all said and done and we were backstage, we all congratulated each other on pulling off one of the most dangerous matches in the business.

Vader slapped my back. "You did pretty good, kid. Nice work."

We knew we'd given the fans in the arena and across the world exactly what they'd paid to see: complete main event carnage. The experience motivated me to do even better the next time I entered the ring.

After we all left the building, Lash and I joined our family for a big homecoming party. All our brothers and sisters—Danny, Carolyn, Gayle, Billie Jean, Donald, and Bonita—had come out to the show and brought little Brandon to see his dad and uncle work. It was a validating moment for sure.

With our first PPV and War Games tucked into our back pockets, Harlem Heat went back on the road, hitting the Southern cities circuit as we geared up for the next big outing. Halloween Havoc 1993 would be at the Lakefront Arena in New Orleans on October 24. We'd take the loss in a Six-Man Tag Team Match with The Equalizer against The Shockmaster, Ice Train, and Charlie Norris. Just like at War Games, I took the big bear hug from The Shockmaster into a huge powerslam that knocked the wind out of me. When someone Fred's size drives you back-first into a stiff mat, nothing other than your body gives. I knew it was coming from the very beginning, so when it was time, I braced myself as if a piano were falling on me.

That was just one of the many hats I wore in Harlem Heat: I was the loser. In our team dynamic, whenever we were booked to lose, there was never a second thought that I'd eat the finisher or submission. It didn't hurt me as a performer or Harlem Heat in general. Lash was a monster in every sense of the word. Being the smaller of the two, I was more believably susceptible to getting caught in a compromising situation. It worked perfectly for our credibility in the ring.

A few days after Havoc 1993, a portion of the WCW main event roster embarked on a tour of England for a few days. Meanwhile, Lash and I loaded up the car and prepared for a Harlem Heat tour of the Midwest.

About a week in, back in Atlanta, we were shocked to hear about an incident that occurred in England on October 27 involving Arn Anderson and our benefactor Big Sid Vicious. This is the story I heard.

After a WCW show in Blackburn, Lancashire, Ricky Steamboat, Flair, The Nasty Boys, Scorpio, Arn, and Sid finally pulled into their hotel in the middle of the night. Tired and hungry, they all piled out and decided to get some food and drinks inside the hotel bar, where some of the boys entered an escalating debate over many aspects of WCW's status as a company. Apparently the conversation between Arn and Sid became the most heated.

Later, after parting in the middle of the night, their fight came to blows. Worse, both men were injured with scissors. Arn sustained a series of slashes to his face and body, and Sid was deeply stabbed in the abdomen. When Scorpio heard from the hall and came in to check, Sid took off for medical assistance.

Vader woke up and came out of his room to meet Sid, who stumbled toward him with blood pouring through his fingers. Vader called employees for help, had Sid sit down, and did what he could with some towels.

Arn's many slashes turned out to be mostly superficial, but he had to get stitches all over his body.

Neither Sid nor Arn pressed charges, and they had to wait to face repercussions at work.

It was a PR nightmare for WCW. A few weeks later, back in the States, Sid and Arn were suspended without pay. It was rumored that a bunch of guys threatened to walk if Sid wasn't released. By December, Sid was let go.

I felt bad for Sid. He'd done so much for Lash and me—bringing us in, putting us up in his own apartment, giving me that first pair of boots, even looking out for our incremental pay raises. I'll always owe a debt of gratitude to the big man for our injection into the mainstream.

However, by the time that confrontation happened, I can say Sid didn't seem to be in a good place. I don't know what he was going through, but there was a shift that most wouldn't have recognized. Something was wrong. Sometimes, without explanation, he would be a no-show at events he was advertised for. Even worse were the times he'd arrive, disapprove of everything they had him booked in, get right back in his car, and leave. The agents and other guys scheduled to work with him were left scrambling to pull something together for the fans.

In one of Lash's and my first shows on the road, in Macon, Georgia, Sid showed up. In the back, everyone was milling around, waiting for the curtain call and there was a big commotion. I wasn't privy to any of the inner workings back then and had no idea what was going on.

Sid walked past me with a look that could kill. He kicked the back door open and was gone just like that. And he was the headliner that night.

I thought, *Wow! When you get to that level, I guess you get to call your own shots. That must be the way the business is.*

But that's *not* the way it is. Unfortunately, although he definitely was big, Sid wasn't *that* big. Nobody is.

Meanwhile, in the midst of all the turmoil surrounding Sid and Arn, Lash and I were gaining momentum in the tag team ranks both on the road and at the TV tapings. We were being booked in matches with a variety of the best talent in WCW. At the November 12 tapings in Orlando, we stepped in against Maxx Payne and the notorious Cactus Jack, where I took the fall courtesy of Cactus's double-arm DDT.

Working with Cactus was always an unpredictable experience. He was a risk taker like I'd never encountered before. He gave every fiber of his being in that ring while stalking with enormous presence. It was funny to listen to him grunt, vocally punctuating every punch and kick, much as Bruiser Brody used to do.

What I remember most about wrestling Cactus was this one move he absolutely had to work into every single match like his curtain call. I'd be there lying next to the barrier gate in front of the ringside fans, and everyone would know what was coming next. As I'd be busy trying to recover from being thrown out of the ring, I'd hear the crowd going nuts. I'd take a quick glance upward and see over three hundred pounds of Cactus Jack airborne and heading my way. I would brace for dear life every time, but surprisingly I'd barely feel anything. That's when I realized the most disturbing part: Jack ate 90 percent of every crash onto the bare concrete. Those were the days way before pads or matted flooring. I don't know how he didn't shatter his hip, ribs, or elbow, and he did that move *every single night.* I don't know if he dropped that to entertain the fans or for his own bizarre thrill. If I had to guess, I'd say the answer rests somewhere in between.

A few weeks later came the most unexpected moment of my life, let alone my burgeoning wrestling career. I was told that Ric Flair had personally requested me for a singles match for a *WCW Saturday Night* taping in Atlanta at Center Stage Theater. I couldn't believe it, and Lash was just as pumped up for it as I was. In my mind, I was still nothing more than the kid from Houston. How could I be in the ring with Nature Boy himself?

I was told Ric had been watching me and was impressed by my athleticism and presence and felt like testing me out to see if I had the chops. This was way before I was even remotely thinking about a singles wrestling career in WCW. My focus was Harlem Heat.

I can remember each detail of that match with Ric Flair.

I had every intention of going out there and controlling the match—that's how confident I was at the time. I was going to lead him through a dramatic story in that ring, play the quintessential heel, and really make him look good like a seasoned veteran.

I'll be damned if all that didn't go right out the window the second he took off his robe and gave me that hazel-eyed glare of a predator. I was in his territory—*Flair country*.

My nervous energy worked against me, and Flair schooled me for a full ten minutes that seemed like ten hours. Flair literally pulled me around by my nose, making me do everything he wanted me to, never giving me a chance to rest or fully be a heel. I tried to get my stuff in whenever possible, but Ric was in total control.

Ric was an amazing communicator in the ring. Without saying a word, he could tell me what to do. For example, I had him in the corner at one point and dramatically with one arm he motioned for me to back off as if he were protesting and scared. But surreptitiously with his other hand, he was signaling me to come in for the attack. When I caught him doing that, I thought, *Man, that's pretty slick right there.*

He used the referee as a communication bridge too. As basic as it sounds, it had never occurred to me before. He'd say something to Randy Anderson, who'd simply come over, act like he was checking on me or asking for my submission, and convey the next move to me while I'd be lying on the mat.

Ric's chops were easily the hardest hits I'd ever taken in a ring. When he applied the figure four on me, I writhed in agony on the mat, making sure the entire crowd knew I was locked into a submission that I had no way of getting out of. It was only a short time before I tapped out. It was an amazing experience to have Ric take me to school.

When the match was finally over and we were in the back, he said, "Good job, kid. Just learn to listen a little more. Know when to follow and how to relax, and let it all come out effortlessly, because eventually it will."

I knew exactly what Ric meant. There'd been a few times I'd pulled against him instead of flowing with his lead. He was the narrator in the ring. I'll never forget that first night working with him, one of the greatest of all time. Now I was ready for the next class in the ring.

4

AN EARFUL FROM CACTUS JACK

About this time I had the opportunity to work with another legendary name in the business. Eugene "Mean Gene" Okerlund was as recognizable as anyone at the top of the professional wrestling world, having been the main interviewer with the WWF during the mid-eighties golden era. I couldn't even think of him without instantly imagining Hulk Hogan towering next to him, shouting, "Let me tell you something, Mean Gene!"

For whatever reason, the WWF hadn't offered him a contract renewal, so in late 1993 Eric Bischoff welcomed him into WCW with open arms. When Lash and I had our first prematch interview with him, his presence alone took us aback, all five feet six of him as well as that little mustache. We just couldn't believe it was really Mean Gene standing there with a mic in our faces, giving us that intent look as he asked about our opponents for the night's *WCW WorldWide* tapings in Orlando —Johnny B. Badd and Mr. Badstreet USA, Michael Hayes.

What can I say about that first encounter? At least it started out great.

Lash blasted off into some of our classic dialogue. "Let me tell you suckas something! We're not going down Bad Street. We're going down 110th Street, fools!"

I jumped in. "We're the Harlem Heat, and we rule the streets! Now can you dig that?" Like a complete idiot, I thrust my arms out dramatically for emphasis and knocked the stick right out of Gene's hand.

He picked it up quickly and shot me a look of disgust, as if he were thinking, *Who the hell are these guys, and why am I wasting my time with them?*

Man, talk about making a great first impression with a legend in the business!

Our first six months in WCW spun by quickly. In December, we competed with Scorpio and Bagwell, traveling to the Georgia towns of Dalton, Gainseville, and Macon.

We closed out 1993 with a Christmas matinee in Denver, which was miserable for this Texas native. It was about five degrees, and there must've been at least a foot of rock-hard snow on the ground. But we were there to put on a show for about a thousand WCW faithful who came out on Christmas to see a good show, so I gave them my best.

By this point in our various runs with each other since June, Scorpio and Bagwell could really cook it up with Harlem Heat in the ring. We easily predicted and followed each other's moves, and the four of us brought the crowd to their feet with one high-flying maneuver after another.

Because we were in Scorpio's hometown, he brought out one of his showstoppers. When it was time for me to go down for the count, I took a clothesline from Bagwell and fell into position near their corner. Scorpio leaped to the top turnbuckle and turned out a perfect 450-degree splash.

Whenever he did that move, to make sure I didn't get the air knocked out of my lungs, I'd make sure my arms were tight across my chest. My hands cupped my groin for safety, too. When it came to aerial maneuvers, Scorpio was effortlessly safe, but there's always going to be risk when a 225-pound man rotates in the air with all that momentum. While his landing looked like a ton of anvils, it was light as a feather. The audience roared as I took the three count for the hometown boy.

After the show, Scorpio brought me to his warm, inviting home to meet his big family and share Christmas dinner. It put me in a nostalgic frame of mind. I thought of the boisterous Christmases at home when all my siblings converged on our little house to enjoy mom's delicious home cooking.

I also thought about Brandon and hoped he'd gotten everything he wanted. As always, I'd sent money to Carolyn so she could check off his wish list for Christmas as well as his birthday on December 29.

He turned ten that year. I called to wish him a special day, but I deeply regretted that I couldn't make it to Houston to see him. He was always on my mind in every town and arena.

The New Year crept in without too much fanfare as Lash and I once again headed up and down the Georgia highways. People didn't usually recognize us yet, but we were gaining some attention with our solid TV matches. Lash and I were doing our jobs and doing them well, but we had a long road ahead of us.

We started the year in Gainesville on January 3, 1994, in another confrontation with Cactus and Maxx. I found myself once again staring up as Jack heaved from the apron with a sickening thud onto the concrete next to me. I knew each of those elbow drops was shaving off the quality of his life, but Cactus was a man on a mission.

The Clash of the Champions on January 27 in Baton Rouge brought a complete surprise to everybody when Bobby "The Brain" Heenan decided to come on board. Heenan was arguably one of the greatest WWF managers and wrestling personalities of the eighties, and here he was on WCW television. Harlem Heat wasn't on the card that night, but Lash and I were there to see the events unfold.

When we saw Bobby walking around backstage, I elbowed Lash. "Hey, look who it is. The Brain."

We had a Mean Gene moment, finding it hard to believe another legendary figure was coming into the company. I thought WCW must've been doing something right to be bringing in more familiar faces from the competition. Little did we know this would soon become a trend.

Bobby joined the commentary team, exuding his typical sarcastic heel disposition that came so naturally to him. The classic one-liners fans were used to hearing from Heenan in the WWF were now enhancing the product of WCW. He was a perfect complement to Tony Schiavone. They had a fun antagonistic banter under the action on TV. They were great both for business and for guys like us.

In fact, every time we would be in the ring, Bobby would naturally side with Harlem Heat, the heels. One time we were walking down the aisle and fans were in our faces, booing. I looked at the broadcast later and heard Tony say, "Is that thumbs-down to Harlem Heat, or is that thumbs-down to the Brain from those fans there? I guess we'll never know."

Bobby didn't miss a beat. "I believe they're giving you the thumbs-down or Okerlund. Because they wouldn't give it to me, and they certainly wouldn't give it to Harlem Heat."

Later during the same match, after I gave a jobber my jumping Harlem Sidekick, Bobby said, "They don't care who you are. They're just going to beat you up! Take a good look! Videotape it, rerun it as much as you want. Slo-mo it, fast-forward—it doesn't matter because you're going to have to get in the ring with Harlem Heat, and we'll see what you're made of then, tough guys!"

Those kinds of lines were exactly why Bobby Heenan was

an asset to WCW, and Lash and I knew we were fortunate to have him.

Soon it seemed new talent came into the company every other week. Not all were seasoned veterans from the WWF; there were some promising newcomers too. Bischoff was looking to develop some homegrown talent, just as Sid had done with us. One of those guys, who went by the name of Terra Ryzing, debuted that February.

When Ryzing came in, I'd never seen or heard of him, but you could tell he'd be a star. In fact, he already was, because somebody had scouted him out and brought him to WCW as a hot commodity. With his look and demeanor, WCW might've even been grooming him as the heir apparent to Ric Flair. He was unquestionably putting in the hard work. At his debut on *WCW Saturday Night*, I saw a lot of Flair's characteristics in him. He wore blue trunks, had the blond hair and the arrogance, and his Indian Death Lock finisher was like a reverse version of Ric's figure four.

With his natural athleticism, great looks, and strong work ethic, Terra Ryzing would go on to solidify his place in wrestling history as Triple H in the WWE. Not only would he end up leading two of the most recognized stables in this business with DX and Evolution, but he'd also go on to become the COO of the WWE.

Even though we passed each other only a handful of

times, I knew I'd see him again.

We spent February in the warmth of Orlando at MGM for a few weeks of *WCW WorldWide* tapings. Match after match, Lash and I focused on getting ourselves over with the crowd with building energy in the ring.

Near the end of the month, on February 20, at Super-Brawl IV in Albany, Georgia, we were booked into a major PPV win over Thunder and Lightning, a muscular babyface team the company was pushing at the time. The guys wore blue singlets and capes that brought Batman and Robin to mind. Lightning, whose real name was Jeff Farmer, was someone I really enjoyed working with anytime we had the chance. A few years down the line, Jeff would find greater exposure and success when Bischoff reinvented his look into one of the most iconic wrestlers ever.

Harlem Heat was hitting our stride and starting to up-grade our look. Gone were the Brooks & Dunn shirts and the standard black-and-red tights. We were now wearing matching one-piece black vinyl long-form tights with custom-stitched red-and-orange flames. I also incorporated plastic rings that rested on our chests and connected fabric straps, leaving our shoulders and backs exposed. We'd keep the do-rags for now and add matching vinyl jackets for our entrance to the ring.

No one had seen anything like our custom look. We were

still 110th Street all the way, but even brutes from the ghetto like to look good. We lit ourselves up into the kind of characters we would've wanted to see on TV growing up. Richard Roundtree of *Shaft* would've been proud.

Going into that match, I had a ton of anxiety. We were starting to feel the pressure of being the only black guys on the roster. It's hard to explain, but on occasion, being in the Deep South as a black heel team and constantly being matched with white babyface teams could be nerve-racking.

It sometimes took me to my school days when Lash would protectively walk behind me, his big palm lightly clutching the back of my neck, letting everyone know they'd have to get through him to get to me. Our travels back then were usually without incident, but there were days when someone would yell, "Nigger!" With Lash there, I'd just look around and shrug it off and we'd make our way onward.

As confident as I was by this time in my career, when I inevitably heard some hillbilly in the crowd yell a crack like that, it just rolled off my back. Whatever their problems were, they had nothing to do with me or Lash, and I was determined to never let attitudes like that hold us back.

By this time, rumors were running rampant about WCW recruiting Hulk Hogan. Hogan had left the WWF in the midst of a steroid scandal that culminated in a federal trial. Hogan testified in exchange for immunity from prosecution. In the wake of the storm, he left the business to pursue opportunities in film and TV. By the spring of 1994, Hogan was doing a show called *Thunder in Paradise* for TNT on set in Orlando, and word reached us that Bischoff went down to offer him big Turner money to return to the ring.

Hulk liked what he heard, and the creative wheels were set in motion. The Hulkster's star power would be a game changer for everyone employed with WCW. The company wasted no time airing vignettes as early as SuperBrawl IV with Mean Gene, The Shockmaster, and Brutus Beefcake on the set of *Thunder in Paradise*, indicating the obvious WCW tie-in and ultimately setting up his return to professional wrestling and, more importantly, a match with Ric Flair.

Hogan versus Flair had been a dream match for fans and the industry alike for years. Throughout the late eighties and early nineties, speculation ran rampant about who would win in a contest between the WWF Champion, Immortal Hulk Hogan, and the WCW Champion, the "Nature Boy" Ric Flair. When Ric jumped over to the WWF in 1991, hype for a match between the two reached unprecedented heights. The world would finally know who was the best in the business, and fans eagerly anticipated the two titans clashing at WrestleMania. The giants did face each other in a series of house shows all over the country, from New York City's Madison Square Garden to San Francisco's Cow Palace. However, they hadn't faced off on the grand stage of

WrestleMania as everyone expected. Now Bischoff attempted to correct history's error.

When Hogan's arrival had been officially confirmed, panic set in with the rest of the boys. "Hey, did you hear?" they'd say. "Hogan's reuniting his old WWF clique and bringing them all over." They were referring to guys like "Macho Man" Randy Savage, Brutus "The Barber" Beefcake, "The Mouth of the South" Jimmy Hart, "Hacksaw" Jim Duggan, and "Earthquake" John Tenta. "Man, this could really mess things up for our spots."

With Mean Gene and Heenan already in WCW, it seemed the WWF's transfer was almost complete. To me, the momentum was a good thing. With the stars coming over, so should new revenue for WCW's house shows, PPVs, and merchandise, which would increase paydays for everyone across the board.

With Hogan's arrival a few months away, I was gearing up for two weeks in Germany. On March 8, we arrived in Ludwigshafen, where I performed a series of singles matches with two of the business's most recognized players, Sting and Ricky Steamboat. Like Flair, these major players had requested to work with me. I was humbled, but this time I wasn't going to let my nerves work against me. I laced up the boots, composed myself, and prepared to make everyone proud.

By this time, Sting and I knew each other from time

backstage and mixed tag matches. My objective was to generate heel heat and make him look as good as he ever had in his career.

We proceeded to get in the ring and light it up, and something occurred to me: *Sting's letting me lead the match.* His confidence in me made me realize just how much I'd learned, and I wasn't going to let him down. Of course, the outcome was for me to get wrapped up like an inverted pretzel in the Scorpion Death Lock, but as the crowd's cheers exploded, the loss felt like a victory.

When we got to the back, Sting congratulated me with a huge smile.

Steven Regal, who'd had his doubts about me and Lash when Sid brought us in, announced to everyone, "I'd like to see anyone in here go and do better than that."

It was an unforgettable moment to receive that validation from the seasoned pros.

The next night in Cologne, Ricky "The Dragon" Steamboat and I went twenty minutes without a net, and it was the smoothest action I'd experienced in a ring. Steamboat was teaching me with a style that contrasted with Flair's. Ricky would have me on the hook in the corner, chopping me across the chest while talking to me in short statements: "Duck the clothesline. Harlem Sidekick. Steal some heat." It was so simple, perfect, and yet completely different from anything else I'd been shown. Flair was a master at making himself and his opponent look good, whereas Steamboat was a pro at making the match look good.

By March 16, the German tour was winding down with just a few more shows to go. We were in Dresden, changing after our performance, and I was talking with Regal. Out of nowhere, Cactus Jack barreled through the curtain, blood covering every inch of his face. He wasn't complaining, and he never even grimaced or made much of a sound. He just avalanched onto a bench, breathing hard.

Just then, WCW announcer Gary Capetta burst in, looking ghostly pale. He held something bloody in one hand, and as he walked toward Cactus, he said, "Jack, this is your ear."

Wait. What was that?

Regal and I looked in Gary's hand, and there it was.

Jack gazed at it with no expression for a couple of seconds, then slowly looked at the rest of us with a smirk on his face. He put his fingers up like little pistols and gave his trademark catchphrase, "Bang, bang!"

I was shocked beyond words.

Regal looked at me as if to say, *What is this madness?*

I thought, *Is this what this business is all about? What have I gotten myself into?*

As it turned out, Cactus had wrestled Vader, and when Cactus went to clothesline him, the big man ducked, sending Cactus out of the ring toward the floor. However, Cactus's neck got caught up in the top and middle ropes, which were rubber-coated steel cables. In an attempt to free himself with the ref's help, the over three-hundred-pound Cactus pulled and scraped his head through, almost completely severing two-thirds of his right ear from his face. He climbed back up to finish the match, and as he was punching Vader, the dangling piece of his ear flew off. The referee saw the curious fleshy object sitting in the ring, quickly picked it up, and gave it to Gary in the corner.

Eventually, Cactus would have reconstructive surgery, but the results weren't ideal.

I couldn't get the whole scene out my thoughts. *Well, Booker T, welcome to Cactus Jack's world of professional wrestling. Bang, bang, indeed.*

5

TAKING THE TAG TEAM GOLD

By April of 1994, we were working fervently on our repertoire of double-team finishers and had developed a new maneuver called the Harlem Heat Seeker. At the close of a match, Lash would pick up our opponent on his shoulders like an electric chair. The second he was settled, I'd climb the top turnbuckle and missile dropkick the guy. It was terrifying to me because by the time I jumped over Lash to kick our opponent, I was fifteen feet in the air for a crash onto my side, hip, arms, and belly. It may have been my most reckless move, but sometimes it was necessary to summon a little of that inner Cactus Jack.

By this time, I was also finishing up a move now known as the Harlem Hangover, which would eventually become my personal highlight move. It was inspired by 2 Cold Scorpio's off-the-top backflip leg drop, but mine was frontward. For quite a while, I'd been doing a move in matches where I'd climb to the top and front flip off as a guy would move out of the way, but it occurred to me I was landing in the same spot ten out of ten times. When I realized it could be modified into an actual offensive finish with a leg drop, there was no turning back.

We were constantly working to improve our performances. From our gear to our moves, fans were drawn into everything about Harlem Heat's presence in the ring. Before every single match, I'd jump rope and use exercise bands to be sure I was limbered up for the challenge ahead. When our entrance music hit, the crowd jumped to their feet, yelling, "Whoop, there it is! Raise the roof!" Fans even started bringing signs with those phrases written on them in bright marker and glitter. The reaction despite our heel status indicated how close we were to making a major breakthrough.

Yet there was one missing piece: our names. We were still Kane and Kole. On May 25, after almost a full year of asking Dusty and Bischoff and anyone else who'd listen, we were finally granted our request to use our Ebony Experience names of Booker T and Stevie Ray. During that night's tapings, as we entered Center Stage Theater, Tony Schiavone announced, "Fans, coming to ring is Booker T and Stevie Ray—Harlem Heat!"

It was the final turning point for the Harlem Heat. Now the vision was complete.

On June 11, the arrival of Hulk Hogan was at hand. The fanfare came in full force during a parade on the streets of Orlando. Hogan sat on the back of a motorcade like the new yellow-and-red president of WCW. He signed his contract during the broadcast, and major media covered it, just as Bischoff had planned.

The first match was set. It would be Hulk Hogan versus Ric Flair at Bash at the Beach 1994 on July 17 from Orlando Arena. Longtime wrestling fans Shaquille O'Neal and Mr. T, personal friends of Hogan's, sat ringside for the event and brought even more hype to the meeting of the business's two biggest names.

WCW World Heavyweight Champion Ric Flair stood face-to-face with legendary rival Hulk Hogan to finally settle the score. It was no surprise to anyone, especially Flair, that when it was time for the match to come home, Hogan dropped the leg and walked away as the new champ.

It was all according to Bischoff's master plan for WCW. He was pulling Turner's top talent and pushing WCW straight to the top of the industry.

Although Lash and I weren't on the card that night, we were there and could feel the energy. I'd once heard that stars made stars. I wondered how bright Harlem Heat could shine with the growing star power at WCW.

Little did I know that Hulk Hogan himself would be the one to put the spotlight on us.

In early August, an elbow injury forced me to take some time off. Meanwhile, Bischoff was hard at work evaluating WCW's talent pool with Hogan. Very hands-on creatively, Hogan was a huge proponent of tag team wrestling and was eager to restructure the division. We later heard that when Bischoff and Dusty sat down with Hogan, they presented all the teams in the company, asking who he wanted to push. He didn't even hesitate to recommend Harlem Heat and say he knew just what to do with us.

When the news got to me in Atlanta, I almost passed out. I needed to get my elbow back in working order, and I trained like a man possessed. When I wasn't training, I was home intently watching the product on TV as guys like The Nasty Boys and Stars and Stripes tore it up in the ring.

It would take until the early fall before I could realistically come back. When I did, nothing could've prepared me for what Hogan had in store for us.

"Brothers," he said, "there's someone I want you to meet. This is Sherri Martel. Get acquainted because you'll be working together, and it's going to propel you guys to the top."

There she was, "Sensational" Sherri herself, the professional wrestling great who, after transitioning out of active performance, had become a very successful manager/valet to major WWF Superstars like Randy Savage, Ric Flair, Ted DiBiase, and Shawn Michaels. She'd been brought into WCW a few months prior as "Sensuous" Sherri, being aligned with Flair during his feud with Hogan. Now her act was being repackaged specifically for us.

"We've got a new name for her. You're looking at Sister Sherri, and the three of you are going to shake up WCW."

To generate buzz, WCW started taping backstage segments of Lash and me talking on a cell phone with a mystery person who was coming to help us. We had started a feud with Brian Knobbs and Jerry Sags, The Nasty Boys, and would meet in a big showdown at Clash of the Champions XXIX on November 16.

I always liked working with The Nasty Boys, who were big brawlers and two of the best in the tag division. Visually and stylistically, our teams complemented each other and delivered the kind of match everyone wanted to see.

At the Clash that night, we went back and forth for ten solid minutes, fists and bodies flying. In the last dramatic moments, all four of us entered the ring at the same time. Lash kept trying to bail out and use the cell to call our secret weapon, but every time he'd get an opportunity, Knobbs or Sags would sandbag him. He did manage to get a call through in the midst of all the interference. I was finally able to hit a double-axe-handle smash on Sags and attempted to drag him into position for the pin when, all of a sudden, out came Sherri, holding the phone, revealing she had been our contact throughout the weeks leading to the Clash.

When I watched it later, I thought Bobby "The Brain" Heenan's description was perfect: "It's Sherri, who's managed more champions than probably anybody! She's taken more men to the top! It's a natural! They're going to win this one!"

It was pure pandemonium as she came out dressed in a low-cut black vinyl dress with flames like ours. With Sherri, it was total Harlem Heat synergy—the winning formula we'd needed all along.

For the rest of 1994, we were in a war around the world with not only The Nasty Boys but also WCW World Tag Team Champions Stars and Stripes, the team of The Patriot and Marcus Bagwell. We made frequent stops in Atlanta for several TV tapings and then traveled overseas yet again. Through all these matches with top teams, WCW was building us up, giving Harlem Heat everything we could handle under pressure. Meanwhile, the three of us worked toward the common goal of becoming the WCW World Tag Team Champions.

On a personal level, Sherri gravitated toward me quickly. She became a true friend, and I cared about her as if she were my own sister. I would have done anything for her. Many nights after she partied a little too hard, I made sure she made it safely to her room for the night. She had her ups and downs, which sometimes affected her ability to perform, but when she was on top of her game in the ring, nothing came close to Harlem Heat and Sister Sherri.

Our team had great momentum, and heading into December, Dusty told us the news we'd been waiting to hear: "You're going over Stars and Stripes at the next tapings for the belts. You boys ready for this?"

I looked at Lash and Sherri and thought, *Oh, yeah, we're ready!*

On December 8, we found ourselves back at Center Stage Theater for the *WCW Saturday Night* tapings. It was time for us to live up to the expectations Hogan had for us.

When Sherri was ready to walk out with us, she laughed and patted our backs. "I knew you guys were all-stars."

We stepped in against The Patriot and Bagwell, and it was a great night with two pros. We'd been working with Bagwell since our entry into the company, and The Patriot had been hugely popular in Global just before we got there. He was a big, muscular athlete who knew how to work a good match and do business. Together, the two of them were another baby-face team like Thunder and Lightning, only Stars and Stripes were super patriotic in red, white, and blue. And then there we were, Harlem Heat, the evil from the streets of New York City about to rain all over their Fourth of July parade.

It felt right, as if we were an arrow that had been pulled back for a year and a half to finally be released into the WCW bull's-eye. We had a steady match, both teams bumping and selling to make each other look strong.

Harlem Heat brought it all home when the ref was distracted. Lash and Patriot collided, and both went down. In the resulting confusion, I rolled into the ring and made the cover for the three count, and the belts were ours. Harlem Heat claimed the WCW World Tag Team Championships for the first time.

On December 27, we headed to Starrcade 1994 in Nashville for the company's biggest PPV of the year. Because our championship win had yet to air, we came to the ring beltless.

We met up with The Nasty Boys for another slugfest with Brian and Jerry. I was always amazed how well Knobbs sold my moves. He took punches to the head like sniper shots, then collapsed and rolled around like a turtle stuck on its back. Sometimes I'd completely miss him, and he'd still fall all over the place and I'd have to stop myself from laughing at his contorted faces. Knobbs enjoyed performing for his opponents as much as he did for himself and the audience.

Sags was less predictable. I was in there with Jerry once and called a dropkick after whipping him into the ropes. He held on to the top rope, pulling himself back and causing me to eat a hard bump to the back of my head.

I stood up quickly and said, "What was that, man? Do it again, and I'm coming at you hard for real."

He laughed. "Ew, I'm really scared!"

I shook my head, but that was the end of it. He knew I was serious.

We took a DQ loss, and that's how we closed out 1994.

We were champions in the wings going through the motions and waiting for our victory to be televised on the January 14 episode of *WCW Saturday Night.*

The year of 1995 started for Harlem Heat with almost an entire month on the circuit with Knobbs and Sags. We hit venues in Arizona, California, Texas, Ohio, and Pennsylvania. In Pittsburgh, we dropped a match by DQ. After our title win aired on TV, we were able to proudly walk out in front of the WCW audiences with those heavy, shining belts strapped around our waists.

After the long circuit, toward the end of January, tensions exploded among the boys in the back. One time, I caught the tail end of a vicious one between two titans in the industry: Vader and Mr. Wonderful, Paul Orndorff.

I heard a commotion coming from the back of Center Stage Theater. When I got there, Orndorff was standing in flip-flops in the middle of a bunch of boys, stomping Vader's face on the concrete.

From what I understood, Vader had shown up late for some promo work, or something to that effect. Orndorff, who'd transitioned to the office as an agent, confronted him about it and they were off to the races. Regardless of how it started, I do know Mr. Wonderful finished it. Orndorff was an old-school tough guy who didn't mind serving up a plate of humble pie if the bell rang for it.

We moved on to Clash of the Champions XXX in Vegas on January 25, where we again defeated Stars and Stripes to retain the belts.

Then we launched into a trip around the Carolinas and back to Atlanta, where I debuted the Harlem Hangover on February 8 against my old WWA pal Mike Davis at Center Stage Theater. After that, we touched down in Florida against The Nasty Boys and Stars and Stripes and won all to DQ finishes, thanks to Sister Sherri. No matter where we were or who we were paired with, Harlem Heat was ready to deliver.

On February 18, we received tragic news. Hot Stuff Eddie Gilbert, who'd given us our shot in Global, had died of a heart attack. He was only thirty-three years old.

Eddie had changed my life forever. He could've believed the rumors about us generated by a miserly promoter. He could've told us to get lost. Instead, he saw something in us and gave us a shot. He was the one who gave Lash the name Stevie Ray in honor of his favorite blues guitarist, Stevie Ray Vaughan, and named us The Ebony Experience. He said, "You're going to be the best tag team anybody's ever seen. You make sure you wear suits wherever you go and hold your heads high. Be respected. You'll never be just some dancing minstrels; I can promise you that." I still lean on Eddie's wisdom today.

Losing him was a shock. We'd give the fans our best in his honor.

At SuperBrawl V on February 19 in Baltimore, we defeated The Nasty Boys yet again and got right back to Atlanta for a *WCW Saturday Night* taping. We were matched up against Sting and a freshly signed talent from the WWF, "Macho Man" Randy Savage.

I'd never met Savage before, but when we locked up, he volleyed for the upper hand. At the beginning, I threw a kick to his chest, and he had no intention of selling it. He caught my foot and backed me up hard into the corner, still grasping at me as if he would cut my other leg out from under me. I quickly reversed Savage and realized this guy was a seriously intense worker. We eventually settled into a groove, but Randy made it clear from the beginning that he meant business, which I liked.

To my surprise, Randy shook my hand afterward. "Hey, kid, we had us some fun out there, right?"

I nodded. I felt the exact same way.

By March, after holding the World Tag Team Championship for three months, Harlem Heat was scheduled to release them at Uncensored 1995 on March 19 in Tupelo, Mississippi, against The Nasty Boys. In doing so, I almost broke my neck courtesy of concession stand condiments.

It was a Texas Tornado Match, where the four of us battled simultaneously all over the place with a no-DQ stipulation in place. We started in the ring, went out on the floor, and then headed toward the side of the ramp, where there were multiple makeshift concession stands set up for our match. Funnel Cakes, Lemonade, Refreshments—it was all there. And, that's where things got seriously out of control.

We were breaking canisters of ketchup, mustard, mayonnaise, and relish. You name it, we smashed it all over each other and dumped it onto the floor. We were slipping and sliding, and when I threw Knobbs into the funnel cake stand, my feet gave out as I slipped on the slick ground. Had I not landed right, it would've been a groin pull with a side order of broken neck.

I wondered, *Who came up with this?*

After taking the spill to the concrete floor, I collected myself, and even though I was annoyed, I carefully got up to continue fighting. During the scuffle, I was impressed with Sherri, who went after The Nasty Boys while trying to navigate that mess. We could barely stay on our feet, but Sherri was out there in high heels punching, kicking, and slapping the two of them in an attempt to give us the advantage. Even with the odds against them, The Nasty Boys would take the win when Knobbs gave me an awkward body slam onto the broken equipment and covered me to claim the belts.

It was my least favorite experience in the business up

until then, even taking Chi-Town Heat into account, and I was glad to head backstage, bruised and covered in mustard and ketchup like a big corndog and fries. I was sure of one thing: for the rest of my career, I'd never allow myself to be booked into another Texas Tornado Match involving concession stands, condiments, or The Nasty Boys.

We spent the rest of March, all of April, and into early May running around the country with Knobbs and Sags. We turned up the Harlem Heat and entered each match with a different psychological approach from when we were the title-holders on the defensive. We had to show the people and good ol' boys of the creative roundtable we were hungry and ready to capitalize on the gold once again.

Throughout Georgia, North Carolina, West Virginia, and Pennsylvania, we pursued Knobbs and Sags with the same frenzy as when we'd hit the road for our very first loops around the circuit a year before. We were ready to see where the WCW roads would take us next.

6

THE NEW WORLD ORDER DECLARES WAR

On May 3, we moved back into the WCW pole position. We took the titles from The Nasty Boys in Orlando at a taping that aired on June 24, becoming two-time Tag Team Champions thanks to the interference of Lord Steven Regal and Earl Robert Eaton, the Blue Bloods. The title changes had just begun.

CHAMPIONSHIPS	
WCW World Tag Team Championship	2

At Slamboree 1995 in St. Petersburg two and a half weeks later, we handed the title back. That particular match was by far my favorite with The Nasty Boys, as all four of us worked hard to deliver a great PPV story in the ring, with Sister Sherri adding the icing on the cake.

Before it all went down, as the story line went, the tag team of "Lord" Steven Regal and "Earl" Bobby Eaton, known as The Blue Bloods, jumped Knobbs, forcing Sags to come out by himself and face Lash and me. He was on his own, and we went to town on him. The fans in attendance and watching at home had no idea why Knobbs was nowhere to be seen. Sags gave his all and held his own as much as possible, but the two-on-one advantage was just too much for him. Based on the beating we were giving him, I'm sure everyone assumed Harlem Heat would finish him off and walk away with our titles intact.

In a last-ditch effort to gain the advantage, Sags reversed a back body drop into a devastating piledriver on me. As we both lay there exhausted and beat up, cheers rose to a deafening crescendo. I looked up just in time to catch Knobbs staggering down the walkway, his ribs all bandaged up, ready to come to the aid of his partner.

All I could think as I saw him was that Knobbs was so out of shape that instead of removing his shirt and taping his ribs, he'd chosen to secure the tape over his Nasty Boys shirt. I silently laughed to myself as Knobbs stormed down to the ring, his subtle comedic genius on display for everyone.

With the crowd in a frenzy, Knobbs took his spot in their corner waiting for the hot tag from Sags. It was obvious from the tape around his waist that Knobbs had been beat up, but the mystery still remained as to who was responsible.

In a moment of great wrestling drama, Sags made the tag, bringing Knobbs in to wreak havoc on Lash and me. He pummeled us both, throwing Lash out of the ring and forcing Sister Sherri, who wore a long satin dress, to come to our aid.

Removing her heels, Sherri climbed the top rope, ready to pounce on Knobbs. But he was too smart for her and caught her on the way down, executing a brutal powerslam that left

BOOKER T. HUFFMAN

Sherri immobilized. Before she could get up, Knobbs picked her up like an old trash bag and tossed her over the top rope and onto Lash, where they both came crashing hard to the ground. A former women's champion, Sherri knew how to take bumps with the best of them. And once again, her presence and talents enhanced the story being told.

With Lash and Sherri disposed of outside the ring, Knobbs picked me up onto his shoulder while backing into his corner for the tag. Sags mounted the top rope as Knobbs drove me into the canvas with a high-impact powerslam. Before I could recover, Sags came down with a heavy elbow drop from the top rope and covered me for the pin. The Nasty Boys were the new WCW World Tag Team Champions.

As we hobbled to the back in defeat, the Blue Bloods came out to stare down The Nasty Boys, implying to the audience watching that they were the ones who'd jumped Knobbs in an attempt to weaken The Nasty Boys.

Though they claimed the title from us yet again, it was worth every minute.

Moving into the summer of 1995, Harlem Heat and Sister Sherri found ourselves in a little feud with old Colonel Parker's redneck-themed duo of Bunkhouse Buck and "Dirty" Dick Slater, who'd been an accomplished performer in the Southern territories for the past twenty years. It was funny to me that two years after our WCW debut, Lash and I would be on TV again with Colonel Parker, but this time we weren't chained up as his team from Chi-Town. We were the badasses from 110th Street, and we were bringing the heat.

One June night, we faced Buck and Slater at Center Stage Theater. Afterward, we went to a bar and saw Slater there. He was hammered and fell flat on his face in front of everyone. Lash and I and some of the other boys ran over and picked him up, but he was out on his feet. We took him to his room and put him down. The very next night, there he was again, two fisted until it was lights out. Some guys were in for a penny, in for a pound.

It seemed creative was reaching for ideas. There were only so many times we could square off with The Nasty Boys, so teams of singles performers were formed for us to exchange the titles with. We transitioned into an endless series of matches with Bunkhouse and Slater, Hacksaw Duggan and Bagwell, and Regal and Eaton.

WCW even brought in teams from the old guard of the eighties, such as The Fantastics and the legendary Rock 'n' Roll Express. We enjoyed working those guys. They could definitely still go and were over with the fans.

Meanwhile, Bischoff was devising methods to launch WCW to new heights. By August, he finally talked Ted Turner into giving him a one-hour block of TV time for WCW to go head-to-head with the WWF's uncontested *Monday Night*

Raw in what would officially begin the Monday Night Wars of professional wrestling programming.

Many of the WCW boys were apprehensive. If the show bombed, it could've been the demise of our company. But Bischoff was a producer on a mission.

The new live show, *WCW Monday Nitro,* debuted on September 4 in the middle of the Mall of America in Minneapolis. There in the midst of the retail atmosphere, Bischoff pulled off a huge promotional show.

Sting defeated Flair, and Hogan dropped the leg on the former Big Boss Man, now known by his old NWA/WCW name of Big Bubba. The huge coup came at the end of the program when Lex Luger walked out unannounced, fresh from the WWF. He claimed he'd had enough of wrestling the kids and was coming for Hogan's WCW World Heavyweight Championship.

The previous night, Lex had been at a WWF house show and decided to take off without notice for his old WCW home at the urging of Sting. The Total Package's WWF contract had expired, though he was still working with them. He jumped ship without notifying McMahon, creating huge self-promotion at WCW and burning his former employer at the same time.

Appearances such as Luger's live defection on *Nitro* would become a regular occurrence, forever transforming the nature of TV competition.

At Fall Brawl 1995 on September 17 in Asheville, North Carolina, Lash and I took home our third WCW Tag Team Championship belts after beating Bunkhouse Buck and Dirty Dick Slater with a little help from The Nasty Boys.

CHAMPIONSHIPS
WCW World Tag Team Championship   3

The following night, on the second *Nitro*, we dropped the belts again, this time to The American Males, consisting of yet another reincarnation of Bagwell and newcomer Scotty Riggs.

Then on October 11 at a taping of *WCW Saturday Night*, we took the belts back. In just a little over two years, Harlem Heat was now a four-time WCW World Tag Team Championship team, but I wondered if this game of hot potato was weakening the merit of the belts.

CHAMPIONSHIPS
WCW World Tag Team Championship   4

Halloween Havoc 1995 crept in on October 29 in Detroit, and we weren't on the card. The PPV was notable for a monster truck race between Hulk Hogan and his protégé. The Giant was brought into the company heralded by Hogan and Jimmy Hart as André the Giant's son, which was completely untrue but a great marketing strategy for the bright new talent. The Giant was seven feet tall, four hundred pounds, and only twenty-three years old. His potential to draw fans was even larger than his physical frame. That night The Giant would walk away with the WCW World Heavyweight Championship around his enormous waist. Little did fans know that he would later become The Big Show in the WWE and one of the greatest entertainers this business has ever seen.

That November, I decided to move from Atlanta back to Houston. I'd wanted to be closer to the WCW, but by now I'd established a steady career in the company and felt secure enough to go home. Brandon needed me more than ever, and it was time to settle where my roots were.

In the Clear Lake area outside of southern Houston, I built a three-thousand-square-foot home, which exceeded my wildest dreams as a kid on the streets. It was hard to believe. I had money in the bank, a house for my son and me, and now we could establish some normalcy as a family.

Brandon was going to be twelve years old. We had a great relationship as father and son and spent a lot of quality time together when I wasn't on the road. I'd enrolled him in a tutoring center, but I was still making regular visits to the principal's office on his behalf.

He needed more guidance from me. When it was time for me to depart, he'd help me pack up my gear but tell me not to go. The problem was it felt like it was always time to go.

I left for the last major event of the year: World War 3 1995 in Norfolk, Virginia, on November 26, a battle royal involving three rings and sixty wrestlers. A guy had to be eliminated from each of them before the night was over. To be honest,

I wasn't too excited about the concept. It felt like an ostentatious display to parade in front of the competition.

When that was behind us, we kicked off 1996 at *Nitro* on January 22 in Vegas, where we dropped the tag titles, which we'd held since September, to Sting and Lex Luger.

We followed that up with a loss in a rematch at Super-Brawl VI in St. Petersburg on February 11. During that night, The Road Warriors finally made their dramatic surprise appearance as Animal ran in and smashed Lash with a lead plate, which cost us the victory. It was great to get a crack at Hawk and Animal, and we soon got another one.

For *Nitro* on February 26 before a standing-room-only Knoxville Civic Coliseum audience, Lash and I walked out to the ring with one thing on our minds: to make a statement against the reunited Legion of Doom. We had the advantage in speed and athleticism and nearly matched them in strength, but Hawk and Animal were still the kings of the mountain in terms of notoriety.

The Road Warriors had been on hiatus since late 1992, when Animal left the business with a severe back injury. Meanwhile, Hawk had been in Japan and formed a new version of the LOD with Kensuke Sasake known as the Hell Raisers.

It was only a matter of months prior to their arrival in WCW that the two joined up again as the Chicago brothers in paint and spikes. After they made their entrance and we were all firmly planted in the ring, my brother stood off with

Animal while I got in Hawk's face.

"You're going down, punk, and there ain't nothing you can do about it." I shoved Hawk and, as always at the beginning of a match, talked like it was going down for real.

Hawk looked at me. "Hey, what the hell?"

We stared each other down, but Harlem Heat would ultimately take the fall. The Road Warriors had to settle for an uncharacteristic finish, though. Backflips were never my specialty, and I was *not* interested in going up for the Doomsday Device. Near the close of the contest, Hawk purposely deadweighted me on a Harlem Side Slam attempt. I proceeded to lift him up and jack him down, clearing the way for a trademark Harlem Hangover from the top. The crowd erupted as I went for the cover, but there was no ref to be seen. He'd left the ring to check on Lash, who'd taken a spill to the outside. While I was leaning over the ropes, looking at the ref and Lash, Animal ran over like a pit bull and gave me a big boot to the face, allowing Hawk to cover me for the pin.

In March at Uncensored 1996 in Tupelo, Mississippi, WCW split up Lash and me for the first time and paired me with Sting, which effectively turned me babyface. Sting and I teamed up for a Chicago Street Fight against The Road Warriors in one of their last appearances with the company before they departed for the WWF. Sting and I won after my brother interfered by hitting Hawk with a chair, allowing me to get the pin.

I was curious why the good ol' boys separated me from Lash. I could only conclude they felt Sting's style complemented my own. Lash was just as strong as both of the Warriors and wouldn't allow them an opportunity to overshadow him with power moves, whereas Sting and I would.

At this time, Sister Sherri was noticeably absent from TV, no longer by our side when we came out. WCW decided to slowly fade her off of programming, though she was still under contract. Unfortunately for everyone concerned, the pressures of being on the road under the spotlight had afforded Sherri the platform to party too much, and she'd been no-showing appearances. Even worse were the times she was there but, when that red light on the camera came on, the look in her eyes said she wasn't fully present.

Sometimes when she was scheduled to work, she wasn't functional. And if she was, it was only because I gave her cup after cup of black coffee in the back. "Sherri, are you okay? How you feeling, Sister?"

She'd slur something and stare at me with her eyes half shut.

Sherri was like family to me, and it broke my heart to see her like this.

Bischoff and Hogan felt Sherri had fulfilled her purpose for Harlem Heat, assisting in establishing us in the mainstream. Rather than watch her run herself deeper into the ground, WCW deactivated her for a while. It wasn't the end of Sister Sherri's run with us; it was just a brief break for her to take some much-needed time to recharge.

By that late spring of 1996, Lash and I had been with WCW for three years, which meant we were finally ready to renegotiate our contracts. We were both very interested in seeing what kind of equity Eric Bischoff perceived Harlem Heat had established. I had no experience in negotiating deals, and when we sat down across the desk from Bischoff it was eerily similar to the first experience with Ole. In retrospect, it would've been in my best interest at least to have spoken to an attorney and discussed how to approach possible leverage strategies. Truthfully, I knew when it came down to it, I'd likely sign anything presented to me as long as there was a noticeable increase from our original 1993 guarantees of seventy thousand per year.

As it turned out, the negotiation started with Eric asking, "Well, what do you think you deserve?"

The mood was light and carefree, so I shrugged. "I don't know. How about two hundred fifty thousand a year for three years?"

Bischoff didn't blink. "You've got it, plus merchandise royalties and PPV bonuses. We'll draw everything up and get the paperwork right over to you."

It was a landmark deal for Harlem Heat.

I was beaming, but it did seem a little too easy.

When we walked out, Lash said, "Man, did you see the relief on his face? I bet we could've asked for half a million each."

When I thought about it, I realized he was probably right, but the figure was generous and more than we'd ever seen in our lives. It was a lesson learned. I thought, *That's cool. Next time I'm asking for seven hundred fifty thousand.*

With our new contracts signed and another three years of security, my confidence was at an all-time high. It was exciting to know Bischoff believed in us as he was making continued power strides with WCW. *Nitro* had been steadily climbing in the ratings, and all the boys knew the live platform was a huge advantage over the antiquated taping process.

Everyone could feel the momentum in the company, and the consensus was that WCW needed only one inspired event to propel us into mainstream culture. Everyone wondered if Bischoff could pull another Hulk Hogan or *Nitro* out of his hat and continue the magic show.

On May 27 in Macon, Georgia, everyone discovered Eric's bag of tricks was filled with plenty of promise. The greatest show on earth was about to begin.

As *Nitro* was in the middle of a live broadcast featuring action in the ring between The Mauler and Steve Doll, a commotion broke out in the audience walkway in the background of the shot.

I was watching on the monitor in the back, and I thought

some fans had gotten into a fight—until they cut from the hard camera to a close-up of a guy walking through, wearing jeans and a cutoff jean jacket. It took me less than a second to recognize him.

It's Scott Hall, "Razor Ramon" from the WWF, I thought. *What the hell is he doing here? Bischoff's pulling off something big again. Business is about to pick up.*

Hall jumped the barricade and interrupted the match by launching into a brief but impactful diatribe against WCW and Eric Bischoff. "Hey! You people, you know who I am. But you don't know why I'm here. Where is Billionaire Ted? Where is the Nacho Man? That punk can't even get in the building. Me? I go wherever I want, whenever I want. And where, oh, where is Scheme Gene? 'Cause I got a scoop for you. When that Ken doll lookalike, when that weatherman wannabe comes out here later tonight, I got a challenge for him, for Billionaire Ted, for the Nacho Man, and for anybody else in WCW. You want to go to war? You want a war? You're gonna get one."

Bischoff had planned it to feel as if WCW had been infiltrated by an unwelcome presence from the competition. It was an unparalleled approach, and even I couldn't wait to see what happened next. We were all kept completely in the dark just like the fans. For the next couple of weeks, Hall kept interrupting *Nitro* with big promises to bring somebody else in to aid him.

On June 10 in Wheeling, West Virginia, Hall finally revealed his partner to be Kevin Nash, the six-feet-eleven former WWF Champion known previously as Diesel. Hall and Nash, now known as The Outsiders, took it upon themselves to terrorize and unleash their wrath on Bischoff, who was establishing himself on-screen as the face of the company.

At their Great American Bash appearance, Eric questioned whether the two were still employed by the WWF. Nash grabbed Eric and Jackknife Powerbombed him off the side of the stage.

The deadly duo soon began mentioning a third member of their alliance. Their mystery partner became the talk of WCW, and The Outsiders' saga escalated ratings.

In the midst of this energy, Lash and I turned our attention toward a different pair of guys, our biggest rivals since The Nasty Boys: The Steiner Brothers.

That summer we'd begun getting booked against Rick and Scott. The dynamic team had destroyed almost everyone in their path over the last six years, including The Road Warriors. Still in their prime in 1996, they were already legends in WCW and Japan and had enjoyed a brief run in the WWF in 1993.

Not only were they brothers like us; they were almost parallel versions of Lash and me in their wrestling style and execution. With their University of Michigan wrestling experience, they could have legitimately beat the crap out of anyone. In the ring, they were fearless brawlers with some of the most unique moves I'd ever seen.

Scott, at six feet one and 270 pounds, might have been the most gifted athlete I'd ever encountered up until then. He invented an array of acrobatic and aerial maneuvers and used every form of Dragon, Exploder, Northern Lights, and belly-to-belly suplex. His Frankensteiner and Steiner Screwdriver finishers were instant showstoppers.

We started our program with them on June 12 in Anderson, South Carolina, where they went over. Then on June 24 for *Nitro* in Charlotte, North Carolina, in a three-way dance with The Steiner Brothers and Sting and Luger, we won our fifth WCW World Tag Team belts. It was phenomenal to finally see the tag division bulk back up with serious heavyweight talent.

CHAMPIONSHIPS
WCW World Tag Team Championship 5

On July 7 at Bash at the Beach 1996 in Daytona Beach, it felt as if the eyes of the world were on WCW's product. And fans would not be disappointed, as it would become one of the most memorable PPVs in wrestling history. That night we saw Sister Sherri return where she belonged: in WCW as part of Harlem Heat. And even though we lost to The Steiner Brothers in a DQ finish, it was great to have her back.

However, the real excitement began with an entrance by The Outsiders, Hall and Nash. For weeks the leading up to the PPV, The Outsiders kept mentioning their secret partner. They were so confident this person would come to their defense that they took on the trio of Sting, Luger, and Savage in a Handicap Match. As the action intensified, so did the anticipation of the crowd and the boys in the back as to who or what was coming. Luger was eventually knocked out with friendly fire by an ill-timed Stinger Splash and taken to the back as both sides evened up to two men. Finally, as all the contenders were lying in the ring after beating each other from post to post, none other than Hulk Hogan made his way down the ramp.

So this, it seemed, was the WCW savior.

There had been talk for a while among the boys that Hogan could turn heel at some point and revitalize his heroic character. But the thought of Hogan turning heel was unthinkable, as he'd been the face of wrestling since the mid-eighties. We didn't know if or when his metamorphosis would happen, until that very night.

Hogan stepped inside the square circle, not saying a word. The fans in attendance and watching worldwide must've assumed this was just another run-in by him to save the day from The Outsiders. Hogan hovered over Savage a moment, as if to protect him from any harm Hall or Nash might cause. And in a moment of betrayal, he dropped a big yellow leg on the Macho Man. The moment he landed across Randy's throat, everyone in the arena jumped up. After two more leg drops, the atmosphere turned into a mob scene. Hogan walked around the ring with a stern expression as the crowd launched garbage and cups, some of them still filled, onto the mat. Hogan had turned his back not only on Savage but on the entire wrestling world.

"Mean Gene" Okerlund entered the ring in disbelief. He demanded an explanation from Hogan for such a callous betrayal. As he held the microphone for Hogan, "The Hulkster" spoke about how the business and the people, including Ted Turner, had mistreated him for years. As the trash continued to fly, Gene was smashed in the face with a full soda, but he maintained his composure like a true professional.

Hogan continued with one of the most memorable and emotionally charged promos he ever cut. He motioned to Hall and Nash and made the trio's intentions loud and clear: "You can call this the New World Order of wrestling, brother! As far as I'm concerned, all of this crap in the ring represents these fans out here. For two years, brother—for two years—I held my head high. I did everything for the charities. I did everything for the kids. And the reception I got when I came out here—you fans can stick it, brother!

And there it was. In one fell swoop, Hulk Hogan ended his twelve-year run as the red-and-yellow beacon of truth, justice, and the American way in professional wrestling and established himself as the self-serving patriarch of the most powerful heel stable ever known to the industry: the nWo.

Hogan comically grabbed Gene.

"Don't touch me," Gene said, recoiling. "I've got a fleet of lawyers!"

Tony Schiavone closed out the show, saying, "Hulk Hogan! You can go to hell! We're out of here. Straight to hell!"

It was an unforgettable ending to an amazing night of wrestling, a full-fledged frenzy no one saw coming. Hogan's arrival sent shockwaves around the world and instantly placed WCW above the WWF, both creatively and culturally. With Hogan repackaged as the villainous Hollywood Hulk Hogan clad in black, our TV ratings spiked to number one above *Raw* for eighty-four straight weeks.

7

SPLITTING WITH OUR SISTER

At Bash at the Beach 1996, another story line was developing: Sting's. In the weeks after the event, Luger and Savage were convinced Sting had been part of the nWo conspiracy against the company from the very beginning. They questioned his loyalty to WCW, which disgusted the protesting Sting so much he walked out on his former allies in a show of martyrdom. He took a vow of silence and disappeared for several months, showing up only for rapid-fire promotionals. Sting had, like Hulk, drastically transformed his image. The California beach boy with short, spiked blond hair now had black hair and white-and-black face paint, his look reminiscent of the undead avenger's in *The Crow*. The repackaging was cool and mysterious and long overdue.

Sting was in seclusion, intermittently showing himself in the rafters during *Nitro*, like Batman in a trench coat, holding a baseball bat. Everyone knew it was just a matter of time before his return for vengeance on the nWo.

Bischoff ingeniously called on my old associate Jeff Farmer

from Thunder and Lightning, who was repackaged as an imposter Sting. With his long dark hair, and mimicking Sting's new Crow-like persona, he was a dead ringer for Sting. Farmer started to appear during run-ins, confusing the WCW faithful and the fans alike as he attacked the unsuspecting WCW roster with the allegiance of Hogan, Hall, and Nash.

However, it wouldn't be long before the real Sting made his presence known, dramatically rappelling from the ceiling on a vertical cable harness to distribute his new form of silent justice with a few swings of the bat.

With the nWo completely unfurled and the excitement of the new Sting and his unpredictable appearances, WCW became the destination for not only wrestling fans but casual viewers surfing the channels or catching the buzz generated by Eric Bischoff's million-dollar ideas.

In the wake of the madness of Bash at the Beach 1996, the rivalry between Harlem Heat and The Steiner Brothers continued, and we traded the WCW World Tag Team Championships regularly. We dropped them on July 24 in Cincinnati and took them back for the sixth time three days later in Dayton.

CHAMPIONSHIPS
WCW World Tag Team
Championship 6

After that, Bischoff decided to take everyone, especially Lash and me, out of our element by developing a PPV like no other: Hog Wild at the Sturgis Rally and Race in South Dakota on Saturday, August 10. The rally is a huge weeklong outdoor gathering of bearded, tattooed bikers. Hog Wild was a free event, a big party Bischoff had invented to capitalize on the rally attendance.

Bischoff envisioned a WCW ring directly outdoors with no seating so the crowd could pull right up on their bikes and, in place of standard applause, hit the throttle. This raucous environment provided yet another unprecedented company spectacle for the attendees and viewers at home.

Bischoff and some of the boys, including The Steiner Brothers, rode their own choppers to the show, hamming it up for the cameras the entire way to Sturgis.

When Lash and I got there, it felt like we'd strolled into the Old West.

When it was time to perform, the electricity in the air was palpable, energizing Lash and me. Having yet another opportunity to work with The Steiner Brothers in this unique setting was great, as we all knew we could really deliver for this crowd. When we came down to the ring with Sister Sherri by our side, Lash and I pushed our 110th Street attitude into overdrive. We stood on the apron as Booker T and Stevie Ray, mixing it up with the bikers in the front row as if we would come down there and smack their beards off and steal their bikes. They loved every minute of it.

It was another bombastic match with the four of us. We delivered, working amid the noise of thousands of revved-up motorcycles. At one funny moment, I gave Rick my hallmark thumb to the eye, a simple but effective heel move inspired by guys like Ric Flair and "Rowdy" Roddy Piper.

Later, during a pin attempt where Rick had my shoulders down, Sherri started screaming at him from ringside at the top of her lungs.

As I kicked out at two, Rick stopped, shot her a look, and barked, "Shut up!"

Not to be outdone, Sherri screamed back, "Make me!"

In the end, Colonel Parker, who'd recently been connected to Sherri in an ongoing flirtation angle, mistakenly threw powder into my face while Scotty and I were in the corner. Sherri then threw a handful of white powder into Scotty's face, allowing Colonel Parker to smash his cane over Scotty's head, setting me up perfectly for the pin. Since the ref was busy making sure Rick was okay, he witnessed none of the cheating, which meant we walked away with our titles intact.

The bikers throttled their bikes loudly, jeered, and threw rocks and garbage at us. Lash and I legitimately couldn't get to the next show fast enough.

Two days later on *Nitro* in Casper, Wyoming, we again defeated The Steiner Brothers by DQ, but the clean win at our fingertips was snatched away by Colonel Parker. After Scotty suplexed me into the ring from the apron, Sherri held his leg down from the outside, allowing me to quickly roll over him for the pin. Parker came into the ring, chased by Rick. Just as the ref's hand was coming down for the three count, he called for the bell. The clumsy Colonel tripped and fell over me, sparking the DQ finish. Lash and I proceeded to verbally dress him down, telling him to stay out of our matches and lives. True to her angle with Parker, Sherri protested and protected him, saving him from us.

The Steiners were great to work with, both in the ring and backstage. They were notorious for ribbing new talent in the locker room. They weren't bullies, but they were pranksters and you might find a new guy stripped naked, gagged, and duct taped to a toilet if they were around. They usually had big smiles on their faces while they either listened to or told crazy road stories.

I remember once seeing Scotty confront Diamond Dallas Page backstage, when he apparently sensed DDP was getting too friendly with Bischoff and the Hogan clique, which, if true, would've rubbed people like Scotty the wrong way. However, Dallas didn't say a word, which was probably in his best interest. Scotty wasn't afraid of anybody, and the entire roster knew it.

WCW's locker room could be an interesting place. The Giant, the seven-feet-tall, four-hundred-pound beast, and I used to shoot on each other for fun back there. He was astonished how effortlessly I took him down and controlled him, but one day the story was far different. No matter what I did, he was able to neutralize everything I threw at him.

Surprised by his newfound ability, I said, "You had The Steiner Brothers show you some stuff, didn't you?"

He just laughed.

Moments like that made the business much more fun, despite the nonstop pace of life on the road.

On Saturday, September 7, I had some much-needed downtime and was excited to treat Brandon to the thrill of a lifetime. Mike Tyson, fresh from prison, was making his big comeback to heavyweight boxing. That night he faced a newcomer named Bruce Seldon in Vegas at the MGM Grand Garden Arena. I was able to lock down some good seats through a WCW connection, and we flew out there for an unforgettable weekend of father-son bonding.

When we touched down at the airport, we were already running late. We hopped into a cab, rushed inside the arena, and got to our seats just as the two fighters were introduced.

Brandon laughed. "This is gonna be great!"

I was catching my breath, settling in for an epic war of Kid Dynamite himself, who was mere feet from us in the ring.

The MGM Grand was a madhouse of deafening cheers and stomps. Michael Buffer made the announcements, capping them off with, "Let's get ready to *rumble.*"

As the bell rang, I looked up in time to catch Iron Mike beating Seldon into oblivion. Boom! He knocked Seldon down. Then boom! Again. Suddenly Seldon was in the corner, and the ref held a hand up and shook his head. It was all over.

What? There was mass hysteria. Tyson looked like he'd barely broken a sweat.

After all the hectic planning and running around to ensure we made it, we saw exactly one minute and forty-nine seconds of a scheduled twelve-round fight.

Brandon was jumping up and down. "Daddy, wasn't that great?"

I wished I were thirteen again.

We went to our hotel and ordered room service, extremely happy to have some time together.

Five days later, I heard rapper Tupac Shakur was shot dead that night in the streets right across from where we stayed. I hadn't followed his work before then, but after his death, I started listening to him. Something about his words, his message of the streets, and his story struck a chord with me, and he's been a mainstay in my playlists ever since.

Back into the mix of things with WCW on September 23 in Birmingham, Alabama, Harlem Heat dropped the belts to Public Enemy. Bischoff had recently acquired the well-known hard-core team of Johnny Grunge and Rocco Rock from Extreme Championship Wrestling (ECW). Fortunately, neither Lash nor I had to experience Enemy's ECW trademark treatment of being smashed through tables from over the top rope. Instead, a simple small package would allow them to take the titles. A week later, we reclaimed the belts from Public Enemy for a WCW record-breaking seventh time.

Finally, it was the moment for Harlem Heat to step up to the biggest main event challenge of our careers when we'd meet with The Outsiders, Hall and Nash, the cornerstone of the nWo.

The New World Order had caught fire since Hollywood Hogan's heel turn three months earlier. Every crowd we saw across the globe was a sea of black-and-white nWo T-shirts. The nWo was great for business. The counterculture of the new faction had completely taken over. The guys everyone loved to hate stormed directly into the imaginations of the watching world and took WCW straight to the top with them.

Bischoff and Dusty decided to adorn the nWo with all the major championship gold, including ours. The Giant, who'd recently joined the nWo, claimed the United States belt, and Hogan was already world champ, so it was time to monopolize the remaining titles.

For us, that meant putting Hall and Nash over. We knew Harlem Heat was being set up to be knocked down like bowling pins, but we were more than ready for a showdown with The Outsiders.

The setting was Halloween Havoc 1996 in Vegas on October 27. We were prepared to bring out a performance no one could top, not even Hogan, who'd wrestle Savage in the main event. When it was showtime, Lash and I came out to an overwhelmingly pro-nWo crowd that showered us with boos and hostility. Even though we were the babyfaces, Hall and Nash were too over for anyone to compete with in a popularity contest.

In the ring, I found it funny to realize Lash's and my red-and-orange outfits matched the Slim Jim sponsorship splattered all over the stage, turnbuckles, and mat. We were unwitting jerky pitchmen.

Hall and I started things off perfectly. Before we locked up, he threw his toothpick at my face. I just stood there staring right through him as he wiggled his fingers at me with a look on his face that said, *Ohhhhh, I'm so scared!* It was the perfect beginning to build anticipation for the match.

Once we locked up, I arm-dragged him across the ring and got in his face: "Come on. It's right here!"

Hall no longer looked so cocky as he got up, glaring at me.

Then I followed it up with a sidekick to his face. As he sat up checking his teeth, I taunted him again: "Come on, sucka! It's right here!" The fans were eating it up.

The four of us had an unforgettable match, and all of us had plenty of opportunities to get our moves in. There was even a great moment near the end when Lash pressed Hall over his head and threw him at Nash, and they both crumpled into a heap.

Over the years, much has been theorized about those two backstage, but I never had an issue with Hall or Nash, and in the ring they were all about doing good business. Scott was an intensely fluid performer who made everything as effortless as it looked, and Kevin was one of the best big guys I ever encountered. He knew exactly how to work light as a feather while making his shots look like a ton.

In the finish, Lash hit Hall with a side slam, setting me up to go to the top rope for the Harlem Hangover. I came crashing down with my leg right over Hall's neck. Lash was still the legal man in the ring, so he covered Hall for what we thought was our victory.

However, the ref was making sure I was okay after the devastating move. So with the ref distracted, Colonel Parker, the bane of our existence, ran into the ring. He tried to hit Nash with the cane, but Nash grabbed him and told him to fork it over. Knowing he was outpowered, Parker gave Nash the cane and ran. Nash turned toward Lash and cracked him hard over the head with the stick. Lash collapsed onto his back just in time for the ref to refocus on the action in the ring and see Hall go for the pin. Three counts later, Hall and Nash were the new WCW Tag Team Champions. The nWo had just claimed every major title in the company, exactly as they said they would.

The match delivered everything all four of us knew we could pull off for the fans and amplified the excitement for the New World Order. Harlem Heat gladly collected our piece of the pie as viewership and revenues continued to soar.

We even ran the loop around the country with Hall and Nash afterward, usually losing by DQ. We headed on to MGM in Orlando for TV tapings and then took another tour of house shows in the South.

Creative even brought in "Rowdy" Roddy Piper, one of the biggest names from the WWF, and the man who fought in the first WrestleMania along with Paul Orndorff against Hulk Hogan and Mr. T, to join the WCW faction against the nWo. By this time, though, the public was losing interest in the appearances of the old WWF guys. WCW in late 1996 was not the WCW of 1994, when Hogan and the rest of the iconic eighties WWF stars came in.

No matter who was brought in and who belonged to which faction, Harlem Heat continued to shine on our own. A month later at World War 3 1996 in Norfolk on November 24, Harlem Heat beat "The Amazing French Canadians," made up of Jacques Rougeau and Carl Oulette and managed by Colonel Parker. It was a fun PPV match with some great moments like the ref getting knocked out, me getting crotched on the top rope, and the ring's steps and a table being brought in. Amidst all the chaos, we took the win when I pinned Oulette with the Hangover.

After all our hard work, Harlem Heat had finally earned some much-needed rest. While WCW went to Germany and ran Starrcade 1996, I happily went home to Houston, dropped my bags onto the floor, kicked off my boots, and relaxed. When I was on breaks, I'd go out fishing, camping with Brandon, golfing, and watching movies. Taking time to do all the things I loved refueled me and got me ready for the ring again.

Feeling refreshed, I hit the road with Lash for the entire month of January of 1997. Little did I know that this would be one of my biggest years professionally.

Harlem Heat went head-to-head with a series of tag teams, some established and well-known, others just two guys put together to give us someone to destroy. I'm convinced if Bischoff had made a team out of a pair of kitchen sinks, he would've thrown them at us too.

During that time, I also had a few singles matches with Scott Hall, which I always enjoyed. Not only was Scott a good worker, but it always helped to have a spot in the ring with a key member of the nWo. However, I had to be extra cautious while working with him, as Scott was still recovering from dental surgery thanks to one of The Nasty Boys, Jerry Sags.

At the beginning of January, during a Sunday house show in Shreveport, Jerry Sags had viciously knocked out Hall in the ring. Sags, whose neck was legitimately injured by that point, had asked everyone to avoid hitting him with chair shots. All the boys were aware of it, but during a match between The Nasty Boys and Meng and the Barbarian, Hall

BOOKER T. HUFFMAN

and Nash interfered. As Sags was on the outside of the ring, unaware, Scott hit him in the back of the neck with a stiff chair shot and knocked him to the ground.

When Sags got up and saw Hall in the ring with the chair, he charged through the ropes and swung left and right. In the end, Hall was seriously messed up and missing teeth, prompting immediate dental procedures. A few weeks later he was back and fairly mended, and the two of us entered into some singles performances.

Hall and I tore it up on January 20 during *Nitro* in Chicago, where seventeen thousand New World Order fans filled the stadium. I took the clean pin with his Razor's Edge crucifix powerbomb, a scary move with me on his shoulders, looking straight up, the back of my head racing toward the mat. But putting it all on the line for a full stadium of WCW fans felt amazing. It felt *right*.

At Uncensored 1997 on March 16 in North Charleston, South Carolina, Harlem Heat faced Public Enemy in a Tornado Tag Team Match, which meant all four of us were allowed in the ring at the same time without penalty. And we were permitted to use anything we wanted in the match. Public Enemy came to the ring with a table and a trash can full of street signs, frying pans, and a toilet seat. It was all legal, and from the moment the bell rang, the weapons were flying. After a hard-fought match, we defeated Public Enemy when I dropped the Hangover on Rocco Rock.

Meanwhile, Sting started to reappear on various *Nitro* episodes and PPVs. I don't know if the creative guys knew where they were going with it, but the visual impact of seeing Sting as this dark, mysterious figure lurking in the corners, stalking the nWo, had the fans glued to their seats as they tuned in each week.

Sting became more visible as time progressed, and his confrontations with the nWo were heating up. Now in the building you'd see not only New World Order T-shirts but black-and-white Sting masks as well.

All signs pointed toward a Sting vs. Hogan showdown. In the meantime, Harlem Heat was helping fill seats and entertain the crowds.

The Spring Stampede 1997 PPV in Tupelo, Mississippi, on April 6 brought an unforgettable moment both in my career and in professional wrestling. Prior to the show, Mean Gene interviewed Lash, Sherri, and me about a Four Corners No. 1 Contender's Match against Luger and The Giant. The victor would get a shot at Hollywood Hogan for the WCW World Heavyweight Championship. Lash and I were well aware we weren't going over for the win, but we were excited to be considered for such a crucial singles main event.

The interview started off typically enough. I stood next to Sherri in sunglasses, my singlet unstrapped, while Gene explained the stakes. Next to being in the ring, promos were the only way to fortify your character, so I always put everything I had into them. In the days before Red Bull, I'd drink about a pot of coffee before these, and it'd feel like rocket fuel was coursing through my veins.

Gene finished his standard intro, explaining the possibility that Lash and I might have to face each other in the match.

Sherri reassured him. "We have everything planned out."

Then Gene turned the mic over to me.

"Let me tell you something, Gene Okerlund," I said. "You're out here talking about a clique. The only clique you need to know about is Harlem Heat and Sister Sherri, see, 'cause what you're dealing with here is the brotherhood! It's nonstop from this point on in WCW! We take what we want, and after we take Lex Luger and The Giant, we want the gold, sucka!"

And then the unthinkable happened. Out of my mouth came a word I never use. "Hulk Hogan, we comin' for you, nigga!"

The second I said it, I grabbed my face and turned.

Sherri rubbed my arms, a big smile on her face, and patted my chin to console me.

Gene didn't bat an eye as he turned to Lash to continue the interview.

I couldn't concentrate on any of it. I was grimacing, trying to figure out how to recover. In a move of desperation near the end of the interview, I said, "Gene, there's a lot of knuckleheads out there been overlooking Harlem Heat, but after tonight, after we got the shot with Hulk Hogan, all the knucklehead suckas can lay to rest 'cause we're taking it all. Now can you dig it?"

I repeated *knucklehead* all those times, hoping people would think that was what I'd called Hogan in the first place.

When we left, all I wanted to do was put my head into the ground while the fallout passed.

When it was all said and done, I had no heat from the boys, although I'm sure they laughed about it for weeks. There was no walk of shame to the office or any repercussions at all, but it weighed on me for the longest time and remains the most embarrassing moment of my career.

The biggest comic relief came when Hogan himself later approached me in the back. I didn't know what to expect and was relieved when he put an arm around me and started laughing. "Well, brother, at least I'm a *good* nigga."

I laughed and felt a little better about it. But thanks to the power of the people at home with their VCRs and now YouTube and whatever entertainment vehicle might be in our future, I'll never live that moment down.

During the actual match with Luger and The Giant, Lash and I were tagged in to face each other in a climactic moment. We squared off, and the crowd jumped to their feet to watch Harlem Heat implode. We took to shoving each other before running the ropes a few times with some tight leapfrogs. Just when the brothers were about to collide, we stopped, stared each other down, gave a little brotherly taunt, and smiled.

There was no way the crowd was going to see Booker T versus Stevie Ray that night.

In defiance, I tagged Luger back in to face Lash. We'd played the stage inside the ropes like fine actors, keeping the fans happy and having a great time ourselves. However, the victory spotlight would be reserved for Luger, who in the end made my brother submit to the Torture Rack.

Back on the road, we wrestled an onslaught of teams. We were all over the place, from Huntsville to Orlando to Nashville to Chattanooga, all leading up to The Great American Bash 1997 in Moline, Illinois, on June 15.

Once again we collided with The Steiner Brothers in another one of our barn-burner matches. We took the win by DQ when Vincent, of all people, an old WWF recruit once known as Virgil, the bodyguard of "The Million Dollar Man" Ted DiBiase, ran in and dropped an elbow on me just after Scotty gave me a top-rope Frankensteiner. Directly after, The Steiner Brothers beat up Vincent with their double-team bulldog.

Our win set us up as the top contenders for another shot at the tag team gold.

Bischoff was constantly looking to add fresh content to the shows, and he had a new idea for a faction of wrestlers themed after the popular *Mortal Kombat* movie and video games. He took Kanyon, Bryan Clark, and Raymond Lloyd, gave them over-the-top costumed roles, and named them Mortis, Wrath, and Glacier, respectively.

Mortis, completely covered in green skeletal armor and wearing a skull mask, resembled the WWF's seven-feet monster Kane. Wrath wore a basic singlet but approached the ring and did interviews wearing a horned, black leather hood.

Lash and I whupped Mortis and Wrath once in Madison, Wisconsin, during a *WCW Saturday Night* taping.

As popular as *Mortal Kombat* was, however, the crowd didn't get those guys at all. And then there was Glacier. Glacier was the best—and by that, I mean most ridiculous—of them all. He was a martial artist who had the icy look of Sub-Zero. While he came to the ring with a blue ninja veil across his face, the production guys dropped confetti snow from the rafters. Raymond Lloyd knew martial arts, so he always incorporated kicks and dramatic karate poses.

Unfortunately, the combination didn't go over. The crowd gave it the thumbs-down, and Bischoff abandoned the concept within a few months.

A better idea Bischoff brought to the table was bringing *luchador* guys, such as Eddie Guerrero, Rey Mysterio Jr., Psicosis, and Juventud Guerrera, into the shows. These smaller, acrobatic performers from various organizations in Mexico tore the roof off every single *Nitro* and PPV we did as show openers. It was the perfect formula to set the pace for the rest of each night during transitions to the midcard before the main event. The *luchadores'* aerial moves were fantastic, and they tried to outperform each other to amaze the crowd. It was the heritage of the *lucha libre* greats who came before them.

Sometimes I got in there and mixed it up with them, enjoying the opportunity to challenge my agility and speed. My size made their moves look even more impressive. The fearless risk takers would suicide dive through the ropes at full sprint toward an opponent outside the ring and then hit a shooting star press from the top turnbuckle to a guy lying on the concrete. It was out of control and completely impressive.

From the back, we used to watch with wide eyes. It truly was one of Bischoff's treasure troves of content for WCW.

The rest of June saw Lash and me take on The Steiner Brothers in losing causes overseas in Hamburg, Oberhausen, and Frankfurt, Germany, before returning to Memphis on July 7 for *Nitro*.

That night, Harlem Heat and Sherri worked together for the last time in the opening bout against Public Enemy. Unfortunately, Sherri's constant interference in our matches, sometimes causing us to lose when we had everything decisively won, was making us look weak, and Lash and I were never stronger as a team than at that period of time. After a planned botched move, where she pushed Rocco Rock off the top into Lash for a pin, we cut a promo and fired Sister Sherri right there in the ring.

As Gene got in with us afterward, it was time to part ways with our sister. Lash stood next to me like an enforcer as she tried to defend her actions, but I cut her off. "I don't know what's going on around here! Last week it was one thing, and before that, it was another thing! All I gotta say is one thing, Sherri. If you can't get your act together, you need to step off team Harlem Heat!"

She screamed, "Wait a minute, brother! You can't fire me, 'cause I quit right now!" She stormed out of the ring.

As the Mid-South Coliseum crowd went crazy, Mean Gene tried to make sense of it all. "Whoa! Is that official? Did she just bail out?"

Lash finalized it. "As of right now, the team of Harlem Heat and Sister Sherri, sucka—it's over!"

It was a bittersweet moment. Sister Sherri had helped establish our careers. She was not only our golden ticket; she was a good friend. But in order for us to go to the next level, we had to move on without her.

8

IN CHAOS LIES OPPORTUNITY

After parting ways with Sherri, we moved on to our next program with Buff Bagwell and Scott "Flash" Norton, the six-feet-three, 350-pound destroyer who'd made a name for himself as a national arm-wrestling champion, now paired as Vicious and Delicious. We faced them at Road Wild 1997 in Sturgis, the same rowdy venue where we'd defeated The Steiner Brothers.

Before that show there was a little excitement that got my adrenaline rushing and provided some deep belly laughs for all the boys. We were in catering outside under a big tent. For some time, tension had been rising between Bagwell and Ernest "The Cat" Miller, Bischoff's former martial arts instructor whom he'd brought in as a performer. The story was that Bagwell had recently discovered Miller was seeing his ex-wife.

While we were all seated and having our meals amidst our loud locker room–style talk, Bagwell jumped up and dove for a sucker punch across the picnic table at the completely unsuspecting Miller, who was just sitting there eating.

Buff completely fell short, and before he had a chance for a second attempt, the rest of the boys held the yelling men back.

Midbite, I stared and thought, *Oh, shit!* I started laughing and almost choked on my burger. It was the perfect way to get amped up for a live event, no pot of coffee necessary.

During the match, Harlem Heat's new manager, Jacqueline, came down to ringside and jumped on Norton's back, punching him in the head when the ref wasn't looking. I pinned Norton with a Harlem Sidekick to the face while Jacqueline held his foot down out of sight of the ref, giving us the victory over Vicious and Delicious.

From the start, Jackie didn't seem to be a great fit or create the type of chemistry we had with Sherri. My personal belief was that because she was black, they thought, *Hm, who can we pair her with? Harlem Heat! It's perfect!*

Unfortunately, not by a long shot. We were an odd trio. It wasn't her fault, by any means. We simply had no team dynamics, but Lash and I went with the flow and tried to make it work.

In my personal life, for the first time in years, I was seriously dating. While living in Atlanta, I'd met this girl named Levestia, and we'd hit it off really well. She had a son about a year older than Brandon, lived with her mother, had a good job with the state, and our relationship seemed to offer the stability I was seeking in my hectic life.

Although I'd moved back to Houston, whenever I came back to the Atlanta area, we were together. She also took plane trips out to my house on a regular basis. When she and her son met Brandon, they got along well. In the back of my mind, I thought maybe someday she'd take on the role of a mother figure in his life. This seemed like the best way to get Brandon through all the troubles he was suffering. It was nice to have someone Brandon and I could count on.

When I got back on the road with WCW, we defeated Bagwell and Norton again on *Nitro* in Birmingham on August 18.

That night, Mean Gene called out Sting, who came through the crowd in his trench coat carrying a baseball bat, pointing to signs in the audience that said *Sting vs. Hogan.* I wouldn't have been surprised if the production staff gave those signs out specifically for the segment. The inevitable clash was on the horizon. It turned out the match to decide the fate of the WCW and nWo war would go down at Starrcade 1997.

The original faction of Hollywood Hogan, Hall, and Nash had grown with many more characters, including Savage, The Giant, Konnan, Bagwell, Norton, Syxx, Brian Adams, and even Vincent. Everybody wanted the big rub of the black and white. The nWo was still way over and selling like hotcakes, but it seemed bloated. It seemed it would've been more sustainable to keep it an elite group. Over in the WWF, for example, they kept Degeneration X exclusive and ultimately outlasted the New World Order.

DX, the faction of Shawn Michaels, Triple H, "The Road Dogg" Jesse James, Billy Gunn, and Chyna, the biggest, baddest female bodyguard to ever step into a ring, was a well-calculated formula. And they were tough. They once filmed an invasion of WCW where they drove a military vehicle, complete with a cannon, to an arena just before a *Nitro* broadcast and yelled on megaphones for us to come out.

The crowd of people, who'd paid to be there, chanted, "WCW sucks!"

Triple H even came up to the doors and gave shout-outs to his boys Hall and Nash.

It was hilarious and well done.

After that, Harlem Heat had a few dates with The Steiner Brothers again. The first was Fall Brawl 1997 in Winston-Salem, North Carolina, on September 14. Lash was the unfortunate recipient of a combination of Scotty's German suplex and Rick's lariat while he was in the air. That was all she wrote for Harlem Heat.

We ran into The Steiner Brothers again at the Battle in Seattle on September 19.

I've always found wrestling ropes to be a little strange, and this night especially they were. Honestly, if you were in a real fight in the middle of a boxing ring and a guy grabbed your arm and tried to throw you into the ropes, you'd take one step and turn around and knock him out, right? Even if you decided to go with it and spring back, would you run toward your opponent and let him knock you into next week with a kick or a clothesline? I know I wouldn't. Long before, I'd concluded the ropes were the most unbelievable aspect of the sport, and that night the audience must've thought so too.

When Scotty threw Lash into the ropes, a loud snap shook the ring, and Rick fell to the floor. When we looked around, we noticed all the ropes were now loose, which made the remainder of the match incredibly difficult. With the ropes out of order, we delicately continued.

When I finally got rolled up for the count, I heard a little boy yell, "Hey, those white guys cheated!" I had to hold in the laughter.

On October 5, I received news that Brian Pillman had died of a previously undetected heart condition. Although Pillman had been most recently wrestling in the WWF, everyone felt the loss of a fellow wrestler in the business. He'd been called The Loose Cannon because he was wild and unpredictable, and the news made me think about how unpredictable and fragile life was. In time, I would lose many colleagues and friends in the business, the shock impacting me every time.

The next day in Minneapolis I defeated Jeff Jarrett in what would be his last WCW match for two years. He was leaving to check out the scene at the WWF. Unlike his arrogant Double J. character at the time, Jeff was a consummate professional in and out of the ring. Anytime we met in a match, the man did everything he could to get the show—and me—over.

Jeff came from a strong lineage of wrestling in the South and grew up breathing the sport. What I remember about him more than anything was his blindness to color in the ring. He treated me like a human being who transcended color, just as everyone treated Junkyard Dog. Everybody, including Klansmen, jumped to their feet for Junkyard Dog when Queen's "Another One Bites the Dust" blasted throughout the building and he came out with the chains. I wanted to be viewed just like him, simply a charismatic performer. That's how Jeff saw me even back then: not as a black guy but as Booker T.

In a world and time when guys were desperate to hold on to their spots, Jeff gave his to whoever was most deserving. And he put me over like a million bucks. He'll always have my gratitude for that.

Working with him that night was as effortless as it got, and no one could blame him for wanting to seek out a better deal with the competition.

On November 17, 1997, Bischoff pulled off a pretty big pie in the face of the WWF during the Monday Night Wars of *Nitro* versus *Raw*. That night, out of nowhere, "Ravishing" Rick Rude walked out on our live program while simultaneously appearing on *Raw*, which had been taped days earlier. His WWF contract ran out. Without warning, and because Bischoff was throwing around serious Turner money, he decided to come back to WCW and pull off a double TV appearance like a magic act: two places at the same time. He came out and cut a promo, calling the WWF the Titanic and criticizing Shawn Michaels. There he was on *Raw* with a full beard, and if you changed the channel to the live *Nitro*, he had his classic moustache back.

I'm sure at Titan Towers, Vince was a little burned, but with everything he'd been through over the years, he knew how to weather a storm. He'd learned wrestlers were a dime a dozen, and one wouldn't stop the show. Still, to have Bischoff one-up him on live TV must've made him dream of having the last laugh.

However, Rude wasn't the same when he came back. Gone were the days of the flamboyant and ripped image that had made him a household name. He hadn't wrestled since his back injury in Japan for WCW back in 1994 and had lost a lot of weight and wasn't as outgoing anymore. I wondered if something was going on with him.

Rude was extremely withdrawn, unlike a lot of the boys who'd roam the halls making jokes or pulling pranks. Even though I didn't get to know Rude well, sometimes I'd see him sleeping while standing up. I didn't recognize them at the time, but these were telltale signs of a big problem. Aside from getting on the microphone and cutting some promos as Curt Hennig's manager with the nWo, he was off somewhere in Rick Rude land, collecting that Turner money.

On November 23, we all went through another crazy Sixty-Man Battle Royal at World War 3 1997 in Auburn Hills, Michigan, which Hall won.

The next day we had a match against the Faces of Fear, Meng and Barbarian, in Saginaw, Michigan. Both men are notorious for being legitimately tough, but one thing about Meng: he's got a legendary reputation. There were multitudes of stories of his exploits, such as biting a man's nose off in a bar for saying wrestling was fake, ripping out a guy's bottom row of teeth with two fingers, and knocking someone out with one slap to the face. One of the boys said he saw Meng get arrested and snap the handcuffs. I heard about him getting into it with Brutus Beefcake in the WWF and lifting him off the shower floor by his neck. Several guys tried to stop him, and Hogan was the only guy to convince him to stop.

I've been in fights personally and professionally and learned to quickly determine whether I could take a person in a real confrontation. Meng was one guy I saw and thought, *No way.* Fortunately, I never saw that side of him, and whether all those legends of Meng are true, I'll never know. I found him

BOOKER T. HUFFMAN

to be a great guy. I guess you just didn't want to make the mistake of offending him.

The Saginaw match set up a series of house shows with the Faces of Fear and even a *Nitro* in Knoxville, Tennessee, on December 1, where Lash took Meng's Death Grip to the mat, giving them the win. Even though it was rare for Lash to take the loss, it made Meng and the Faces of Fear look even stronger.

On December 15, I had a stiff back-and-forth singles battle with Randy Savage in Charlotte. It was great working on the fly with Savage due to his intensity and explosiveness.

On December 28, Starrcade 1997 featured the anticipated return of Sting versus Hollywood Hogan for the WCW World title in D.C. Harlem Heat was left off the card, but we were there on call for the event.

When those two finally met, it was the payoff fans had awaited for over seventeen months. Hogan pulled out all the classic heel tactics, sending Sting outside and throwing him into the barricade and post.

My pal Nick Patrick, who'd been playing a crooked nWo-favored referee, was officiating and was supposed to quick count Sting after Hogan dropped the leg at the end. Something got confused, though, and Nick didn't count it as quickly as was planned to give a screw-job-type finish.

Bret "The Hitman" Hart, who'd just signed over to WCW and had been the victim of a shoot screw job himself in the

WWF the month before, came out and had them restart the match. Sting grabbed Hogan and applied the Scorpion Death Lock, getting the improvised submission, and won the belt.

It was a weird situation, and the company worked in a story line over the botched finish and rebooted the concept by vacating the belt.

The two met again a few months later, and Sting won the title with authority, claiming victory over the nWo and vindicating his position with the WCW faithful.

On December 29, the day Brandon celebrated his fourteenth birthday, I stumbled into my biggest triumph in WCW. That night at the Baltimore Arena on *Nitro*, I simply filmed some pre-taped interviews and wasn't scheduled to wrestle. I was on my way out with Lash when one of the agents approached.

"Hey, Booker, get your gear on. You're wrestling Disco Inferno tonight for the WCW World Television Championship, and you're going over for the belt."

"Win the title? What are you talking about?"

He explained that Rick Martel, the former AWA World Champion and WWF Superstar, had forgotten his gear and lost his opportunity.

"You've got to be kidding me."

But they were dead serious. Martel thought he was doing only promo work in the back and hadn't brought his bag. My win would be a temporary solution, and after the New Year,

I'd drop the belt to him so he'd hold the title as originally planned. They decided I was the right performer to get Martel over during our potential match, making me their choice for that night's break against Disco.

When my music hit, for the first time I came out wearing only the bottom half of my purple-and-yellow-flamed gear. I'd always wanted to wear just trunks and boots, but as Harlem Heat we'd developed our uniform to perfect our dual image. I'd made a calculated decision that night while dressing to transition out of the double-strapped singlet top to indicate my transformation into a singles competitor.

The match went off perfectly. Disco had a great seventies look and a ton of charisma, and he was over with the crowd. He was flawless to work with and really brought it. We intuitively worked together, knowing both of us would seamlessly hit our entire standard repertoire. It was a textbook example of how two performers can go out in front of an arena and tell a powerful psychological wrestling story.

When I watched the playback, though, the commentary bothered me. Schiavone and Heenan talked about everything but the action in the ring. There Disco and I were, tearing the place down with a title match, and those two were talking about Hogan, Flair, and the nWo.

That was one thing I felt WCW often didn't get right. The commentary team was supposed to get the talent over as they were in the ring, not advertise Doritos or split screen to action from a match two weeks before—all of which they seemed to do for the undercard matches.

I think they spoke about Disco and me for three minutes of our six-and-a-half-minute contest, but right there in the ring, Disco and I were over with the crowd. It seemed they could sense my big moment coming. In the end, when Disco was laid out after a Harlem Side Slam, I pointed up and the people knew what was coming. I climbed to the top and hit the Harlem Hangover, grabbed his leg, and got the pin.

I was the new WCW World Television Champion. When the ref handed me the belt, I was overcome with emotion and looked right into the camera for a close-up. "Brandon, this is for you, baby! Happy birthday! Daddy's coming home!"

The people in the stands were jumping as my music played. When I turned around, Lash was already in the ring for a giant bear hug. It was an incredible moment I'll never forget.

CHAMPIONSHIPS	
WCW World Tag Team Championship	7
WCW World Television Championship	1
Total	8

Going into 1998, I was rising to the top tier. WCW's plan was to take the belt from me and give it to Martel, but my plan was to go out and perform even harder to show them the title was around the right waist. All I needed was a couple of weeks to go out and put on shows that would make them forget all about Rick Martel.

I was going to create a demand with the crowd for me to remain champion. If they'd give me two weeks defending the title on *WCW Saturday Night*, nobody could question the right decision had been made that evening when I'd faced Disco.

My World Television Championship didn't mean Harlem Heat had divided. Lash and I were still riding the roads as the badasses from 110th Street. This just meant double duty for me, and I'd often perform with my brother and then defend the belt in the same night.

I was able to renegotiate my contract for more money as well. Since the beginning, Lash and I had always made the same amount, but when my checks became larger, Lash never showed any animosity.

When we'd started out with the WWA in Houston and Global in Dallas, Lash was always the one getting the push because of his size. He was a big man with the power of a tank and even became the North American Heavyweight Champion.

Back then, I was the one who was overlooked but was always backing my brother, telling him, "Bro, go for it!"

Even though I wasn't on the championship radar back then, I did receive more than my fair share of support. Many guys pulled me aside in the back with words of encouragement. "Hey, Book, truth be told, your brother works well but not the way you do. You've got that extra fire."

I only hoped that if my day came, I'd make Lash as proud as he'd always made me.

Just a couple of tag team matches into January with consecutive wins over High Voltage, the team of Robbie Rage and Kenny Kaos, Lash was injured. He tore a part of the arch muscle in his right foot and was out of action for a few months, sitting at home in Houston.

Meanwhile, I stayed focused on defending the TV title from Rick Martel.

My first stand was at the Georgia Dome against Prince Iaukea on January 5, when I won in high fashion before moving on to The Forum in Rome, Georgia, for another victory over Disco. I was lighting the crowd up and keeping the office impressed.

Meanwhile, Bischoff was expanding the empire by creating an entirely new two-hour show called *WCW Thunder*. It was taped on Tuesdays and aired on TBS Thursdays at 8:00 p.m. Here was another chance for me to climb the company ladder.

On January 18, we stopped off at Shreveport, where I defended my TV title and beat the mighty Meng while managing to *not* take the Tongan Death Grip. Because Shreveport wasn't far from my birthplace of Plain Dealing, I could always count on family members to come to shows there: aunts, uncles, and even a ton of new faces claiming to be cousins. They couldn't believe the hometown kid had made it, famous and on weekly TV. Even I found it hard to believe.

The next night at the Superdome in New Orleans, an angle with Martel and me started. After I beat Mortis with the Hangover, his partner, Wrath, came out and attacked me as I was celebrating. While I was getting beaten down with stomps to the head, Rick Martel came running in and made the save and cleared the ring.

As a result, I told him he deserved a shot at the TV title at Souled Out 1998 in Dayton on January 24. It was now going to be the babyface challenger Martel against the baby-face champion in a showdown for the gold, just as the company planned.

When it was finally go time at the PPV, we had a blistering match. It goes without saying that Rick was a stellar athlete with amazing conditioning. I'd really been working on so-lidifying certain go-to maneuvers in my matches and used ev-erything available to me in that particular performance. For example, I had Martel down and bounced off the ropes for a simple elbow drop, which I'd always miss because that set me up to immediately corkscrew right back up with my break-dancing backspin, yet to be named the Spinarooni, up to my feet and right into the Harlem Sidekick.

When it was time to bring it home, I gave Martel the Harlem Side Slam and raised the roof to the audience before going for the Harlem Hangover and the resulting pin. When it was over, in a show of respect, Martel took the belt from the referee, handed it to me, and raised my hand. It was an epic showdown I was proud to be a part of.

Martel and I still had unfinished business with the TV title, which we would address again three weeks later.

In the meantime, I defended the championship a couple of times against the talented and hard-hitting Perry Saturn in Fort Wayne, Indiana, then again in Memphis, Tennessee. Each time his stable, known as The Flock, consisting of Raven, Kidman, Sick Boy, Lodi, and Riggs, interfered, prompting Martel to come in and make the save.

Then in Boston on January 31, I squared off with Mike Rotunda, who was going by the name Michael Wallstreet in WCW, a play on his famous WWF character, I.R.S.

Mike was a world-renowned talent and one of the greatest performers the business has ever seen. To be in the ring and see him work his craft was awesome. He did business and, when I pinned him with my spin kick, put me over like a true professional.

A week later, *Nitro* broadcasted from the Alamodome in San Antonio. I looked out at twenty thousand screaming nWo fans and finally faced off with Steven Regal. With a style all his own, he had an amazing arsenal of signature moves, including a weird European uppercut and, of course, his double-standing knee smash, which made it look like he'd killed a guy.

At first, realizing how good he was, I followed his lead. But when we were ready, he quickly switched gears and let me take over with a Harlem Sidekick for the loss.

Regal was equally entertaining to watch, which was the case when I had the pleasure of seeing him put on a well-known display with one of the biggest company stars to emerge during that era.

Bill Goldberg, WCW's six-feet-three, 280-pound answer to the WWF's "Stone Cold" Steve Austin, had debuted the previous September with a UFC look and feel. Goldberg found out firsthand what Regal was all about.

In the ring one week after our Alamodome bout, Regal decided to school Goldberg on national TV. I think he simply felt Goldberg couldn't wrestle his way out of a paper bag and wanted to introduce him to the business with a shoot. Steven unloaded some pretty stiff shots and twisted Bill up like a pretzel. Goldberg was visibly shaken and neutralized.

When it was over, the boys in the back were in awe that Regal had the balls to do it. Privately, they patted him on the back, and to my knowledge, Goldberg never said a word.

On February 16 in Tampa, Rick Martel and I had our rematch from Souled Out 1998. I dropped the TV title to him but not without incident. Things went awry when I gave him a hip toss out of the corner. He landed awkwardly on one of the ropes and tore his right ACL. He didn't indicate he was injured, and we continued as Saturn interfered and was up on the apron antagonizing Rick, who went over and clocked him to the floor. We finished the match with me tapping to the Quebec Crab, making Martel the new, injured champion.

Afterward, we talked about it in the back and Rick expressed no hard feelings, but I felt horrible about it.

Due to the extent of his injury, Rick would soon need to give the title up to me. At SuperBrawl VIII in San Francisco on February 22, Rick geared up for his last time in WCW. Even in pain and with limited movement with the torn ACL, he went out there and gave his heart and soul in a ten-minute performance to put me over and allow me to regain the WCW World Television title.

CHAMPIONSHIPS	
WCW World Tag Team Championship	7
WCW World Television Championship	2
Total	9

There was a pre-match stipulation that Saturn, who was sitting at ringside, would get an immediate shot at the TV title at the conclusion of our match. As soon as I pinned Martel with the Harlem Sidekick, that little wolverine Saturn jumped the barrier and put the Rings of Saturn on me.

It was grueling back-to-back work. I'd told Saturn before to control the pace until I got my second wind and then I'd be ready. "Try to beat me, man, as hard as you can. Pull it all out."

And that's what he did, testing me to the absolute limits in a performance I still consider one of the most mentally and physically challenging of my career.

As planned, I disposed of Saturn with a Sidekick and retained my WCW World Television Championship.

9

THE BEST OF SEVEN

After the marathon challenge of Martel and Saturn, I couldn't wait to get home and decompress while awaiting my next line of booking. It turned out that subsequent assignment would be WCW stationing me in the cruiserweight division with the likes of Saturn, Raven, Chris Jericho, Chris Benoit, Dean Malenko, and Eddie Guerrero. I think after the company witnessed how versatile my performances could be from working with guys as big as Kevin Nash down to smaller talents like Saturn, they saw a new avenue for me. I was a heavyweight at around 240 pounds, but my agility and speed could match, if not supersede, any of the wrestlers under six feet tall and around 225 pounds.

I loved getting in there and working matches like the February 26 *Thunder* taping, where I teamed up with Malenko against Eddie and Jericho. We went a little under eight minutes as if it were eight seconds, and we had so much fun. I remember club-clotheslining Eddie right in the face and picking him up for a rare overhead press. I'd never done the move before, but because of his size, I was able to improvise all day just to entertain the fans and myself.

The crowd was all over Guerrero, shouting, "Eddie sucks! Eddie sucks!"

He ate it up like the great heel he was.

I still had the belt, so there was meaningful weight behind every match. The TV title kept me grounded with the prospect I'd be moving up to a more powerful position if I just kept going out there and giving the fans my best.

And so my singles odyssey began. I started looping the country in matches with all the cruiserweights, defending the TV title four or five days per week at house shows, on TV, and on PPVs.

The rest of the late winter into early spring was a blur of wrestling not only the cruiserweights but the Mexican *luchadores* as well—Psicosis, La Parka, Mysterio, all of them. I enjoyed every moment, especially because the new challenges developed my skills. The people loved the diverse mixture of athletes I faced, and I knew the boys in the back, including the agents and office staff, got a kick out of it too.

It was hot, explosive action serving as a segue in the middle of the card that drew TV ratings, keeping viewers tuned from the *luchador* openers to the main event scene with Hogan, Hall, and Nash. That was my job for the time being.

All through March, I defeated Chavo Guerrero Jr., Saturn, and Raven. I even pinned Eddie at Uncensored 1998 in

Mobile, Alabama, with a missile dropkick, my top-rope alternative finisher to the Harlem Hangover. I started reserving the Hangover not only to preserve my body but also to make it more dramatic when I used it in a big event like a PPV or title match.

I kept up the pace day after day, going to a ten-minute time-limit draw in Louisville on March 23 with Chris Benoit, one of the toughest guys I'd ever worked with. He was a relentless performer who could go all day, and it was a good thing because we were about to be shackled together for almost three months. Starting at Spring Stampede in Denver on April 19, where I pinned Benoit, we went straight into a rivalry and championship trade-off unlike any the business had never seen.

CHAMPIONSHIPS	
WCW World Tag Team Championship	7
WCW World Television Championship	3
Total	10

CHAMPIONSHIPS	
WCW World Tag Team Championship	7
WCW World Television Championship	4
Total	11

In Augusta on April 30, Benoit submitted me for the title with the Crippler Crossface, only for me to pin him in Greenville, South Carolina, on May 1 to regain it.

The next night in North Charleston, South Carolina, he again defeated me for the belt with the Crossface only to lose it the next night in Savannah. I thought the competition was interesting and kept the elements of realism and surprise alive for the fans. It wasn't the typical scenario where a guy had a belt and seemed to keep it forever, as Hogan and Flair had in the eighties. Even Chris and I didn't know what creative would have us do. The unpredictability was far from the professional wrestling standard.

Finally on May 4 in Indianapolis, while Benoit was distracted at ringside, I dropped the title to the take-no-prisoners Irish brawler Fit Finlay, courtesy of his inverted tombstone piledriver.

This would ultimately lead to a seven-week smash-mouth drama to determine the top contender for Finlay's TV title. What unfolded between Benoit and me challenged us and drew out some of the very best work either of us would ever be known for.

Dusty came up to Benoit and me after one of our matches and said he had a great idea. "You guys have been stealing the show out there every night. We want to take it to the next level and create something really special, something historic, for the people. We're going to have you enter into a Best of Seven Series leading up to The Great American Bash where the winner will beat Finlay for the belt."

Chris and I looked at each other, wide-eyed. I think we were both wondering, *Why not best two out of three?*

Dusty, always being old school, was likely thinking of paying homage to his old buddy Magnum T.A.

Back in 1986, Magnum had an intense rivalry with

Nikita Koloff, which culminated in a Best of Seven Series for the United States title.

Arn Anderson was another proponent. "You guys will be doing something that hasn't been done in a long time. It'll be great!"

I was thinking, *Man, who's gonna want to see this?*

In all honesty, both Benoit and I thought they were doing it to get rid of us because they didn't have any better angles at the time. It was like being shoved into wrestling purgatory. I didn't think we could pull it off. Wouldn't it get repetitive to the viewers seeing the same two babyfaces out there on *Nitro* and *Thunder* and then a major PPV like the Bash? We could come up with some different ideas for each match, but I didn't know if the viewers would stick with us.

But that was the challenge put before us, and we'd have to go out there and get the job done. We needed to strategize to work harder and smarter to put on the best performances possible.

The series began on May 19 in Portland at a *Saturday Night* taping, where Chris beat me with a German suplex. Getting a feel for the showcase Dusty and Arn were trying to present, we turned up the heat. Over the next couple of weeks, it started having the vibe of the World Series.

We were all over the place. Indiana, Tennessee, D.C., Illinois. At every venue, our goal was to put on the greatest show on earth. The people started getting invested in it, and the ratings indicated a huge spike during our matches.

We kept trading wins with different finishes. Chris pulled out his Crippler Crossface, flying headbutt from the top, and triple German suplex. I demonstrated my missile dropkick, Harlem Sidekick, and the Harlem Hangover.

We used multiple near falls, high-flying maneuvers, eye pokes, low blows—everything we could think of to heighten each other's performance and trade the role of the heel. We turned up the volume by putting me at a three-to-one deficit to give the underdog element to it all.

Together, we kept the crowd's interest soaring.

Right in the middle of all this, I got married. When I'd first started dating Levestia, marriage was the last thing on my mind, but the more I thought about it and looked at the married men around me and imagined Brandon with a dependable mother figure in the house, the more I'd convinced myself it was the right step.

Levestia and I exchanged vows in an elegant but small ceremony in her hometown of Birmingham, Alabama. Only our immediate families were invited, and afterward, I whisked her away to the Bahamas on a relaxing cruise.

It was hard to believe that in the midst of the chaos of the Best of Seven Series, Levestia and I were sipping champagne on the beach. I was a married man, in the fiercest competition I'd ever faced, and for a frozen moment in time, everything was crystalline.

While I was away and we were on a short break, Chris tended to an elbow injury he'd been working through. By the time The Great American Bash 1998 arrived on June 14 in Baltimore, we were all tied up at three wins each. It was the only way to book it properly for the whole concept of the series. I defeated Chris that night with the missile dropkick.

After a brief rest between matches, I went right into the championship affair with Fit Finlay. Ironically, I beat him with his own move, the tombstone piledriver, which was Fit's idea. I wanted to win with one of my own moves, but when we discussed things in the back, he was adamant about that finish. Out of respect, I agreed. He put me over, and the WCW World Television Championship came back to my waist for the fifth time. Lash even came into the ring to congratulate me, just as he had the first time I'd won against Disco, which meant a lot to me.

CHAMPIONSHIPS	
WCW World Tag Team Championship	7
WCW World Television Championship	5
Total	12

Though it had begun as a ridiculous idea to Chris and me, the Best of Seven Series resulted in some of the best work we'd both ever done. Having gone through that experience, so psychologically entrenched together, made it feel almost like we were war buddies.

As Lash continued to recuperate and heal from his foot injury,

I was still on my own and Harlem Heat seemed to be fading in the rearview mirror. In such a short time, I'd gone from competing in a tag team with my brother to consistently facing competitors alone.

Now there was no one but myself to rely on to put on a dynamic show. I had to take destiny into my own two hands the way I'd learned to in Houston while growing up.

It's easy to get comfortable with the security of a supportive partner or family, but if you woke up one day and they were gone, what would you do? Could you handle it, or would you fall apart? It reminded me of a trip that I'd taken before my singles career began.

It was shortly before Sherri's TV firing about two years earlier, and we were still running strong as the Harlem Heat trio. Bischoff had been developing a relationship with New Japan Pro Wrestling and thought the three of us would be a perfect showcase of the WCW product over there. My brother and I would come from 110th Street to destroy teams and take names, much as The Road Warriors did when they debuted there in 1985. Plus, we had planned to bring Sherri back with us, which would've shocked them since it was unorthodox to have a female manager. Imagine Sherri going over there screaming her head off at ringside. It would've been completely out of place to them. So the idea was set, and we were ready to go.

But then Lash got injured and couldn't wrestle.

Bischoff said, "You and Sherri go by yourselves, and you'll perform singles matches and still pull it off."

That was fine with me. I got to the airport and was waiting for Sherri to arrive. When she did, her bright red lipstick was applied like a clown's—literally all around her lips in a big oval. She was a mess.

The agents took one glance at her and cancelled her trip.

They looked at me and said, "How would you like to go by yourself?"

"Hell, yeah, I'll go by myself!"

And so I did, but the unique team dynamic had degenerated into a potentially dull one-man show. Instead of Harlem Heat and Sister Sherri invading Japan like American monsters, I went over there and did my best to entertain the Japanese audience, losing battle after battle.

In the end, I just made sure that even in defeat, I shined in every match. I tore the house down at the Tokyo Dome, pulling out everything in my arsenal before taking the nightly fall for whatever hometown guy they threw at me.

Bischoff was watching. Late after a show, at about two in the morning, he was good and drunk but had something on his mind. He came to my hotel room and said, "Book, I'm going to make you a rich man after what I saw you do out there tonight. I saw the reaction. I saw everything. The people were amazed. *I* was amazed."

Right then and there in that room, I felt validated in

everything I'd ever done in professional wrestling. I'd made the right choices, maintained a professional attitude, shown respect, but even more importantly, I'd been patient. I'd always told myself that in due time, my talents and character would be recognized. And now it was happening in a big way.

While being defeated night after night in Japan, I still won. That's when I knew my breakout time was at hand. In the summer of 1998, it was just starting to come into view.

Another indication I was headed in the right direction came after the Best of Seven, when Bret Hart came into the picture. Bret had debuted for WCW the previous December on *Nitro*, pledging allegiance to the nWo after having signed a contract with Bischoff to leave the WWF. Because he was the WWF Champion nearing the time of his departure from the company, according to rumors, he was the victim of a legitimate and infamous controversy known as the Montreal Screwjob at the Survivor Series on November 9, 1997.

Even though I was in the business, I knew as much about the infamous moment as any other fan did. As the story went, the WWF was concerned that Bret would bail to WCW, taking the WWF Championship belt along as a hostage trophy and making a mockery of it on *Nitro*, much as Madusa did when she left with the WWF Women's title.

To prevent that, in the middle of Bret's match with Shawn Michaels, the decision was made to have referee Earl Hebner make a false call for the bell due to a submission. The second Shawn Michaels applied Bret's own Sharpshooter hold on him, it was over. Hart was declared the loser. They gave the belt to Michaels, and Bret got up legitimately shocked and upset, motioning with his hand the huge letters *WCW*. Fans everywhere knew exactly where he was headed.

I always wondered if the whole thing was a work developed between Bret and Vince to generate some huge publicity for the WWF and Hart himself. They easily could've pulled that off and played it as if it were a real situation. It was fairly convenient, as Bret had been filming his *Hitman Hart: Wrestling with Shadows* documentary, which captured the events before, during, and after the whole thing went down.

Nobody knows. After all, the whole business is about telling a story to sell the product. Only Vince, Bret, and Michaels know for sure, and I think they'll take that answer to the grave.

During the last of my Best of Seven with Benoit on *Nitro*, Bret Hart came down to interfere on Chris's behalf and help him beat me. His goal was to convince him to join the nWo. I have to admit, Bret's presence in a WCW ring was even more impressive than when Hogan, Savage, or Hall and Nash hopped over. When Benoit realized what went down, he told the ref. He didn't want to win the belt that way. Bret was disgusted and berated Benoit. Since Chris failed to take the TV title,

Bret decided *he* was going to take my gold, and thus our angle was established.

That was one nobody saw coming. Bischoff and that Turner money had worked their wrestling voodoo yet again. At that point, anything could've happened and it wouldn't have surprised me in the slightest. The Undertaker or Shawn Michaels could've walked in backstage and I wouldn't have blinked.

Looking around WCW at that time, I felt like the company had flipped upside down. All the ex-WWF inmates were now effectively running the place, but it felt like we were the unbeatable business model in professional wrestling at the time.

Working with Bret was an honor. Like Flair, who'd wanted to perform with me at Center Stage Theater back in 1993, Bret had requested to work with me. I'd admired Bret as a craftsman since his WWF days in the eighties with Jim "The Anvil" Neidhart as The Hart Foundation and when he broke away into his own singles career in the pink-and-black attack gear. He understood storytelling in the ring as few others did, and when we met in San Diego on July 12 at Bash at the Beach 1998 in his first WCW Championship Match, his in-ring craftsmanship blew me away.

Before we tied up, we stared each other down, and I shoved him to set the tone for a fight. Instead of pushing me back, he walked around the ring with his classic hands-out expression, saying, "So much for being Mister Nice Guy."

He kept that shove in mind, and later he pushed me.

I retaliated with the same, never letting him get the upper hand. He was playing the outpowered but never outsmarted heel the whole time, and that's what he did best. The Excellence of Execution didn't disappoint, and our match was exactly what we expected. I hit him with everything I had, and he bumped and rolled around, biding his time until it was opportune for him to stretch and test me. It's what he was taught by his father, Stu, in the famed Hart Family Dungeon in the basement of their home in Calgary.

After I hit him with the missile dropkick and nearly got the pin, he hung his foot on the ropes, stopping the count, and rolled to the floor. Not one to let him recuperate, I launched myself over the top rope, hoping to land on Bret with a flaying body press. But Bret had grabbed a chair, and while I was in midair, he slammed me with it, causing me to come crashing to the ground. While I lay there, Bret continued his assault by slamming me with the chair again and rolling me into the ring so everyone could see him pummel me. As the chair came crashing down on me again, Bret remembered my injured leg and began attacking it mercilessly with the chair.

Earlier in the spring, I'd sustained a legitimate injury when Psicosis's baseball slid out of the ring and into my right knee. As soon as it had happened, I realized something was wrong but continued to wrestle over the months, even in the Best of Seven. It was just some cartilage damage, but sometimes during a contest, my knee would lock out and I'd have to shake it to snap it free. I needed a story line departure to be able to set up surgery. As it turned out, the match with Bret was my perfect out.

After working over my knee, Bret hit a hanging upside-down figure four on me against the ring post. It's a painful-looking maneuver that really stretches your legs and hyperextends your kneecap. It felt like I was locked up there, writhing in agony, forever before the crowd erupted. Lash was calmly walking down to ringside to break up the assault. When he finally got to the outside corner, Bret released the hold and slowly walked away.

Lash looked at me with disappointment, never once trying to help me up. After a few minutes, he rolled me out of the ring as the ref yelled for him to take it easy on me. Lash looked at the ref and said, "Shut up!" as he dragged my body out of the ring and loosely assisted me to the back, with the ref helping to support my weight.

It was classic wrestling drama between two brothers. With me out of the picture and Lash's foot recovered, it was decided that in my absence, he would assume control of the TV title and defend it in my name.

Bret lost by DQ so I could take time off to get the procedure taken care of and rehabilitate for a return. That finish made him look like a hideous heel who would resort to the most vicious tactics to hurt somebody, and he was really happy with the results. I was satisfied too because if there had to be an angle to write me off TV, having my knee destroyed by Bret Hart on a PPV was the way to do it.

After my knee surgery, I sat at home for almost four months. I was thankful Levestia was there helping me through the process. Now we could focus on establishing our new life together. I was trying to be a good dad to my fourteen-year-old boy, who was becoming a young man before my very eyes. Levestia's sixteen-year-old son, who lived in Mississippi, visited sometimes. He seemed good-natured enough at first, but I began to have concerns about the way he talked to his mom. The four of us weren't exactly a perfect family, but we were doing our best to make it work.

I was also having a rough time trying to rehab my knee. Instead of getting physical therapy, as any professional athletic entertainer should, I slowly started working out again on my own until it felt stable. I felt like I just needed to get back to work as quickly as humanly possible to avoid losing the ground I'd been gaining in my singles career. I found myself getting depressed about it and questioning whether I'd ever be able to perform the same again. Could I jump as high? Could I hit all my signature kicks or the Hangover?

I'd watch Lash on TV doing his best to capture my essence as champ, but the people weren't buying it. They remembered his callous attitude toward me when I was attacked by the Hitman, and when he wrestled Chavo, the people were all over him: "Stevie Ray sucks! Booker T! Booker T!" I knew it ate him up, and I never really understood why creative put him in that awkward position. But since he was a natural heel, his intimidating presence would eventually be welcomed by the nWo.

I was also watching the WWF to see what the competition was up to. I'd see guys like The Rock, whom a lot of people considered to be my counterpart. He was already a huge household name, and his stardom made me question myself. "Man, that guy's really good. Would I measure up if given the chance?"

I never doubted my physical talent. That wasn't the issue. It was just that the WWF stars were bigger than life in the mainstream media. I was only Booker T making my way up the ladder at WCW. Despite everything we'd done to build our name and following, WCW was always seen as the smaller group from the South, while the WWF came off like an impenetrable megalopolis of slick Hollywood production.

Because I was so impatient to return to the ring, I even went to shows here and there to check in with the story lines, also letting Bischoff know how my knee was coming along. I didn't want to be a complete stranger upon returning, so it was good to sit around with the boys and absorb the product again.

While I was out, I missed the bulk of the return and dismissal of the very last of the big old-school WWF names to join WCW: the Ultimate Warrior, though by then he was simply called Warrior. From what I remember, he wasn't much of a people person. He simply came in, did his thing, and left. His promos were cut in private at select times, and he had his own personal dressing room with all his Warrior gear in there. Keeping the Warrior mystique intact, he'd come in to lose to Hogan at Halloween Havoc 1998 in Vegas on October 25. Later we'd hear he'd left the company after a dispute with Bischoff.

I made my own way back to work on October 30 at far less than 100 percent. My first match was in Lubbock, Texas, where I defeated Wrath. I was afraid I'd blow out my knee on my first spin kick or even a simple leapfrog, but thankfully the knee held up without any issues. I could lay my fears to rest and concentrate on fully getting back in the game.

10

THE DOWNWARD SPIRAL BEGINS

After I got that first comeback match out of the way with Wrath, my motivation kicked in. I wanted as many performances as possible to finish out 1998 strong and show the world I was standing tall once more.

On November 2 in Fort Lauderdale, I beat Hall by DQ and never looked back. Four and five nights a week, I was going in there and putting on displays with Disco Inferno, Konnan, Brian Adams, and Jericho. Even Bret and I squared off again. No matter the circumstances, whether it was a PPV or a Saturday night house show, Bret and I always stole the show.

On November 22, the separation of Lash and me was succinctly stated at World War 3 after his match with Konnan. Lash was now with the nWo, and during his match, his ally Vincent accidentally hit Lash in the head with a metal object called the slapjack. He went down like a ton of bricks, and Konnan pounced on him, punching him over and over again. When the ref tried to stop the beat-down, Konnan shoved him and was immediately disqualified. It didn't matter to

Konnan, though, as he continued pummeling my brother. When I ran in to help, Konnan stopped the assault and backed off. I began to help Lash up, but he shoved me away, pointing to Vincent and saying, "That's my brother right there! I don't need your help!"

I stood there acting it up with a confused look on my face.

The two of them walked away with the distinct music of the nWo blaring, leaving me alone in the middle of the ring.

The fans understood the story being told: Harlem Heat was dead. The separation was necessary for our careers to move forward, but Lash and I definitely had each other to thank for how far we'd come.

There was a transitional period for me to close out the year as I maintained midcard singles matches. I wasn't in on the action at the company's showcase PPV at Starrcade 1998 in December, but I knew I was incubating into a new form. With the New Year at hand, there was no question in my mind I'd make big things happen in WCW.

When 1999 hit, there was a lot of talk about the looming new millennium. Theories flew around that everything would malfunction when Y2K hit. For me, though, the future looked bright.

Unfortunately, as I aspired to rise to the top of WCW, the company fell into a downward spiral it could never reverse.

Straight out of the gate on the January 4 edition of *Nitro* from the Georgia Dome, Bischoff, Hogan, and the rest of the power holders backstage cut the legs right out from underneath WCW. By this time, the WWF's programming ratings had eclipsed ours.

While Bischoff was spending loads of Turner money to bring Vince McMahon's talent to our side, the WWF mogul quietly rebuilt his empire. In the meantime, the nWo, which was responsible for skyrocketing us to number one, had lost its edge. Instead of a unified, unstoppable force destroying the WCW roster from the inside out, the nWo became a parody of itself. Nash and Hall formed their own clique called the nWo Wolfpac, along with Savage, Sting, Lex Luger, and Konnan as a group of babyfaces. Meanwhile, nWo Hollywood remained a heel stable with Hogan and guys like Bischoff, Norton, Brian Adams, Horace Hogan, and my brother.

Those two groups had been feuding with each other since the spring of 1998. However, January 4 on *Nitro*, they cooked up a plan to reunite as a solidified stable. The plot backfired.

Nash, the WCW World Heavyweight Champion, squared off with Hogan that night for the title. Just as they were about to lock up, Hulk poked Kevin in the chest. Nash fell as if he'd been shot by a sniper, and Hogan pinned him for the belt. Nash jumped up, and they hugged and laughed.

The fans didn't buy it. The incident became forever known as the Fingerpoke of Doom, and people's interest in the nWo fell by the wayside.

That was only the half of it.

During the broadcast, because the WWF's *Raw* was still taped days in advance, Bischoff knew that Cactus Jack, then performing under a leather mask as Mankind, had already won the WWF Championship from The Rock. He thought it would be a great idea to have Tony Schiavone make an announcement.

"If you're even thinking about changing the channels to our competition, fans, do not," Tony Schiavone said, "because we understand that Mick Foley, who wrestled here one time as Cactus Jack, is going to win their world title. Ugh, that's going to put some butts in the seats."

And it did. The TV ratings indicated nearly six hundred thousand fans immediately switched over to *Raw* to watch Foley win the title, and many never came back to WCW programming.

With those two massive backfires, our year began. The breakdown would continue in WCW over the next twelve months.

At the same time, Bischoff and WCW continued to invest in me. I was ready to go out and blow the roof off of every challenge they put in front of me. My first big match of the year was on January 25, and it was with my man Bret Hart on *Nitro*. When I came out, it was with a bang—literally. The production crew rigged up an amazing explosion of fire and flash pots to go off as I came down the ramp with my single-leg, stutter-step, raise-the-roof, double-arm gesture. Man, the adrenalized pop immediately set the mood for me to take over with some serious heat. For extra drama, I held the pose for a second while the flames burned behind me.

I was a maestro with the crowd as my orchestra. As I walked down the aisle, the people went crazy, and I saw Booker T signs everywhere. While scanning the audience on my way around the ring, I even noticed Chuck Norris standing in the front row, cheering.

Bret and I started the match similar to the way we'd kicked off Bash at the Beach 1998. When he went for the Mr. Nice Guy handshake, I slapped it away and said, "Get that shit out of here!"

Bret, the master showman, walked away, shrugged for sympathy, and we were off. It was another great match with tremendous chemistry. He was the WCW United States Heavyweight Champion by this point after beating DDP the previous July, and I was in the running for the belt.

Bret worked smart. When I kept turning up the speed and took too much control, he'd duck out of the ring. It was a perfect heel tactic. We finished out the performance with him getting the pin after hitting me with the belt when the ref wasn't looking.

Another memorable meeting was logged in the books.

At SuperBrawl IX in Oakland on February 21, I beat one of the nWo members, Disco Inferno, yet again with the Hangover. In fact, Disco may hold the record for taking the most

Harlem Hangovers in WCW.

The next night on *Nitro* in Sacramento, I faced off with Bret one more time in a full twenty-minute match. It was another classic that ended when I went to the top for the Hangover, but Bret quickly got up and caught me on the ropes. He delivered a huge top-rope superplex on me that shook the entire ring and popped the crowd.

We both lay there, our broken bodies not moving as the ref began to count us down. "One! Two! Three!" Still neither of us moved. If the ref made it to ten, we'd both be counted out and the match would be a no contest.

"Four! Five! Six!" Still no movement as we used the precious seconds to catch our breath.

By the time the ref counted, "Seven," Bret was on his way up.

"Eight!" Bret, now fully to his feet, grabbed my legs and rolled me over for the Sharpshooter.

Thankfully I was near the ropes, and before I could submit to the pain, I grabbed the middle rope, causing the ref to break the hold.

Closing in for the kill, he picked me up and whipped me into the ropes, but I reversed. He came toward me and went for a sunset flip. As he went over, he tried to hook my legs for the sure victory, but I stopped his momentum and sat on his chest, cradling his legs for the clean three count, and walked away the winner and the number-one contender to the United States title.

Unfortunately, when I watched the match afterward, right in the middle of it, the program cut for about a full minute to some angle unfolding in the back with Disco Inferno wanting to pirate the WCW broadcast for the nWo. I was disappointed and brought it up to Bret the next time we met backstage.

"Did you see what they did during our match with that cutaway?"

He shook his head. "I don't get it, Book. What are these people doing?"

But we'd never get an answer about the way WCW conducted their broadcasting.

In February, another disappointment came when The Giant left. He didn't like the atmosphere in WCW anymore and saw great opportunity and a lucrative contract at the WWF. He debuted first as his real name, Paul Wight, and received a huge push right out of the gate in a match against Mankind at WrestleMania XV.

The Giant was a huge talent, literally, and he'd slipped right through Bischoff's fingers to become a WWF Superstar. The role reversal had begun. WCW had become obsessed with luring away all of Vince's old talent, but now he was coming for our younger, disillusioned guys.

Almost two weeks later, after my match with Bret on *Nitro*, I was in Winston-Salem, North Carolina, at *Thunder* and teamed up with Rey Mysterio against Scotty Steiner and Bagwell. I hit Bagwell with the missile dropkick from the top, immediately followed by a big splash from Rey, but the real angle was Scotty attacking me with a steel chair directly after. We were setting up for another run like the old days, only without our brothers.

Since our last encounters a couple of years prior in the tag division, Steiner had made a dynamic career transformation. A year earlier, he'd turned total heel on his brother, attacking Rick in a tag match at SuperBrawl VIII, and joined the nWo. Then he started appearing with short, bleach-blond hair and matching goatee with a black strip down the middle of his chin. Instead of the usual amateur-wrestling singlet, he wore tight shorts with a Superman logo. But the biggest change was his attitude. The formerly reserved babyface now took center stage with an egomaniacal rage. He referred to himself as Big Poppa Pump and the Big Bad Booty Daddy and cut loud promos about beating people's asses and getting all the ladies, complete with a new catchphrase: "Big Poppa Pump is your hookup. Holler if you hear me!" He kept it funny and exciting and still pulled off all the same devastating moves, only now he was the jacked-up and evil Man of Steel.

Scotty was the TV champ at the time, and we were booked into a program that started on *Nitro* in Worcester, Massachusetts, on March 8. I lost after Bagwell pushed me from the top turnbuckle. The kids in the front row were all over Scotty, chanting right in his face, "Steroids! Steroids!" I think if he'd had the chance, he might've gone over there to smack them all across their faces.

The Worcester served as a great warm-up for our impending match at Uncensored 1999 in Louisville on March 14. That night I took the belt after Bagwell tried to hit me with a steel chair shot, but I ducked and he hit Steiner instead. That win gave me the WCW World Television Championship for the sixth time.

CHAMPIONSHIPS	
WCW World Tag Team Championship	7
WCW World Television Championship	6
Total	13

With the TV title soundly around my waist yet again, my exposure was maximized on WCW programming. Afterward, they entered me into a tournament for the vacant United States title, and I won my first-round match against Saturn on March 18 in Lexington. Then I beat Jericho in the semifinals on April 5 in Vegas. Finally, at Spring Stampede 1999 in Tacoma, Washington, on April 11, I lost to Scotty after he nailed me with a foreign object during a suplex attempt on him.

On April 20, we were all hit with the news that Rick Rude had died. He'd been on my radar since returning to WCW, when I'd seen him regularly incapacitated outside of the ring. Sadly, Rude died at the age of forty and left behind a wife and three children. Rude was a legend in the business. His passing served as another warning of untimely deaths in the business.

Back on the road as TV champ over the course of the next month, I beat guys like Norton, Meng, and Hennig on the way to Slamboree 1999 on May 9 in St. Louis.

My right knee was locking out on me again, and I knew right away the cartilage damage had returned. I had no one to blame but myself for not seeking physical therapy after surgery the previous summer. There was no way to escape having surgery again, so I had to put Steiner over for the title.

It seemed like I was well on my way to a win against Rick. Then Scotty, who'd since reconciled with his older sibling, appeared and tripped me while running the ropes. His brother picked me up and delivered the bulldog for the pin.

Written off TV for another few months, I went home to go under the knife. I had my knee scoped and cleaned out for the second time, but it wasn't as bad as the first experience. Over the course of the following seven weeks, I made sure to take my time, visit my physical therapist, and work through the pain the right way to ensure a proper return.

While I recovered, more tragic news came May 23 when Bret's brother, Owen Hart, fell from the rafters of the Kemper Arena in Kansas City. It was for the WWF's Over the Edge 1999 PPV. Appearing as the Blue Blazer, he was scheduled to rappel seventy feet down to the ring, but he stepped off the main beam without the cable harness secured. He plunged to the ring, and his body suffered insurmountable trauma upon impact. He was taken to the hospital, but attempts to revive him failed. At the age of thirty-four, he left this world far too soon.

Hearing the news made me feel nauseated. I'd met Owen only once, but I'd heard nothing but amazing things about him as a human being and family man.

I immediately thought of his brother. I could only imagine the pain of his loss. Bret took a leave of absence to mourn and help with his brother's final affairs. He eventually returned in the fall, but he wasn't the same. It was as if a piece of him were missing.

Between physical therapy sessions, I was obsessed with watching all the wrestling programming on TV, from *Thunder* and *Nitro* to the WWF's *Raw* and *SmackDown* (*SD*), and I didn't like what I saw. Not being involved with the product at the time gave me the perspective of a fan I wouldn't have had otherwise. The WWF's shows were much more compelling than our presentations.

I knew I had to return to action in the ring and do my part to help WCW get back on top, so I called Bischoff. "I'm almost healed up. Can you line something up for me?"

To my surprise, he said, "Nah, don't worry about it. Just take a couple more months and heal up. Everything's fine. Take it easy, and we'll bring you back when the time's right."

"Okay," I said, but I thought, *The time is now. We're*

getting whupped.

While I sat and got aggravated over the state of affairs in WCW, my home life was also falling apart. After a year, my marriage was already getting strained. I don't think Levestia anticipated what being married to a full-time professional wrestler on the road would be like. Every time I was on the way to the airport, Levestia seemed to feel like I was going to a big party she wasn't invited to. She'd call me after a show. I'd be at a restaurant or a bar, and she'd want to know who I was with, what I was doing, and whether I was telling her the truth or just what she wanted to hear. And it continued when I came home. I started to dread going back to Houston at the end of the week. Something had to give.

The stress of our marriage only exacerbated my uneasiness about WCW when I watched the company losing its edge on TV. Meanwhile, the WWF had now emerged with some of the most irreverent and creative booking in their history, with performers like Triple H, Mankind, Kane, Stone Cold, The Rock, D-X, and Kurt Angle. Sometimes I'd be so impressed, I'd think, *Man, I wish I was in the WWF! I need to get back on a winning team.*

The last thing I wanted was to get blown back to WCW's past of bingo halls, state fairs, and VFWs. Honestly, though, I felt I could help WCW get its edge back if I had the chance. I wanted to hang around and find out, so I called Bischoff again. "I've got to come back and get to work. I can't sit around here at home anymore."

Finally he said yes, and they had an idea to get me back in motion: the reunion of Harlem Heat and the WCW World Tag Team Championships.

A trip back to 110th Street? I was all in. I packed my gear and headed out for the opportunity.

It had now been about six years since Lash and I had stepped foot into WCW for that first meeting with Ole, and now it was contract renewal time again. Our service and loyalty to Bischoff and WCW were undeniable. I kept all this in mind during renegotiations. In those days, guys like us still didn't have attorneys or agents to represent us. We negotiated for ourselves.

Although it was obvious Bischoff wouldn't give me Hall or Nash money, which was probably about seven figures per year, I knew it was time to bump it up to significantly more than the two hundred fifty thousand we walked away with in 1996.

Eric and I sat down fairly informally and spoke almost like friends—only this time, Bischoff surprised me. "Booker, you're respected around here because of your performance ability and, more importantly, your loyalty to this company. And remember I promised you in Japan I'd make you a rich man. How does seven hundred fifty thousand sound? You've earned it."

I was elated. It was an amazing gesture of trust. Eric was

securing my future not only in the company but financially as well. Just like him, I was committed to WCW, and now we were moving forward together.

About that time, I was contacted by the WWF. An agent called and said, "Mr. Huffman, we understand you're coming to the end of your current commitment with WCW. We'd like you to know the door's always open up here for you."

I politely thanked them and let them know I was happy with WCW and had no plans to leave. It was gratifying and reassuring to know I was on the WWF's radar, but WCW was home and I was more than satisfied with that now.

With the security of three more years, a generous salary, and the WWF kindly knocking at my door, I felt a sense of accomplishment that allowed me to relax. Now I could get back to real business.

According to the story line, Lash and I were still at odds with each other, so Bischoff developed a series of singles matches that gradually unified us. At that time, the WCW World Tag Team Championships were divided among The Jersey Triad, the trio of DDP, Kanyon, and Bam Bam Bigelow. Their stable was permitted to utilize any combination of the three of them to defend the titles. From July 2 through July 7, I was sent to Louisiana, Alabama, and Florida for singles victories over Kanyon, DDP, and Horace Hogan, one of Lash's principal nWo allies.

On the July 19 *Nitro* in Rockford, Illinois, Lash defeated Kanyon. However, when DDP and Bigelow came down to beat him, I ran in and made the save.

On a later show, I took Bigelow out by DQ. When the rest of The Jersey Triad tried to jump me, Lash returned the favor and cleared the ring. The fans sensed what was coming and started showing up to the arenas with Harlem Heat signs. During those moments when Lash and I were in the ring alone after The Jersey Triad dispersed, we'd stare at each other and nod in recognition of the bond forming again.

The last variable of the Harlem Heat equation was for Lash to remove himself from the disintegrating nWo. On *Nitro* in Memphis on July 26, Vincent called Lash out on the mic. My brother stepped into the ring and destroyed Vincent. Horace and Brian Adams got involved, and I made an appearance. The Mid-South Coliseum chanted, "Harlem Heat! Harlem Heat," while I ran down with a steel chair.

Everything solidified on an episode of *Thunder* when I told Lash to get out of the clique and get with the Heat. Lash stood there, looked around at the audience going berserk, hesitated, and took off his nWo T-shirt. We hugged, and the Huffman brothers were united once again.

Also around this time, feeling like he'd hit the ceiling in WCW, Chris Jericho jumped ship just as The Giant had. I was in awe as the WWF pushed him to the moon right away as Y2J in his debut countdown promos.

I didn't like these departures tearing our company up. It made me think, *WCW had this talented guy stuck as a mid-carder, and now look at him. I wonder what the WWF could do with me.*

While things like that were running through my head, WCW paired me with Sting in a series of warm-up house show matches against DDP and Bigelow. From July 30 through August 1, we defeated them in Flint, Grand Rapids, and Battle Creek, Michigan. I hadn't been in tag matches in quite some time, and it was good to get in there and get acclimated again.

Lash and I officially reentered the ring as Harlem Heat on the August 2 at *Nitro* in Sioux Falls, South Dakota, against Bigelow and Kanyon. We beat them down in a non-title match by DQ when DDP interfered.

It was as if Lash and I had never disbanded. Every move, characteristic pose, and double-team finisher was there, and it felt like 1993 all over again. Deep down, though, I knew this was our farewell tour. As soon as the window of opportunity for another singles breakout opened, I knew I needed to jump through it.

I imagined a resurgence of WCW, but I started losing my optimism fast. On the August 9 *Nitro* in Boise, Idaho, Hulk Hogan abandoned the black-and-white nWo Hollywood Hogan image and returned to the yellow and red.

The transition demonstrated how dry the creative well in WCW had become. There were times I reconsidered making the leap over to the WWF, but despite it all, I kept the focus on doing my best in the ring for our fans.

At Road Wild 1999, Harlem Heat returned to the Sturgis Rally on August 14, where we beat two-thirds of The Jersey Triad, Kanyon and Bam Bam Bigelow. DDP tried his best to thwart our efforts by running up to the apron and interfering, but Lash Irish-whipped Bam Bam into him, causing DDP to tumble to the floor. Reeling from the impact, Bigelow staggered back to the center of the ring, making him the perfect target for my missile dropkick from the top rope, hitting him square in the face with both feet. Bigelow collapsed as Lash covered him for the pin. In the heat of Sturgis and in front of all those raucous bikers, Lash and I became eight-time WCW World Tag Team Champions.

CHAMPIONSHIPS	
WCW World Tag Team Championship	8
WCW World Television Championship	6
Total	14

Nine days later, Harlem Heat entered into a feud with another team of brothers, Barry and Kendall Windham, on *Nitro* in Vegas. We dropped the belts to them but claimed them for the ninth time at Fall Brawl 1999 on September 12.

CHAMPIONSHIPS	
WCW World Tag Team Championship	9
WCW World Television Championship	6
Total	15

My head was already spinning from all this title trading,

but another huge change was happening at the same time. That month, Bischoff was called into question for exorbitant spending, bad business decisions, and our failing TV ratings, especially with *Thunder*.

After being given the position of executive vice president some six years earlier and taking WCW to the very limits of success, Bischoff was demoted to a creative position. He was no longer the go-to guy for decisions, and we were all in for an enormous transition.

11

DOMESTIC DISASTER

In the wake of Bischoff's demotion, WCW sought out the very guy responsible for writing the WWF's angles and story lines during the dawn of The Attitude Era. Vince Russo left the WWF, eyeing our company as his new frontier. I didn't know anything about the guy except that he was Vince McMahon's right-hand man and was extremely talented. He came in at massive speed, focused on WCW's creative process, and only time would tell if he was positioning us for astronomical success or catastrophe.

During the transition, Harlem Heat kept trading the tag titles. At *Nitro* in Philly on October 18, we lost to The Filthy Animals, the team of Rey Mysterio and Konnan. However, Rey had sustained a legitimate leg injury, which forced WCW to vacate the titles and put them up for grabs at the next PPV.

The new champs would be determined at Halloween Havoc 1999 in Vegas on October 24 in a three-way street fight, where pin falls counted anywhere. The teams consisted of us and The Filthy Animals, now made up of Konnan and

Billy Kidman, and The First Family, Brian Knobbs and Hugh Morrus, who were managed by "The Mouth of the South" Jimmy Hart.

The First Family all came to the ring wearing rubber Halloween masks. Knobbs wore one that looked basically like a demonized version of himself. Ironically, if he had kept it on the entire match, it still would have looked like Brian Knobbs.

It was a funny street fight where I got the pin backstage on my old comedic buddy Knobbs when Lash hit him with a life-sized prop mummy.

Tony Schiavone and Bobby Heenan added to the humor.

"He hit him with a mummy! He hit him with a mummy!"

Heenan said, "His mummy's there?"

After the three count, Lash and I triumphantly raised our hands as I declared, "We beat them suckas!"

Now the Huffman brothers were ten-time WCW World Tag Team Champions, by far the most decorated team in the company's history, followed by The Steiner Brothers, who had seven.

CHAMPIONSHIPS	
WCW World Tag Team Championship	10
WCW World Television Championship	6
Total	16

Already by the next night, WCW had us hand the title over to Konnan and Kidman.

Seeing Knobbs at Havoc 1999 made me think of how much of a prankster he was outside of the ring. True to fashion, he was again up to his unforgettable antics, even if it was at his own expense.

One night around this time, we were in Germany, all getting on the bus in the middle of the night when Knobbs, beer in hand, took a seat in the middle. I was in the back when suddenly Don and Ron, The Harris Brothers, six-feet-seven-inch twins, came on board.

Although I couldn't see his face, Knobbs' body language told me he was planning something.

I shook my head and smiled as I waited for it all to unfold.

As The Harris Brothers headed down the aisle, they made it no farther than Knobbs' seat when we all heard, "Oh, look! The Harris twins. You know, if you put your bald heads together, it would look like a big ass, complete with a crack!"

One of the Harris boys jumped right on top of him and pummeled his face. "Now what do you think of that? Got anything else to say?"

Knobbs got up, undaunted, beer still in hand, and strolled to the back of the bus. After composing himself for a second, he leaned over to me and said with his high-pitch squeal and a scrunched-up expression, "So how'd I do?"

By November, I was in on some singles action. The creative team had established a WCW World Heavyweight Title Tournament. On *Nitro* in Minneapolis on November 1, I lost in the first round to Jeff Jarrett, who'd recently returned from the WWF. Then it was back to the drawing board for me, but the month turned out to be one of the most memorable periods in my career.

It was announced that Warner Bros. was going to produce a major motion picture called *Ready to Rumble*, featuring WCW as its primary backdrop. Many of us, including me, were going to have on-screen roles and for all of November, we'd be put up in a luxurious hotel on Avenue of the Stars just west of Hollywood. It was about the most unexpected news I could've heard.

We all touched down in Tinseltown, and when we entered the studio, it was like walking into Center Stage Theater in Atlanta or our setup in Orlando. They'd constructed a miniature version of our *Nitro* set, complete with full seating capacity, the ring, entrance ramp, and the Jumbotron—the works.

While there, we saw the stars of the film, including David Arquette, Scott Caan, Oliver Platt, Rose McGowan, the legendary Martin Landau, and even Joe "Joey Pants" Pantoliano. I don't get starstruck, but I definitely felt out of my element while visiting their world. All of them were friendly and approachable, especially Arquette, who hung out with us to gain insight into our craft as performers.

After a day of shooting and collecting a per diem, we'd all depart and crash at the hotel. To make dates for WCW, we flew in and out of LAX on a weekly basis. During one trip, I stopped in Houston to check in with Levestia and Brandon for the day before heading to the *Rumble* set.

After landing in Los Angeles late one night, I went to check in at the hotel, but the employee at the front desk informed me they'd given my room away and were all booked up.

"What? How did that happen? I'm booked here with WCW for a movie shoot all month."

She didn't know how the mistake had happened, but there was nothing that could be done.

I stood there frustrated, wondering what to do.

All of a sudden, a voice from behind said, "Booker, you can stay in my room on the couch if you want."

I turned around, and it was Storm from the Nitro Girls, whose real name was Sharmell Sullivan. The Nitro Girls were WCW's dance troupe version of the Dallas Cowboys cheerleaders and one of Bischoff's concepts in 1997 to further the entertainment value of *Nitro*. They were responsible for either starting or concluding a segment of the show, doing choreographed dance routines to house music.

Sharmell had become a Nitro Girl in 1998, and although I'd seen her around, I'd never gotten to know her.

I looked at her, still upset about what happened, and asked, "Did you see that?"

"I heard everything. I'm so sorry. But you don't have to leave. Just come up and stay in my room. It's no big deal. You can crash on the couch."

I was hesitant, feeling a little awkward about the whole arrangement, but I was exhausted. "You know what? I'm going take you up on that offer, and I'll make it up to you sometime.

Thank you."

So we went up together, and we wound up talking into the night. I was impressed to find out she was Miss Black America 1991 from Gary, Indiana, just houses down the street from where Michael Jackson grew up. She'd also been one of James Brown's stage dancers for almost four years. I promised her a lunch for being my Good Samaritan.

After that night, I started noticing her more both on the *Ready to Rumble* set and on the road for *Nitro*, where we'd talk backstage. I thought she was great but kept a safe distance.

By the end of the month, the WCW performers' shooting for *Rumble* was a wrap, and we all had to bid a fond farewell to the glam and glitter of Hollywood to return to full-time professional wrestling.

Back into the swing of things on November 21 at Mayhem 1999 in Toronto, I lost to Scott Hall with the Razor's Edge. They also paired Lash and me with Midnight. After the match was over, I was being triple-teamed by The Harris Brothers, now known as Creative Control, along with Jarrett. Then my music started playing, and the lights flickered to reveal Midnight, a black female former bodybuilder. Midnight, who'd been trained at the Power Plant and was strong but lean on experience, came to the rescue and I escaped the beating.

Midnight also appeared with us at Starrcade 1999 on December 19 in D.C., where the three of us lost to Curt Hennig and Creative Control. Lash criticized Midnight in the ring and wanted to kick her out. My role was to come to her defense.

Soon after on *Nitro*, Lash forced me to choose between him and Midnight and attempted to hit the Slapjack on her, but I broke it up. My brother even challenged her to a match to decide whether she could stay, but he lost in a quick and embarrassing surprise small-package roll-up.

After that, Lash and I had a fictional falling out, which led to not only the end of the reunion but of Harlem Heat. Our six-and-a-half-year creation from 110th Street was officially gone, once and for all.

Because I'd been written in as Midnight's ally, she came out with me for a few singles matches in my corner. As the new millennium approached, I defeated Norman Smiley, Rick Steiner, and a few other guys, with Midnight grandstanding in the background, but the last thing I needed in my singles performances was company.

When the New Year of 2000 hit, people watched the clock strike midnight in each time zone and waited for the predicted blackout to sweep the world, but you already know what happened: absolutely nothing. It was back to business as usual and, for me, that meant mixing it up in the ring and putting on another thrilling show for the fans.

The first major event of Y2K for me was a grudge match at Souled Out 2000 in Cincinnati on January 16. Lash and I met for the first time as opponents since our days back at the WWA in Houston.

Before our entrances, they played a vignette where Lash was walking around our old streets of Houston, portrayed as Harlem, saying, "This the ghetto. This is where I come from. This is what I'm proud of, and I know *this* is what you want to forget! But Booker T, I ain't ever gonna let you forget, because this is what we are!"

I went out to the ring and cut a heartfelt, scathing promo on him, telling him our relationship was over. "When we were little kids, you used to call me Junior. Well, it ain't Junior no more. It's Booker T. So come out here and get your ass whupped like it's supposed to be done! Now can you dig that?"

When Lash got into the ring, he looked over at Midnight and waved her off dismissively. We went at it as if it were a real fight, laying it on thick. I took charge with a Harlem Sidekick, sending him rolling out of the ring. He got in some power moves, and we mixed it up outside, using everything at our disposal.

Later when I watched the broadcast, it was weird to hear Schiavone and Heenan talk about what it must be like for our parents to be watching the two of us going at it. You'd think those two would've been informed our parents had been gone for years.

We slugged it out, and near the end of our stiff war, I gave him a new move, the Book End, which The Rock was using as the Rock Bottom around the same time. I was closing in. Then Tony Norris, known a few years earlier in the WWF as Ahmed Johnson and now called Big T, ran down and tore into me, causing the DQ finish.

Tony knew Lash and me from the old days in Houston. Back then, the three of us would moonlight around an apartment complex as security vigilantes taking out petty criminals. He'd been out of work for a while, and Lash was able to land him a job in WCW, but by now he was about fifty pounds heavier.

They beat me down pretty good and left me in a heap while Midnight helplessly watched outside. Tony got on the mic and called her "a piece of fish," a classic line that made me laugh when I heard it, and it set up an entirely different angle as a new team began to form, starting with Stevie Ray and Big T: Harlem Heat 2000. Tony struggled in the ring due to his lack of conditioning, but we would run the course of the story line, and in the end, it proved to be the exit door for Midnight.

Also gone after Souled Out 2000 were Chris Benoit, Eddie Guerrero, Saturn, and Dean Malenko. In a move of solidarity, the quartet bailed on the politics and creative direction of WCW and signed with the WWF. All four of them debuted on *Raw* on January 31 as The Radicalz, appearing as guests of Mick Foley. They were all given opportunities to win contracts with the company by competing in a variety of matches.

That week on *SD*, during his tag match with Saturn against Road Dogg and Billy Gunn, Eddie went for his frog splash finisher and gruesomely dislocated his elbow live on TV. It looked like he'd broken his arm sideways. Thankfully he would eventually come back to tremendous success.

That unified defection from WCW was a huge statement to the company and had everyone talking. In less than a year, we'd lost The Giant, Jericho, Benoit, Guerrero, Saturn, and Malenko to the WWF, and I privately wondered if I should've gone there too.

The Radicalz weren't the only loss to strike WCW in January.

Bret Hart, the WCW World Heavyweight Champion at the time, was supposed to wrestle in the main event at Souled Out 2000 but pulled himself out of the PPV. Back in December at Starrcade 1999, Bret had defended his belt against Goldberg, eaten one of Bill's back thrust kicks square in the head, and gone down hard. You could see him lying there holding his face in real pain. At the conclusion of the match, Bret went for the same upside-down figure four he used against me on the outside ring post, but he slipped on the move, fell, and hit his head on the concrete floor. He got up and continued the rest of the match, which involved a closing beating on Goldberg with Nash and Jarrett. He didn't realize the extent of his injuries.

Over the next few weeks, he was losing his equilibrium and getting horrible headaches. Doctors determined he'd sustained concussions from both the kick to the head and the fall from the figure four. Bret vacated the WCW World Heavyweight title and retired from the business.

It really affected me. A performer of his rank and professionalism shouldn't have had to go out that way. I regretted that I'd never be able to get into the ring with Bret again, and I would really miss having him around.

In addition, Scott Hall, who'd appeared on *Nitro* and formed the first and most lethal version of the nWo, was on his way out. Hall's performances and reputation had suffered from his reckless approach to life, and he was sent home.

Toward the end of the year, WCW ultimately fired him and he took a couple of matches in ECW before taking off for New Japan. Hall left a huge void after being a staple in main events for almost four years. For a moment in time, he'd been the best in both the WWF and WCW with his slick, heel craft within the three ropes.

Harlem Heat 2000 toured the country into spring. We revolved in and out of singles performances between Lash and me, Tony and me, or tag matches pairing me with Kidman against the two of them. They were mostly forgettable matches. In fact, I thought the whole angle stunk.

That wasn't the only stench in the air. After one

particularly long run on the road, my brother's gear began to lose its freshness. The odors emanating from his bag, locker, and gear were so bad that some of the boys complained. I remember Sting asking, "What's going on with your brother's tights, Book? Did something die in there? Is he okay?"

Another story line with Harlem Heat 2000 had Lash laying claim to the *T* in my name and the copyright to our Harlem Heat theme music and outfit designs. He brought this attorney out on TV with a legal order, stripping me of rights to the *T* in my name, music, and pyro entrance and the ability to wear my custom gear.

When I faced Tony at SuperBrawl 2000 as just Booker, I finally made the full transition out of my Harlem Heat tights. In accordance with Lash's ownership of Harlem Heat, it made sense to come out in all black trunks, kneepads, and gloves as well as my new black-and-white buckled boots. Because my music was also stripped from me, when I came out for the match, the production guys played a *Leave It to Beaver* theme song knockoff and didn't launch any pyro. The fans were laughing, and I tried to maintain a stern expression as the ridiculously wholesome-sounding song blared.

SuperBrawl 2000 also saw Mark Madden's entry into the commentary team with Mike Tenay and Tony Schiavone. It was Madden who officially coined the term *Spinarooni* around that time after seeing my trademark corkscrew backspin.

After Big T took control over me at the beginning of the performance, I threw him over the top ropes. As I postured on the apron, preparing to attack, Madden referred to me on the broadcast as "one of the greatest athletes in WCW and a possible future World Champion, even."

When I heard that on the replay, I was beaming. It was the first time someone had mentioned the possibility, and I wondered if it would come true.

After I landed the missile dropkick, the ref counted, "One! Two!" Before he could count to three, all the lights in the arena went off. After a few seconds of total darkness, the lights came back on to reveal the four-hundred-pound behemoth known as 4 x 4 standing on the ring apron. While I was distracted taking in the sight of this monster, Tony was able to hit me with a forearm to the back and T-Bomb me for the win. After raising Tony's hand, J. Biggs announced the new Harlem Heat Inc., saying the scales of justice were just too great for me to overcome.

I realized that no matter what direction Russo was planning to steer the angle, it was doomed. While contending with Harlem Heat Inc., I couldn't live out Madden's prediction of my World Championship.

While my focus was narrowing on that World title, WCW's vision was blurring. Major performers had left us in droves due to frustration, injury, or personal issues, which assisted the WWF in blasting past us. The turbulence caused a ton of unrest in all the guys on the roster.

As a result, Vince Russo brought in new talent to stop the hemorrhaging. Although he had yet to impress anybody with his creative direction, at least he recognized the panic around him and tried to do something about it.

There were guys like Vampiro from Mexico, Tank Abbott from the Ultimate Fighting Championship, Chris Candido from ECW, and some fresh young faces like The Wall, a performer with powerful, reckless moves and a billed height of six feet ten. They even acquired a licensing deal with the rock band KISS and developed a character for wrestler Dale Torborg called The Demon, which involved full Gene Simmons makeup to capitalize on the band's fan base.

It looked as if major efforts were being made, but the jury was still out on these decisions. All I knew was that Russo was booking my matches in a rush, with time limits at five minutes or less, which didn't work for me.

I found him backstage one night and said, "Russo, I need more time out there to do anything."

He looked surprised. "I had no idea, Booker. I'm sorry. We'll start extending your matches in the next broadcast. You're one of the bright lights around here, and I want to make things work for you."

That was cool, and I really appreciated Russo's support and faith in me. I really hoped we could find our way as a company again.

BOOKER T. HUFFMAN

Back in Houston, Brandon, who was now sixteen, presented me and Levestia with more challenges. One time when I was on a short break, I came home and noticed traces of cigarette smoke, which led me straight to the garage, where I discovered beer cans in the trash. I suspected he was throwing parties when we weren't home. When I confronted him about it, he denied it.

Another time, I arrived after a long week on the road and sifted through the stack of mail. When I opened one of my credit card statements, I found some charges for the local movie theater and a nearby restaurant. My card had been stolen from my own home. I headed straight for Brandon's room.

"Hey, did you take my credit card?"

Brandon was startled. "No way, Dad. Not me."

I showed him the bill, and he still tried to deny it. I told him he was grounded until I figured out how to handle it.

When his girlfriend called the house, I picked up. "Did Brandon take you to the movies and use my credit card?" I said. "Tell me the truth. I need to know because he's already in big trouble."

She admitted he'd tried to use it with her at one point, but she said it hadn't worked.

I was sorely disappointed. My own son had stolen from me. Brandon had crossed the very last line available in my house. I gave him three choices. One, straighten up and stay.

Two, go to military boot camp and learn some discipline. Or three, move out.

To my surprise, he chose the third option. I called my sister Billie in Dallas and asked if he could stay there. She agreed and brought him to her house, just as she'd taken me in at about the same age. History was repeating itself as I'd feared.

I helped Brandon pack and gave both Billie and him enough money to take care of all the necessities.

He trudged out the door, and we didn't directly communicate at all for a couple of years. I was mad and sad and broken up about the whole thing, and I'm sure he was wrestling his own emotions about it all as well. Billie kept me updated on Brandon, who continued his plummet as I had, dropping out of school, not working, and getting a girl pregnant.

Between stressful parenting and my wrestling career, Levestia and I were also on the rocks. She couldn't adjust to my constant absence, which was understandable. Worst of all, the romance was dead.

Finally, we agreed to a divorce. It wasn't ugly. She was just brokenhearted and wanted to get on with her life and move back to the East Coast. I wanted the arrangements handled quickly and amicably, so I offered her a generous settlement. She accepted the deal, we signed the papers, and our marriage was over.

In just a few months, I'd gone from having a family of four to being on my own. I sat around, lost and broken, for a while. I couldn't fix the marriage. I couldn't fix my relationship with my son. It seemed as if there was only one thing I could do: pour myself back into my work in the ring.

12

WORLD CHAMPION BY CHANCE

Although shaken by my failed marriage, I didn't completely give up hope that a good relationship could be in my future. Sometimes during my darkest moments at home, I'd call Sharmell, a good friend who always lifted my spirits. Slowly but surely, we began to see each other in a different light and started dating. We were very tight, but I took my time to make certain she wasn't just a rebound.

Meanwhile, back at WCW, the Harlem Heat 2000 Inc. angle ran its course. I found a partner in Kidman to end the story line at Uncensored 2000 in Miami on March 19. Kidman did a diving sunset flip from the top on Big T as he tried to suplex me, and we defeated Lash and Tony once and for all. After that, the team pretty much dissolved. I once again had control over my full name, music, and entrance pyro. Tony would eventually fade away from the WCW scene as well.

Russo and Bischoff had united their creative efforts backstage since the New Year, and after Uncensored, they came up with a plan to reboot WCW. On the April 10 *Nitro* in Denver, with the entire roster in attendance, the two of them prepared to address everyone from the ring. Then Jeff Jarrett, Steiner, Vampiro, Kidman, The Wall, Van Hammer, Ernest Miller, and I joined them at the front.

Jarrett grabbed the microphone and called Russo to the ring, where he cut a long, vicious promo on WCW. He ranted about how he left the WWF after six years of singlehandedly taking them to the top. He'd come here to personally destroy Vince McMahon. In a shoot that caught me off guard, he started smashing all the guys in the back trying to protect their jobs by keeping down the younger guys, The New Blood (TNB), as he called them.

I felt Russo was making a mistake. He was a writer nobody knew about in the first place. I thought he took the segment too far, and it felt like desperation.

Russo continued, ranting about Hogan and management and their politics, which he said caused The Radicalz to take off and Steiner to be suspended.

In his promos, Scotty had recently gone off script and called Ric Flair "a backstabbing, ass-kissing old bastard . . . with more loose skin than a shar-pei puppy," and "WCW sucks, and so do you."

As a result, Scotty had been legitimately suspended.

During his continued diatribe, Russo even called Flair a piece of shit.

Then Bischoff shockingly came out after being gone for

months, hugged Russo, and then drove us further into the ground. In a self-deprecating monologue, Bischoff said he'd been blinded and put the vision of the company into the hands of guys like Nash, Sid, DDP, Sting, Luger, and especially Hogan.

I was standing there in the ring thinking these two should've been in the back writing compelling story lines and developing dynamic new stars to ensure the security of WCW—anything but this.

Russo said in order to reboot the company, he wanted to vacate all the championship titles and conduct tournaments with all the talent, old guard and TNB. He asked for all the champs to hand over their belts on the spot.

Reluctantly, the guys gave up their gold. Jarrett dropped the United States belt; Knobbs, the Hardcore; The Harris Brothers, the World Tag Team titles; and my old benefactor Sid, who'd returned after a near seven-year absence to become the World Champion, even gave up the Big Gold belt.

Bischoff went as far as to insult Sid, referencing the bloody Arn incident and asking him if he had a pair of scissors.

Through the whole meeting, I scanned the approximately five hundred guys under contract sitting there clueless. To wrap it up, Russo and Bischoff divided the roster into two major factions. The Millionaire's Club would consist of all the veterans, such as Hogan, Nash, Sting, Luger, DDP, Sid, and the rest of the old guard. TNB were all the younger talent, including Kidman, Mysterio, Goldberg, Bagwell, Steiner, The Wall, Kanyon, me, and about fifty other guys. The concept was to pit the two factions against each other to elevate TNB talent and draw some viewership back to WCW from the unstoppable machine of the WWF.

Tournaments started between The Millionaires and TNB right away to crown new champions, and I was entered into the United States tournament.

By Spring Stampede 2000 on April 16 in Chicago, I had made it to the quarterfinals. Based on Russo and Bischoff's new philosophy, it didn't make a lot of sense that I'd lose to Sting, but I did cleanly after he countered my suplex into a Scorpion Death Drop for the pin. In a show of respect, I had Sting step back in the ring and we fist bumped.

The next night on *Nitro* in Rockford, Illinois, as part of the show, Bischoff came out and berated a group of TNB, including Hugh Morrus, Lash LeRoux, Chavo Guerrero Jr., and me for not performing well against The Millionaires at the PPV. I also got involved in the World Title Match between Jarrett and Steiner, giving Scotty the scissor kick to get back in Bischoff's good graces.

The following week on the April 26 edition of *Thunder* in Syracuse, I wrestled Mike Awesome, who'd hopped over from ECW and was known for a reckless running powerbomb. When Steiner came out and distracted me, Awesome picked me up for his Awesomebomb in one corner and ran me in the seated position toward the opposite side.

Just before he released me, I tried to look up to the big screen to determine my position, but it was too late. He threw me headfirst into the bottom turnbuckle. For an excruciating moment, I thought my neck was seriously injured and my career was over. Scotty, not realizing I was in legitimate pain, came in for more and stretched me into the Steiner Recliner. Then, once again, he choked me too hard and dumped me on my face. Morrus, LeRoux, and Chavo, now known as The Misfits, came to clear the ring for my save as I lay there motionless.

When I made it backstage, the trainers checked me out and applied an ice pack to my neck.

Across from me was David Arquette. He'd been around for the last couple of weeks to promote the April 7 release of *Ready to Rumble* and had just won the World title in a match with DDP against Jeff Jarrett and Eric Bischoff. On his lap rested the legendary Big Gold Belt that Flair made famous in the eighties.

David looked at me, excited beyond belief. "How many times have you won the World title, Booker?"

I casually stared back. "Not once."

He looked down. "Oh."

I hadn't meant to take away from his moment. He was justifiably having the time of his life.

I'd liked David since the day we met on the set of *Rumble*, but giving him the WCW World Heavyweight Championship to promote the movie was another example of Bischoff trying to bring in some mainstream media but ruining the credibility of our product.

A couple of days before on *Nitro*, David beat Bischoff in a singles match, which I think should've been the extent of his wrestling career, with the same media goal having been achieved. Arquette's claiming the World title was taking it way too far. It wasn't David's fault. He hadn't asked to be involved in WCW programming but reluctantly agreed after Eric and DDP convinced him it was best for *Rumble*'s exposure.

The same affable and humble guy he was on the movie set, he donated all the money WCW paid him for his appearances to the families of Brian Pillman, Owen Hart, and Darren "The Droz" Drozdov, a WWF performer paralyzed from the neck down after being dropped by D'Lo Brown during a running powerbomb attempt—the same move from Awesome that night that was giving me a lot of pain in my neck.

Directly after my chat with David in the locker room, I went to the emergency room to get it checked out. They gave me a series of scans and determined there was no break.

The incident made me doubly aware of the risks I was taking day in and day out in the ring. One wrong landing, and I could've been in a wheelchair for the rest of my life.

One week later in Birmingham, Alabama, on *Nitro*, Bischoff

put Hugh Morrus in a three-way dance with Jarrett and Steiner, threatening to fire him if any of the other Misfits interfered. Morrus won the match after Jarrett smashed Steiner in the face with his guitar. Meanwhile, Scotty applied the Recliner on Hugh, then allowed him to cover for the pin. Afterward Bischoff, according to the story line, went back on his word and walked up and smugly fired all four of The Misfits even though the other three stayed out of the match, as he demanded.

To circumvent Bischoff's firing and reappear the following week, all in the creative master plan, The Misfits signed contracts with new military personas. In fact, it was my own design to reintroduce my old G.I. Bro character from my first days in the WWA.

Hugh Morrus became Captain Hugh G. Rection, Lash LeRoux became Corporal Cajun, Chavo Guerrero became Lieutenant Loco, and Van Hammer became Major Stash, transforming themselves from The Misfits to The Misfits In Action (MIA).

Hammer had initially wanted to call himself Private Stash, but everyone knew he was dealing with addiction, and we argued about it. "Bro, you want to go out there with a dumb name you think's an inside joke, but everyone knows you're messed up. You're going to get fired trying to use a drug reference on national TV. And besides, private's not even a ranking; it's a nothing. You've got to have status, man." Sometimes Hammer just didn't use his brain.

To continue the setup of my G.I. Bro return at *Nitro* on May 22, I lost a match to Ernest Miller when Shawn Stasiak ran in with a chair for the assault. I fought him off and gave him the scissor kick and started going to town on him with the chair, but Miller cartwheel kicked it into my face. They started beating me down, and The MIA came to my rescue. Then Bischoff fired me as he had The Misfits, giving me the same segue to repackage myself and introduce G.I. Bro to the world for the first time on a national stage.

Ever since I got to WCW, I imagined there'd be a day I'd be able to bring G.I. Bro out and display him at least once. On May 29 in Salt Lake City, I came out to full pyro. I was in army fatigues, a camouflaged vest, war paint, and my green army cap. I couldn't contain my big smile. Great memories of the WWA and Cowboy Scott Casey, one of my first mentors, who'd encouraged the military persona, flooded my mind.

I grabbed the microphone and addressed the crowd. "Everybody's been asking me, 'Why, Booker T, have you gone back to G.I. Bro?' Well, when I first got into this business, this is who I was, and this is who I am now!"

I also addressed Stasiak's attack on me with the chair and laid the challenge down for a Boot Camp Match at The Great American Bash 2000 in Baltimore on June 11. Then I went straight into revenge mode in an Ambulance Match with slapdash neck-breaker Mike Awesome. I won with the help of DDP when he came out and smashed Awesome in the back with a chair on the ramp, prompting a double Book End off the side and through a table ten feet below. We went down, grabbed him, dumped him into the waiting ambulance, and slammed the door as I claimed the victory.

G.I. Bro climbed through the ranks to the national level with a five-star general win. Now I was on my way to war at The Great American Bash.

The Bash was on June 11, and Russo came up with the idea of having me zip-line from the top of one end of the Baltimore Arena to the ring. It was something Shawn Michaels had done years before in the WWF. We tested it out a couple of times prior to the match, and it worked out pretty well.

When it was go time, I was in full G.I. Bro force. My music hit, and the lights went down as they clipped me to a safety wire. I took off all the way down to the ring, scared out of my mind. All I kept thinking was, *Come on. Come on. Please don't let me get stuck halfway down there, dangling over the audience.* Murphy's Law came into play about halfway down as I did start losing momentum. In a panic, I kicked my legs together and made my landing on the top rope.

After a pinpoint landing inside, I unhooked, ready for the boot camp battle to begin. Stasiak came out in combat pants and camouflage face paint, as I had during my war a couple of weeks prior, but his looked almost like a sloppy homage to KISS. I ran up the ramp and dove in with heavy punches. The way you win a Boot Camp Match is pretty straightforward. Anything goes, and the last man standing after a ten count wins. We spent the first five minutes outside as I smashed Stasiak into the posts and the barricades before he grabbed me and tossed me back inside.

After fifteen minutes of warfare, Stasiak's WCW World Tag Team Champion partner Chuck Palumbo ran down. Palumbo started hitting me with the Lex Flexer, an exercise bar Lex Luger had been carrying around with him. They both started in with the boots, but when they threw me into the ropes, I came back with a jarring double clothesline and did the Spinarooni back to my feet.

Mark Madden went insane. "Spinarooni! Spinarooni!"

I gave both of them huge Harlem Sidekicks, grabbed the Flexer, and knocked Palumbo down and out of the ring. Then I knocked Stasiak out for the ten count for the win. G.I. Bro had completed his mission.

After the Bash was over, I went straight into a short feud with Kanyon, who was always great competition in the ring. He was technical, smooth, and had a vast arsenal of innovative moves. We began on the June 19 *Nitro*, when I entered the ring as G.I. Bro for the last time. I tore away the camouflage warm-up pants to reveal my white Booker T trunks and boots. At the end of the match, Kanyon and DDP doubled up and gave me a twofold Diamond Cutter that continued our program over the ensuing weeks.

All this was leading up to our final match together at Bash at the Beach 2000 in Daytona Beach, where the most unexpected occurrence in my professional wrestling career would take place.

About a week before the PPV, I got a call from Russo, who told me he and Bischoff and all the other top office guys had just had a huge creative meeting. "Booker, we're trying to figure out exactly what direction to take WCW, and so far the decision is to make you WCW World Heavyweight Champion." They were still mulling over other options, but he wanted to place the title on me at Bash at the Beach.

Although I was beyond excited, I was also aware of how indecisive WCW could be. Because of their last-minute creative changes, I could only hope for the best and, to avoid disappointment, expect the worst. However, nothing could ever prepare me or anyone else for what occurred that infamous night in Daytona Beach.

Still holding on to the sands in his hourglass, Hulk Hogan, who'd since reverted back to nWo Hollywood Hogan, made it clear he wanted to defeat Jeff Jarrett that night for the World title and carry the torch for WCW and the old guard. He'd had full creative control written into his contract since day one, and he was pulling that ace for the Bash, driving Russo insane.

I was right there in the back amidst the continuing chaos,

and now I wondered if I'd be wrestling at all, let alone for the belt.

At the very last minute, an exasperated Russo came in and said he'd booked a haphazard match between Kanyon and me just so we could be on the card. He had no idea what would happen with Hogan and Jarrett, but it was easy to see his mind was racing for a solution. I was a little disappointed at the situation but definitely not surprised as my music hit and it was go time.

Kanyon and I went out there and wrestled an intense match with all the crowd-pleasing moves the fans had come to see. Just as I was going up for the missile dropkick, Jarrett surprised me by arriving on the scene and smashing me over the head with his guitar, shattering it to pieces.

What's this about? I wondered. *Why is Jeff here?*

I took a Kanyon Cutter from the top and lost the match.

I went to the back, thinking that was the extent of my evening. However, I and everyone watching had another big surprise coming.

In a live turn of events, Russo decided to supersede everything Hulk wanted to do. It was more real than anyone would ever imagine.

After Hogan and Jarrett made their entrances and introductions, it was time to lock up. Instead, Jarrett simply lay down on his back in the middle of the ring, making everyone, especially me, watch and wonder what was going on.

Hogan was visibly shocked and walking around the ring,

looking at the announcers and the crowd.

Russo came stomping down to ringside and grabbed the Big Gold, yelling, "Is this what you want? Then pin him and get it over with!" He threw the belt in the ring next to Jarrett, who lay there like a corpse.

As Russo made his way backstage, Hogan grabbed a microphone and yelled, "Is this your deal, Russo? That's why the company's in the damn shape it's in—because of bullshit like this."

With his hands on his hips, Hogan walked over and put his foot on Jarrett's chest and scored the pin fall.

The moment the three count was made, Jarrett jumped up and ran through the ropes as quickly as possible, hightailing it backstage, never even making eye contact with Hogan.

Schiavone, Madden, and Scott Hudson sat at the announcers' table with their mouths wide open, scrambling for something to say.

After Hogan finally left the ring, he went to the back with the belt, grabbed his gear bag, and walked out of the door and WCW for the last time.

One thing many people don't realize is that Hogan walked out of WCW with one of a few exact cast replicas of the Big Gold that the company had made for the boys. When Hulk had grabbed it from the ring and stormed from the building, he successfully took one of the new belts Jarrett had been given. Jeff had come out that night wearing his fresh copy. The original—the actual twenty-pound gold belt with the bent top nodule and missing jewels—was in the back.

Finally, Russo came down with a microphone and explained the actions everyone had just witnessed. "There's only one way for me to do this, and that's to tell it like it is." He went silent and rested his head against crossed arms on the top rope.

The crowd shouted, "Russo sucks! Russo sucks!"

The commentary team still sat in silence, fully aware that what was happening wasn't on a sheet in front of them. Finally, Schiavone muttered, "This is real life here, fans."

Russo then went on a seriously emotional monologue about the frustrations of dealing with "the bullshit and politics behind that curtain." He went on about how he left WCW a few weeks before and only came back because of guys like The MIA, The Filthy Animals, Jarrett, me, and everyone else who cared about the company. Then he blew his stack, yelling about Hogan and his creative control, saying people "will never see that piece of shit again." Russo called the belt Hogan walked out with the Hulk Hogan Memorial Belt that didn't mean anything and that he'd created a new WCW title for the one guy who never screwed anyone backstage: Jeff Jarrett.

I was shocked. Russo was committing career suicide.

Then Russo suddenly announced Jarrett was defending the World title against the one guy who deserved a shot more than anybody: *me*.

I looked around at the other guys, thinking, *This is out*

of control.

"Booker T and Jeff Jarrett are the two reasons why I'm in this damn stinking business to begin with," Russo said. "And, Hogan, you big, bald son of a bitch, kiss my ass!"

My heart was pounding. The moment happened so fast that it was hard to grasp the announcement. I was about to face Jarrett to go over for the belt, as he'd proclaimed a week earlier.

I quickly grabbed my gloves from the bench, realizing it was a good thing I'd left my boots on.

As soon as I had my remaining gear in hand, I heard ring announcer Michael Buffer yell, "Let's get ready to *rumble!*"

My music hit, and my mind went blank as I walked to the curtain.

Jarrett and I had never even seen each other, let alone had a minute to discuss what we were doing out there. We'd have to call it on the fly. I took a deep breath and burst out to the ramp, psyching myself up. *This is it. Everything you've been working so hard for is happening here in living color. Be cool. You've got this.*

I made it down the aisle to the ring, still trying to put my gloves on.

Instead of using my usual brawling style, I wrestled Jarrett very technically with a ton of grappling moves and counter-moves, taking the time to rest by working outside of the ring as well.

The action moved from inside the ring to deep into the audience and all the way up to the concession area. A sea of fans patted me on the back and cheered for both of us. I had control of Jarrett the entire way, until he took advantage and led me back through the audience and over the railing, where I landed at ringside.

Giving everything he had, Jarrett hit me with a chair and threw me onto the announcers' table for a piledriver. When he picked me up vertically and dropped backward, the table didn't break, and I bounced onto the floor. We made it back into the ring and went back and forth until the referee got knocked down and Jarrett went for his guitar.

Once he had it gripped, he climbed to the top turnbuckle to attempt to smash me over the head, but as Jeff leaped off and landed, I caught him with a Book End and the pin to score my first WCW World Heavyweight Championship.

CHAMPIONSHIPS	
WCW World Tag Team Championship	10
WCW World Television Championship	6
WCW World Heavyweight Championship	1
Total	17

The entire Ocean Center in Daytona Beach erupted, raising the roof in unison.

At the same time, Mark Madden, the guy who'd predicted my World title a year earlier, was busy announcing on TV. "Hard work pays off! Booker T busted his ass for fourteen years and is now the Heavyweight Champion of the world. This is what it should've been like a long time ago! Finally, the new WCW *is* the new WCW!"

I was never sure where Madden got the part about the fourteen years, because in total it was going on ten, with the last seven being in WCW, but it sounded good anyway.

I just couldn't believe I held Flair's original Big Gold belt, custom-made for Jim Crockett Promotions in 1986 by the late Nevada belt maker Charles Crumrine on behalf of the NWA. It was an unforgettable moment as my emotions took over and the show closed out on a close-up of me perched on the ropes, the look of disbelief captured on my face, and the belt on my shoulder.

Backstage, everyone—Lash, Sting, Steiner, and even Flair himself—came up to congratulate me, but I was still too overwhelmed to really grasp it all. Ric grabbed my shoulders and, in an unexpected and humbling moment, said, "I'm passing the torch of this belt to you, Booker. You deserve it, and *you're* the man!"

That night was a series of flashing images, as if I were under a strobe light. I would have to piece it together later. Right then, I was physically and emotionally exhausted and went straight to my hotel room.

As I sat on the edge of the bed with the Big Gold across my lap, I pondered my career up until that point. I was now representing WCW at its very top rung. Sure, wrestling is a work and a business, but the enormity of being the trusted figurehead is as real as it gets. I was grateful beyond words.

A couple of weeks later, I was off and running as the defending champion. In Cleveland on July 24 for *Nitro*, I faced Bill Goldberg in the ring for the very first time, though I'd known him as a friend in the business. I knew Goldberg had viewed me as one of the only guys he could sit down and talk with since his monstrous debut back in 1997. I was always honest with the boys, and it put people like Goldberg at ease. He had a reputation of being a brick wall to most everyone else, but he was able to put his guard down with me.

I'd been looking forward to working with Goldberg, but when I told him I'd be going over on him, he didn't seem too happy about it. The story was that he'd recently renegotiated his contract and told the office staff, "The only person I put over is God."

I thought, *Well, I don't believe I'm God, but the Big Gold's staying put, brother.*

Whether he'd actually said that or not, Goldberg did an outstanding job of putting me over when the time came. The angle was that I was supposed to wrestle Sting that night but Goldberg attacked him backstage and substituted. We went at it in a stiff power match with a false finish when Lash came down and threw the towel in on me. Bill wiped his face and underarms with it before throwing it into the crowd.

Ernest Miller, acting as WCW commissioner, came out and said that although Bill was the winner, I was still champ because I never tapped and wasn't pinned.

I demanded an immediate rematch.

In the finish, Bill told me to really lay into him, so when I Harlem Sidekicked him, it was directly in the mouth with my right knee brace.

He ate it harder than anyone I've ever seen, and then I Book Ended him for the clean pin.

As I was getting up, to keep his image strong in the face of a loss, Goldberg stood and speared me, then went for the Jackhammer. However, things went awry for him. As he got me up and slammed me down, he visibly popped his collarbone out of place and immediately rolled over, clutching the injury and screaming.

Much like Steiner, Bill hadn't known his own strength and it could be a liability not only to his opponents but to himself as well. I felt really bad for him as I walked out of Cleveland the defending World Champion and one of the very few people to score a three count on the once seemingly indestructible Goldberg.

Where WCW would take us next was anyone's guess.

13

DAWN OF THE IMPERIAL TAKEOVER

On August 2 in Terre Haute, Indiana, on *Thunder*, I had my one and only opportunity to step into the ring with one of my idols and a true legend in the business, The Great Muta from Japan, when he came into WCW for a quick run for the first time since 1990. Sting, Wrath, Brian Adams, and I took on Muta, Jarrett, Vampiro, and The Demon in an Eight-Man Tag Team Match.

The Great Muta was one of the guys I'd emulated in my early days. His calculated, sweeping martial arts approach had inspired me all those years. When I met him, I was surprised to see he matched my size. With the way he moved, I'd always thought he was smaller. If we were ever in a real fight, I'd have a problem. The Pearl of the Orient exceeded my expectations in the ring, and it was a true honor and career highlight to meet and perform with him.

A couple of weeks later, I defended the World title against Jarrett at New Blood Rising 2000 in Vancouver, British Columbia, on August 13 in a crazy fifteen-minute match. At one point, the referee was out and Jarrett went for the guitar smash. I Harlem Sidekicked the swing, taking the shot to my right knee. He kept trying to injure me with the figure four, and I gave him a huge Book End through a table off the ring apron. In the end, I Book Ended him out of his boots in the ring and kept my title.

My victory against Jarrett turned into a vengeance angle as he came for some payback during my match with Nash on the August 28 *Nitro* in Las Cruces, New Mexico. Nash had Russo and Steiner in his corner, and Jarrett had been assigned as the special guest referee, stacking the deck against me. When I was getting the upper hand and nearing a finish, Russo tossed Jarrett his loaded particle-board guitar and exploded it over my head. They always had that thing loaded with talcum powder for extra dramatic effect, and it sprayed all over me, setting me up for Nash's Jackknife Powerbomb.

Taking a powerbomb from anybody is always a little scary. Anything could go wrong. You could be knocked out and wake up paralyzed. Getting hit by a guy standing six feet eleven is terrifying, but Kevin was always a pro and took care of me when pulling me up for the big release. It was almost like he floated me down as I took the massive fall.

With that, I lost my World title after only a month with it.

It turned out the Big Gold did come back to me a little sooner than expected when I got the rematch against Nash at Fall

Brawl 2000 in Buffalo on September 17 in a cage. Steel Cage Matches still completely took me out of my element and limited my range as a performer. Everything from simply being whipped into the ropes to trying to climb the top turnbuckle became trying.

In this case, the cage was implemented as an equalizer in my favor due to all the interference I kept getting in my matches from Jarrett, Steiner, and Russo. Now they couldn't meddle in my affairs.

Kevin and I lumbered around inside that chain-link fence for about ten minutes, getting all our moves in before he saw an opportunity for the Jackknife, which I countered into a Book End for the pin.

I was the WCW World Heavyweight Champion for the second time!

CHAMPIONSHIPS	
WCW World Tag Team Championship	10
WCW World Television Championship	6
WCW World Heavyweight Championship	2
Total	18

I thought I'd seen the last of the inside of a cage for a while, but I was wrong. For *Nitro*, at the Nassau Coliseum in Long Island, Russo booked himself against me in a cage for the World Heavyweight Championship.

I thought, *What's this all about? David Arquette the sequel, only worse?*

Maybe Russo was feeling insecure. I know there were wrestling editorials out there giving him a hard time every week. That garbage would wear anyone down. Russo wanted their approval so desperately, and I'd seen that obsession ruin people over the years. Maybe Russo became so fixated on winning fans over that he figured he'd insert himself into on-screen angles, as Vince McMahon was successfully doing.

Russo entered the cage wearing an entire New York Giants uniform and helmet. The match was a mess, with everyone getting involved. The Filthy Animals and The Natural Born Thrillers slugged it out on the floor. Luger handed Russo a pipe to beat me senseless with. Sting rappelled from the ceiling. Flair ran in dressed as an EMT. Steiner slammed the cage door in my face as I kicked it back into his. Last, the now-healed Goldberg came in and speared Russo through the structure just before I walked out. Since he was technically the first one through the cage, I lost the belt to Vince.

I thought the whole event was another embarrassment for the World title and WCW.

The following week, Russo realized there was no way he could hold on to the belt and declared it vacated. It was official: in my opinion, Russo had no idea what he was doing. He tried to fix the problem by simply giving the title back to me in San Francisco on October 2. On that *Nitro*, Jarrett, Steiner, Sting, and I faced off in a four-way dance with the first two performers.

Jarrett pinned Sting while I got the best of Steiner, setting up a ridiculous contest called The San Francisco 49ers Match, involving poles with wooden boxes on them positioned in each of the four corners. The belt was hidden inside one of the boxes, and the first man to locate it was the new champ.

Jarrett got the edge in the beginning and scrambled for the first box to find a blow-up doll. Then I controlled him enough to open the second box and found a framed picture of Scott Hall, a backhanded reference to his firing. Jarrett and I had no idea what was in each of the four boxes other than the title one, so the image of Hall caught me off guard as the cameraman zoomed in for a close-up.

The third box held the Coal Miner's Glove used in the Spin the Wheel, Make the Deal Match from Halloween Havoc 1992 between Sting and Jake Roberts, months before I was even in the company. Just as it seemed Jarrett would get the fourth and final championship box, Beetlejuice, a black man of short stature from *The Howard Stern Show*, came out of nowhere and started punching Jarrett in the balls as he was reaching for the box. He went down, and I capitalized by leaping up, grabbing the box and the belt to become a *three-time* WCW World Heavyweight Champion.

CHAMPIONSHIPS	
WCW World Tag Team Championship	10
WCW World Television Championship	6
WCW World Heavyweight Championship	3
Total	19

Although it was great to go over again, I felt the winner should hold on to the belt and establish credibility for himself and the company.

For me, Russo's writing and booking skills left a lot to be

desired. I decided to talk to him about it. "Man, you're killing me and my career with this stuff. What are you doing?"

"Don't worry. I've got this," he said. "I completely understand where you're coming from, and I'll make it right. I promise."

I'm not really sure he understood what I think everyone backstage did. Time was running out for WCW if we didn't make drastic changes fast.

"Big Poppa Pump" Scott Steiner was the contender to step up for my next feud over the WCW title with our first PPV brawl happening at Halloween Havoc 2000 on October 29.

We were in Vegas, and setting the tone of the match from the beginning was ring announcer Michael Buffer. With his distinct voice and trademark intro, he asked the audience, "Are you ready?"

They applauded.

"WCW fans, are you *ready*?" He drew out the last word.

They cheered even louder.

"Then, for the thousands in attendance, and for the millions watching around the world, ladies and gentlemen, *let's get ready to rumble!*"

And the crowd erupted as my music hit.

As I stood at the top of the ramp, my pyro went off, bringing the crowd to a frenzy. They were ready to see me defend my title, and I was ready to entertain.

The match with Scotty was as brutal as any I'd ever been

in. We hammered each other from start to finish. At one point, the match spilled out over the guardrail and into the crowd, with Scotty hammering away on me. Careful of the ten count-out from the ref, Scott rolled back into the ring and back out again to reset the count.

As I lay there trying to recover from his assault, he picked me up and slammed me through the announcers' table, right in front of my brother, who was doing commentary.

Steiner took advantage of the moment by berating my brother while I was down. "You're next, you son of a bitch!"

"You haven't even beat him yet!" Lash yelled back, pointing to my crumpled body on the table.

As the action made its way back to the ring, Steiner would get the advantage by delivering a turnbuckle fall-away slam on me. He showboated with some push-ups and double-bicep poses while I lay there, broken.

The fight continued with Scotty pummeling me back to the outside and then again into the ring, where I finally got the upper hand. Mounting the top rope, I connected with a perfect missile dropkick, covering Steiner for the two count. We both got up, and I bounced off the ropes, delivering my scissor kick, and we both collapsed to the ground in exhaustion.

Scotty used the moment to roll toward the ring apron, where his valet, Midajah, handed him a lead pipe. WCW Championship be damned, Scotty hit me with the pipe as I went for a kick. He then dropped it and went after the referee, kneeing him in the stomach and hanging him upside down in the corner of the ring.

From that point on, it was pure chaos. Numerous officials came in to stop him, but Scotty grabbed his pipe again and began beating each one who entered the ring.

I rolled out onto the floor, where Steiner continued to assault me with a metal chair.

When all was said and done, Scotty and I put on a compelling and brutal match that saw me keep my title due to Steiner being disqualified.

Unfortunately, my knee was acting up again, and after my match with Scotty, it got to the point that I knew I'd need surgery for the third time. Because of this, it was decided that Steiner would win the title and become the new WCW World Heavyweight Champion. I was looking forward to doing the honors for my friend, but I was a little worried about the knee locking out and hyperextending. Still, this was business, and everyone counted on the champ to step up.

So at Mayhem 2000 on November 26 in Milwaukee, Scotty and I finally squared off in a messed-up Straitjacket Match in a steel cage. The point was to grab the hanging jacket, put the other guy in it, and get a submission or pin. We were all over each other in a blur of heated punches, kicks, and slams. Scotty got the jacket down but tossed it to the side. I finally got him down with a spin kick and went for the jacket myself. I had him pretty well stuffed into it before he recovered and put an end to his fitting session. He hit me for a backflip with a Steiner Line, tore the jacket off, and eventually hit me with a steel chair, knocking me out before locking on the Recliner for the submission victory. Scotty then dropped me and started ripping at my leg brace, repeatedly striking my knee, effectively writing me off TV.

Just like that, Scott Steiner won his first WCW World title and ended my third championship reign. I'd be gone from the scene for the better part of three months, until February 2001.

I was genuinely happy for Scotty. He deserved the company recognition. He'd been working consistently and always took it as hard as he gave it in the ring. I thought it was long overdue for Big Poppa Pump to have the Big Gold around his waist, and I made sure to congratulate him backstage on my way out.

Relieved to have some time off, I seriously pondered retirement. As I healed up again with a scoped-out knee, feeling like the six-million-dollar man put together again, I concentrated on fishing. I'd bought myself a nice big bay boat, and I took it into the Gulf of Mexico as often as possible. There I was, the three-time WCW World Heavyweight Champion of leisure on the open seas with a Corona in hand, line in the water, and sunshine on my face as the New Year rolled into view.

By the time the Sin 2001 PPV arrived on January 14 in Indianapolis, I'd been coming around to some of the shows and hanging out with the boys backstage. It was close to two months since I'd been sidelined. I was feeling rested, and thoughts of retirement were behind me. In fact, my fever for the ring was soaring. It would be another six weeks before I was cleared to come back, but it was nice to be around the sights and sounds of the action.

During my absence, Mark Madden was fired, apparently for making on-air references to the possible sale of WCW as well as Scott Hall's release.

For quite a while, there'd been rumblings about the company's financial problems. I heard several companies were making offers to buy us out, including Bischoff himself and his new group, Fusient Media Ventures. A big merger was about to take place with Ted Turner's Time Warner and AOL.

At the time, though, I wasn't aware of most of this information, and like anyone else in the locker room, I had to sit and wait for something to happen.

While at the Conseco Fieldhouse before Sin 2001 started, I walked around saying my hellos and shaking hands as usual and decided to see what was going on in the ring area.

As I walked down the ramp, I noticed Sid practicing a jump from the second turnbuckle, something I'd never seen him do. He was simulating a giant right boot to the face while coming down flush on his left foot alone. Sid was a monstrously tall power performer with long legs definitely not meant for any flat-footed landing from even as high as the first turnbuckle, let alone the second. It didn't look right at all.

It turned out one of the agents in the back wanted Sid to hit that jumping boot to the face on Steiner during their Four Corners Match for the World title with Jarrett and Road Warrior Animal. Apparently Sid had protested trying the unorthodox maneuver, but the agent had eventually convinced him to do it.

When the match went down and it came time to deliver the move, Sid jumped onto the second turnbuckle and went for the flying boot to the face. While landing on his left leg, he completely compound fractured it in a perfect right angle to the left.

I was watching in the back and jumped up. It was like seeing a skyscraper pancaking on top of itself. Sid was lying there with his leg literally dangling up and down as if it were severed, only his boot keeping it attached. Steiner didn't even notice it at first and started stomping him, going on with the match as planned while Sid held his knee, writhing and in shock.

It was the worst injury I'd ever seen in my life, period. It was insane to watch Scotty, even after realizing Sid was messed up, keep going over and crushing his throat with the boot until the mystery fourth opponent showed up. It turned out to be Road Warrior Animal, and even he ran over and kicked Sid in the head before Steiner covered him for the pin.

I don't know how Sid kept from passing out or why medics didn't immediately come down with a stretcher.

After Sid was out, it was the talk of the locker room for weeks. I felt terrible for him, trying to imagine what was going through his mind while he was in that ring staring at his leg.

It would be years before Sid made a full recovery. Shockingly he even started wrestling again on the independent circuit. But neither Sid nor anyone who saw the incident at Sin 2001 will ever be able to erase that image from memory.

I finally made my return to the ring in New Orleans on February 26 for *Nitro* in a Six-Man Tag Team Match with DDP and Ernest Miller against Steiner, Bagwell, and Luger. It felt great to be back. I had the energy of ten men and pushed myself to the physical limits. In the end, I cracked the back of Steiner's head flush with my scissor kick and scored the pin.

Afterward, the three of us left through the crowd and stopped at the top to celebrate with the fans for my Louisiana homecoming. A couple of weeks later, I faced off with Scotty's brother Rick for his United States title at the Greed PPV in Jacksonville on March 18. A guy could always count on a rough one with The Dog-Faced Gremlin, who punched like a mule kicks and clotheslined like a jackknifed eighteen-wheeler.

We beat each other up, and at one point he yelled, "You ain't getting shit," in reference to his title, but he was wrong and he knew it.

After he climbed up on the top for his flying bulldog, Shane Douglas came from behind and whacked him to the mat while the ref was down.

I picked him up for a Book End and won my first WCW United States Heavyweight Championship.

On March 23, the news we all feared reached us. The rumors about WCW being bought out by another company after the AOL-Time Warner merger proved to be true, but what was shocking was the identity of the buyer.

Unbeknownst to any of us, Vince McMahon had thrown his hat into the ring. He'd secured the purchase of his own competition. After seventy years of existence in various formations of Georgia Championship Wrestling and Jim Crockett Promotions' Mid-Atlantic Championship Wrestling, WCW had just been placed under the thumb of the WWF once and for all. For each of us performers, the future was now in the center of Vince's palm.

When I heard the news, I took a deep breath and braced myself for the changes ahead. I considered my options and where my talents could take me. I knew I could go to Japan or even Mexico, where my style and reputation could carry me to the highest echelon in their professional wrestling companies.

But from the onset, I suspected I was WWF-bound,

heading to those cold cities up North and reinventing myself with a brand-new cache of performers. It seemed destined from the beginning of my career, but I'd always placed the dream on the back burner in favor of the security and familiarity of WCW.

At the last *Nitro*, known as The Night of Champions, three days after the sale on March 26 in Panama City Beach, Florida, there was no formal meeting presided over by Bischoff and Russo. There weren't any farewell speeches. We weren't given WCW memorial plaques. It was just gloomy everywhere I looked. The news meant the end of the mainstream period for most of our careers. Even the production crew and creative guys faced the possibility of career changes.

I ended my performances with WCW with a final match against Steiner by jumping out of a powerbomb attempt into a Book End for the pin, giving me my fourth World title and unifying it with the United States belt.

Immediately after, a couple of guys asked me to hand over the belts as they were now commodities of the WWF. I later heard Steiner, who had an exact replica belt cast from Flair's original Big Gold, had swapped his out for the original while he was champ. Aside from that rumor, I have no idea where the first

CHAMPIONSHIPS	
WCW World Tag Team Championship	10
WCW World Television Championship	6
WCW United States Championship	1
WCW World Heavyweight Championship	4
Total	21

BOOKER T. HUFFMAN

incarnation made by Crumrine now rests.

From there, I went back to Houston and waited for a call. Although I wasn't sure when, I knew an offer from the WWF was coming.

During the last *Nitro*, Shane McMahon had pulled me aside. "Booker, it's going to be great working with you. We've looked forward to bringing you over for years. Both my mom and my dad knew you'd be one of the key acquisitions from this place when the time came."

Because of that, I knew my place with the WWF was secured. It was just a matter of when and how.

Most of the marquee-value guys in WCW like Steiner, Goldberg, Flair, Nash, and Sting had significant time left on their original contracts with Turner's Time Warner, which still had to be honored even after the merger with AOL. The offer was made that anyone could take a 50 percent buyout in order to take jobs elsewhere, or they could stay at home and collect their full contractual salaries. All those particular guys decided to ride it out and sit pretty—but not me. With only about a year left on my contract, the buyout was the only answer. Waiting around was not an option for me.

I remember Flair telling me once, "A wrestler's worst enemy is time off. The adage of *out of sight, out of mind* is absolutely true."

If the WWF called and had an immediate offer and angle

for me to step into, I'd be ready and willing. To me, standing still would've been tantamount to sprinting backward.

With that decision made, I talked to my brother about whether he'd take the buyout and go with me. Maybe someday the WWF would reunite Harlem Heat.

"Nah, Brother," he said. "I'm not interested in starting all over and having to prove myself again. What we did in WCW's good enough for me. I'm hanging up my boots."

And that's exactly what he did. He went back to Houston and used some of his savings to open up a car wash and invest in a trucking company. It suited him well. And if it made him happy, it was fine with me too.

As it turned out, I was the only one of the WCW performers to take the AOL-Time Warner buyout. Other guys, such as DDP and Bagwell, were able to move to the WWF right away because they were at the end of their contracts.

My first official contact from the WWF came from Director of Talent Relations Jim "JR" Ross. He called to tell me I was at the top of a short list of WCW performers the company was interested in. He was all business and stated I wouldn't be making the same amount of money as I had in my last run in WCW. But he did explain I'd have a guaranteed amount subsidized with PPV and merchandise revenues and that the sky was the limit to make even more than I had back in Atlanta.

"It's all up to you, Booker. Your international stage and branding are at your disposal. What you do with those elements is up to you."

"That's all I need." I'd make my own way through hard work and determination.

"Sit tight," he said, "because even as we speak, creative is fleshing out the plan to bring you in."

That sounded good to me.

As much as I was excited about my own career, there was someone else who'd signed with the company whom I had quite the vested interest in.

Just before the sale of WCW, Sharmell had been one of the first performers released from her contract. The WWF had contacted her and signed her to a developmental deal and sent her to Ohio Valley Wrestling (OVW) in Louisville, Kentucky. OVW was the company's farm system for training new wrestlers where they lived, ate, and slept every aspect of the business in preparation for a prospective call to the big show on *Raw* and *SD*. I was so proud of her.

We'd always discussed the possibility of being on the road together again someday. The idea was a real possibility now that I was going to be part of the WWF.

In May, JR called again to explain how they were going to assimilate WCW performers into the WWF's roster. They planned an invasion angle where they would gradually introduce the main players who came over, such as DDP and me, week after week on *Raw* and *SD*.

Soon, I answered the phone to hear JR saying they had something really big for me. My official surprise debut would be at the King of the Ring (KOTR) 2001 PPV on June 24 in East Rutherford, New Jersey. The rest of the details were vague, but my WWF stage was set and I was ready to step onto it.

14

THE INVASION

The first official appearance of a WCW faithful happened on June 18 in Tampa for *Raw*. As The Undertaker's entrance played, a masked figure rode a motorcycle down. When he hit the ring, the rider stood for a moment in the center of the squared circle, allowing the fans to soak up the mystery. After a dramatic pause, he tore the disguise off to reveal himself as DDP, who declared he was there to make an impact by going after the biggest and baddest wrestler in the WWF at the KOTR: The Undertaker. It was the official kickoff to the impending Invasion angle by us WCW expatriates looking to make a deadly impact behind enemy lines.

On June 24, it was time for my own inaugural WWF appearance at the PPV at the Continental Airlines Arena. I was asked to stay in the hotel right up until about an hour before the show to maintain the element of surprise. While waiting, my nerves kicked in.

When staff came to take me to the arena, my anticipation was at fever pitch. I still didn't know what was going on for the show.

Finally, Vince, JR, and Bruce Prichard, the former Brother Love and a chief agent in the back, gave me the outline. I'd be interfering in the Three-Way WWF Championship Match featuring Austin, Chris Jericho, and my old Best of Seven Series fellow war veteran, Chris Benoit.

The pressure was on. What if I ran out there and fell flat on my face like The Shockmaster had in his big debut?

I was told to walk down from the concession area and through the crowd, then jump the barrier, put Stone Cold through the Spanish announcers' table with a Book End, and hightail it back through the audience. The screens and the top of the table were all going to be cleared before I got down there to ensure it would collapse as planned, leaving Austin buried on the floor.

But while I watched the match on a monitor and it got closer to my time, they still hadn't removed everything from the table. I knew I couldn't personally do it once I was down there, and I thought, *They'll take that stuff off by the time I'm out there, won't they?*

When I got my cue, I ran out the door to the top of the concession area and stomped down the steps toward the ring.

The fans around me stood and pointed. "Look! It's Booker T!" They were going crazy.

I picked up the pace.

Austin was in position on the floor near the table as I

raced toward him.

Boom, boom, boom! I lay in hard and gave him the scissor kick before getting him up on the table.

Although the monitors had been taken out, the entire top frame was still there! Instead of a Book End, I gave Austin a sidewalk slam and the table crashed as planned, but he kind of bounced off the top piece onto the floor instead of crashing through. I hopped the barricade and retreated hastily through the fans and straight to the back, sweating.

After their three-way dance was over, I anticipated seeing Austin to congratulate him, but he never came. I figured he was just the kind of guy who took off after matches and kept to himself.

As I was in the car later on my way to New York City for the next night's *Raw*, my phone rang.

It was Prichard. "Booker, what happened out there tonight? Steve broke his hand."

I stared at the road in disbelief. "What are you talking about? Why didn't anyone tell me while I was there? Steve ran out before I even got a chance to see him."

"You should give Austin a call and check in. Maybe you could pack his bags for him for a while and do whatever you can to help out while he's injured."

I was sitting there, thinking long and hard about the situation. *Are these guys working me? I ain't packin' nobody's bags. I'm not even gonna consider that! I can't believe I came out for my first performance and caught this kind of heat already.*

The next night at Madison Square Garden, I saw Steve and walked toward him.

"Listen," he said. "When you're out there, you've got to know what you're doing or people are going to get hurt."

I listened and apologized, never mentioning that the table-top frame had erroneously been left in place. I just ate it, aware I was the new guy and couldn't overreact to a WWF Superstar on my second outing.

After that talk, nobody said a word about it. I also noticed Steve's hand didn't seem to be bothering him at all. There was no cast, brace, or even Band-Aid, and he didn't miss any dates. To this day, I still wonder if the whole thing was a test to see how I'd react. I think I passed.

The next night, *Raw* was live from Madison Square Garden in New York City, and I was awestruck by the sprawling metropolis. I'd performed in Manhattan only once before—with WCW at the Paramount—so navigating the city by myself was daunting. I had a GPS, which at the time was a huge boxy contraption, and I wouldn't have made it there without it.

I finally got to the building, found the locker room, and settled in, making the rounds. I shook everybody's hand out of respect that was immediately returned in full. No one ever gave me any problems.

Over the years, I'd heard that if you couldn't make it in

the WWF locker room, you wouldn't make it in the WWF ring either. The boys would ensure it. I knew I had no special privileges or a band to attach myself to, even though Big Show, Jericho, Benoit, Saturn, Eddie Guerrero, and all the WCW alumni warmly welcomed me. My talent and my legs for the business would prove to be my ticket in the WWF, and I was more than willing to put in the work, listen, and learn, which would show them more about who I was than any accolades of the past.

From the beginning, The Undertaker gravitated toward me, maybe because we were both Texans. One time he saw me looking a little tentative before going through the curtain. "Just relax and be yourself," he said. "Everything will come natural to you."

Another time The Rock came up to me with his big smile and said, "If you ever have any questions or need some advice, please don't hesitate to come to me. I know you've never done one of these before."

I smiled and thought, *This bush-league boy's going to school you before it's all said and done.*

There was no doubt The People's Champion from the WWF and the World Champion from WCW were eyeing each other, but I knew it was all part of the process of proving myself to the WWF locker room.

Then there was Hardcore Holly, who had a reputation backstage for being a hard-ass, getting in people's faces, and even taking liberties with job guys or young new talent. I was never afraid of him, and around me he was never hardcore, just a playful guy. I knew we wouldn't have any problems, and over the years Holly and I have remained friends.

My initial meetings with Vince were extremely friendly. "Welcome aboard, Booker! We're very pleased to have you with us. Here's my cell phone number. Feel free to use it or call my office anytime you have something on your mind."

I never planned to use it and wondered if it was another test. And unless he personally summoned me to the WWF headquarters in Stamford, Connecticut, I wouldn't go there for the guided tour. It was enough for me to share mutual respect as businessmen focused on the common goal of WWF showmanship.

That night on *Raw* we continued my story line with "Stone Cold" Steve Austin. Shane McMahon, who was the acting onscreen owner of the newly acquired WCW brand, introduced me to the audience at their WWF New York–themed restaurant in Times Square. On camera, I challenged Austin to come and get me as he watched live on TV with the audience back at the Garden. He got fired up and took Kurt Angle to Times Square only to find we'd pulled the old switcheroo on him and were on our way back to the arena. When we got there, Vince was cutting a promo in the ring and Shane interrupted him at ringside as I slid in behind him.

Then without warning, Vince got a really good right-handed shot on me that burst my left eardrum. All I could hear was ringing as I tried to regain my composure.

As scripted, I heavy-handed him several times with right fists of my own and scissor kicked his head before hitting a whirling Spinarooni back up to my feet.

Before the show, Vince had approached me with specific commands. "When you go out there tonight, I want you to really lay it in stiff. Make it look good by making it real."

"You're the boss," I said, and I delivered. As a bunch of the WWF guys ran out to intervene, I bailed out through the audience.

JR lost his mind on the commentary. "The legacy has been trampled!"

Taking that hard shot from Vince was my true initiation into the company.

I was really enjoying my position being with Shane-O Mac. I was partnered with him to manufacture the invasion story line. We formed a bond right away. More than anybody, he looked out for me from the very beginning and treated me like family. Anytime I needed to talk, he was available.

The next night, we were still at Madison Square Garden for the *SD* taping, and we filmed another segment where I came through the crowd and attacked Austin. After cracking him upside the head with the WCW title, I jumped back into the audience for my escape to Shane's limo, which waited in the underground parking lot.

It was a multiple-hour production with the WWF roster chasing me to the car. It was an eye-opening experience.

The path to the limo was downhill. The first time we shot it, I was running ahead as planned when The Godfather caught up to me. He swung and connected with a shot, causing me to hit my head on the top of the doorjamb while trying to get in.

"Cut!" The producers had to explain to Godfather, "Although you're supposed to be *trying* to catch Booker, you're not going to catch him."

"All right," he said, apologizing.

"Action!"

I started running for the limo again, and Godfather ran after me so hard that he got tripped on the downhill ramp and tore both his hamstrings right there and fell over.

He was out of action for three months. I felt terrible for him.

With the scene in the can and work for the night concluded, I found my way back to the hotel near LaGuardia Airport. My nerves were shot, and my ear was ringing as I tried to rest. All in all, it had been another amazing day in Manhattan, and I couldn't wait to get back to work.

The following *Raw* on July 2 in Tacoma, Washington, was another day of infamy for my arrival in the WWF as I took on fellow WCW transplant Buff Bagwell for my WCW World Heavyweight Championship. It was my first one-on-one action in the WWF ring, and beforehand I went out to get familiar with the structure itself. The WCW ring was eighteen-by-eighteen feet compared to the WWF's larger twenty-by-twenty, which meant I had to adjust the timing of my steps or I'd misfire on all my moves.

But as it turned out, the ring should've been the least of my concerns.

When they let me know about the match between me and Bagwell during the previous week, I thought, *This isn't going to be good. Bagwell's got nothing left in the tank*. I even told the producers my concerns, but they fell on deaf ears. I was told that it was out of their hands.

I knew right then and there that this was setting up WCW to look as bad as possible. No matter, though. As with everything else, I was going to do my best to shine.

I'd had a hundred matches with Bagwell over the years in WCW, and he could always go, but that night in Tacoma, he had stage fright and, just as I'd been concerned about, no stamina.

The night of our WWF match, nothing went right. Many times I wrestled and carried guys when they were off their game or injured and needed me to compensate. Buff was struggling so much that night that there was nothing I could do to salvage the match. The crowd was all over the mess.

Mercifully, in the end, Austin and Angle came running

down and, along with Bagwell, gave me a triple beat-down, walked me backstage, and threw me out of the arena.

I was sure all the WWF guys and the viewers worldwide were now convinced WCW performers were the worst. I was embarrassed to have misrepresented what I was all about in a performance.

When it was all over, the agents pulled Buff and me into the back. "What was that?"

Bagwell said, "Well, I'm just going to be honest. My timing was off. Booker's timing was off—"

I cut him off. "Whoa, wait a minute. Your timing was off. I can work every time."

The situation was disappointing. I'd considered him a talented friend, but sadly he was becoming a virtual shadow of his WCW self.

After that, the writing was on the wall for Buff. He was fired a few weeks later, and I wondered if I was next.

After the discouraging match with Bagwell, I tried to settle into the WWF schedule and pick up where I'd left off in WCW. I was still the defending WCW World and United States Heavyweight Champion, which meant Vince could pull out any story line for me anytime. In two successive weeks, July 9 and 16, I stole victories from both Kurt Angle and Chris Jericho with the assistance of WCW referees Charles Robinson and Nick Patrick. They were both working as officials with a natural bias toward WCW and routinely found themselves in altercations with Dave and Earl Hebner, the longtime WWF refs.

On July 22, we had the official Invasion PPV in Cleveland. All the WCW talent merged with the existing ECW performers already in the company. We became Team ECWCW, later changed to The Alliance, and we were led by Shane McMahon in the clash with his father. Every match on the card pitted us against members of the WWF roster in a struggle for supremacy over the company.

The main event was a 10-Man Tag Team Match featuring Rhyno, DDP, The Dudley Boyz, the team of Bubba Ray and D-Von Dudley, and me with Paul Heyman, Stephanie McMahon, and Shane McMahon versus the team of WWF Champion Austin, Jericho, Angle, The Undertaker, and Kane with Vince. It was one of those matches where in-ring time was extremely limited for each guy, which I didn't prefer but understood. Vince was trying to find a way to get us all on the show at one time to get his money's worth.

I scored the pin on Angle after Austin turned on Team WWF and gave Kurt a Stone Cold Stunner. Vince even tried to get involved after it was over, and Shane ran in and knocked him out, giving Team ECWCW the first blood drawn in the war.

I felt The Invasion angle was running out of gas. The true invasion had occurred in 1999 when Jericho, The Giant, Benoit, Guerrero, Saturn, and Malenko all defected and showed up on WWF TV. But by 2001, the WWF was still trying to salvage it. Maybe if Bischoff had come over with Sting, Goldberg, Steiner, DDP, Mysterio, my brother, Hogan, Hall, and Nash, we could've created something for the history books, but those boys sat and collected their Turner money, and The Invasion fell flat.

Thankfully, I had a three-year contract and a spot, but all those matches with Austin, Angle, and the rest of those guys were the most pressure I'd ever been under, all while adjusting to the new culture of the WWF.

Kurt Angle defeated me on *SD* for the WCW title in Pittsburgh on July 26 after tapping to the ankle lock. It wasn't a good night for me. Earlier in the show, they had me relinquish the United States title to Kanyon without even wrestling him in a show of Alliance unity. Dropping both the World and United States Championships in one TV taping left me wondering, *Now what are they going to do with me?*

The WWF always kept me guessing without revealing any kind of long-term plans, so it was a welcome surprise to win the World title back from Angle four days later on *Raw* in Philly. It was a No DQ Match, and Austin interfered by hitting a Stunner on Angle while the ref was knocked out. I reclaimed the Big Gold

CHAMPIONSHIPS

WCW World Tag Team Championship	10
WCW World Television Championship	6
WCW United States Championship	1
WCW World Heavyweight Championship	5
Total	22

BOOKER T. HUFFMAN

once more, now officially the *five-time* WCW World Heavyweight Champion.

From there, I wasn't exactly sitting around twiddling my thumbs. When they started booking me into a long-anticipated, inevitable feud with The Rock, it was apparent the championship wouldn't be mine for long.

It all began on August 2 on *SD*. The Rock ran in on The Undertaker and me in D.C., which led to my retaliation during a match he had with Shane in Anaheim on August 6 for *Raw*. While The Rock was pinning Shane, I came in for a shot to the face with my belt, setting up McMahon to elbow him from the top through the announcers' table.

On August 16 in Salt Lake City, we fought to a no contest. Shane was the one making his presence known by distracting The Rock enough for me to get the advantage and put him through the table myself with a Book End.

All this was a setup for SummerSlam 2001 in San Jose on August 19, when I dropped the WCW title for the last time in the title's illustrious history. I was trying to grow roots in the company for strong positioning for the future, knowing it wasn't the end of The Rock versus Booker T saga. Unfortunately, I didn't take control as much as I should've to make us both look even better than we did. The Rock was the face of the company, and his particular style of working took me out of my element. I wasn't the Booker T people usually saw, and I was aware of it the whole time.

Bradshaw and Faarooq, my old WCW mentor Ron Simmons, known together as The Acolytes, came down the ramp for Shane, who'd just hit The Rock with the belt. While they beat up Shane, I hit The Rock with the scissor kick, but instead of following it up with a pin, I performed a Spinarooni right into The Rock's waiting hands. He gave me an electrifying Rock Bottom and pinned me to win the WCW gold.

Afterward, we shook hands on what we'd accomplished out there, but I was disappointed with my middle-of-the-road performance, which is never what I wanted to give the fans.

The next night on *Raw*, The Rock made fun of me by bringing out Mini Booker T, called Booker Wee, a play on the Austin Powers character Mini-Me. He did a little Spinarooni and some other dances until Lance Storm came out and superkicked his head. It was then that I understood how Goldberg felt back in WCW when the WWF had this skinny little jobber named Gillberg come out dressed like him, mocking his mannerisms and attempting to perform his moves. Goldberg was so hot about that.

I have to admit, though, working with The Rock was some of the most fun I ever experienced in my career. Once we got past the competitive tension, we were really cool, each realizing what a charismatic worker the other was. In the business, all it takes for two guys to bond is to get in the ring together and test the ability to control, follow when it's time, and tell the right story for the both of you.

By then, the boys in the locker room were much more aware of how I conducted myself in and out of performances, and although I still wasn't considered a WWF guy, everyone was welcoming. From my vantage point, though, there was so much more to prove.

After I lost the title, I wasn't booked in the singles championship picture for the time being. No matter where I'd go, even if the Big Gold never found its way back around my waist, I was determined to make sure everyone remembered exactly who I was.

DDP had been using the catchphrase "It's me, it's me, it's DDP" at the beginning of his entrance music, and an idea came to me. I borrowed his concept and started raising the fingers on my right hand, exclaiming that I was, in fact, "the five-time, five-time, five-time, five-time, *five-time* WCW Champion!"

With the self-aggrandizing announcement, no one could ever forget my accreditations. For the rest of my career, I simply wouldn't let them.

15

THE ROAD TO WRESTLEMANIA

On Tuesday, September 11, 2001, we were scheduled to tape *SD* in my hometown at the Compaq Center in Houston. Nick Patrick had stayed at my place the night before to be ready for the taping. That morning, we awoke to devastating news. When I turned on the news, on the screen One World Trade Center was engulfed in flames. Overwhelming disbelief flooded me.

"Hey, Nick, get down here," I yelled.

We both stared in horror when the second plane flew into view and struck the other tower. We sat there dazed in my living room with the images on constant replay.

Later that day, a lot of opinions flew around the WWF about how we should respond. Everyone agreed it was right to postpone the show. We would convene Thursday, September 13.

When the day arrived, of course the entire country was still in shock. Vince pulled us into a meeting for a pep talk. He said we needed to go out and perform like never before, bringing some much-needed joy to the people.

And that's what we did. There were no promos, angles, or story lines, just match after match of pure physical action in front of a sold-out crowd at the Compaq Center.

It's tradition in the business that a guy wrestling in his hometown is booked to lose. I walked out in front of my city to wrestle Big Show, and we poured it on heavy in an emotional and high-impact contest that lasted under three minutes. It was a fast-paced match where I hit Big Show with two devastating scissor kicks in a row. When I couldn't keep him down for the three count, I took advantage of his lying on the ground by delivering a running, newly renamed Houston Hangover, for the rare hometown victory.

That was an event I'll never forget. I'm proud we made the right decision to go out and do what we did best to give the nation as much consolation as professional wrestling could. I believe it was just as therapeutic for the hometown and TV audience as it was for us. It felt like we were breaking the ice for America during what would become a long hibernation of mourning, anger, and innumerable negative emotions that we knew wouldn't loom forever. There had to be a restarting point, and I like to think we were part of that resurgence of hope in some small way.

After wondering for some time what my fate would be, I was paired with Test and added to the tag team division again for the first time in years. I liked Test. We got along and had great chemistry working together. Our first feud was with WCW World Tag Team Champions The Undertaker and Kane.

On September 23 in Pittsburgh, I had an opportunity for a rematch with The Rock at Unforgiven 2001 in a Handicap Match along with Shane-O Mac.

Before the match, they showed a vignette where I mused about what it would feel like to be the *six-time* WCW World Champion. After I left, they shifted to Shane staring at himself in the mirror, imagining himself winning the belt as well.

We double-teamed The Rock the majority of the show, and Test even interfered right in front of Nick Patrick, who was still my loyal WCW official. Then it all fell apart when WWF ref Mike Chioda intervened against Nick, giving The Rock time to recover and slam me with a Rock Bottom to retain the Big Gold.

On September 25 in Dayton for the *SD* taping, Test and I scored the WCW tag titles after nailing The Undertaker with a chair as Shane distracted the referee. The win made me an eleven-time WCW World Tag Team Champion, and this was the first without Lash and me together as Harlem Heat.

CHAMPIONSHIPS	
WCW World Tag Team Championship	11
WCW World Television Championship	6
WCW United States Championship	1
WCW World Heavyweight Championship	5
Total	23

Another new development for me was being invited into the WWF TV dressing room where all the veterans stayed and the production guys did their camera and screen checks. Because there was always a ton of space, it was where the top guys like The Undertaker, Austin, The Rock, Triple H, Angle, and Kane opted to change.

The Undertaker saw me once while I was headed to the standard locker room and said, "From now on, you're welcome to come into our space."

It felt great to be welcomed. I knew there were still more than a few degrees of separation between us, but at least I wasn't an outcast anymore. There was a strong network of supportive guys there who helped me not only become familiar with the new roster but develop my own character.

I wanted the viewing audience to be dazzled by not only my in-ring performances but my persona in interviews and vignettes as well. I wanted them to be invested in Booker T the man, not just the thug with fists and high-flying kicks.

Fortunately, people like Blackjack Lanza, Pat Patterson, Jerry Brisco, or Mr. B as I call him, and especially Freebird Michael Hayes were there to give me advice. They'd say, "Be yourself, be natural, and don't hold back. Run with it, have fun, and you'll see what happens."

And night after night, I found out they were right.

Back on the road, I had a series of singles matches with Kane, usually getting the pin after a Test run-in on my behalf. Kane was an amazingly big guy who knew how to work light and make his opponents look great. He was freakishly strong, and he'd effortlessly pick me up for the chokeslam or grab me with one hand and throw me into the corner for some shots. I felt like a little kid against The Big Red Machine.

Whenever I was going into the ring with the giants of the business, I had to think about how to best approach the match. My power moves didn't enter the equation. I wasn't going to try to slam a guy close to seven feet tall and over three hundred pounds. I'd have to pepper around with my arsenal of kicks, punches, and high-flying moves from the turnbuckles, which was the safe, believable way to handle someone like Kane.

On October 8 in Indianapolis, Test and I were scheduled to drop the tag titles to Matt and Jeff Hardy, The Hardy Boyz. The Undertaker got involved and slammed me with the Last Ride, a super powerbomb where once you were in the seated position up on his shoulders, he'd pick you up by your trunks over his head for an extra foot of height before mercilessly dropping you. Aside from Mike Awesome's terrifying running powerbomb, The Undertaker's Last Ride is the scariest of them all.

I didn't know what to expect from The Hardys before getting into the ring with them. From my initial perspective, they were nothing but another pair of babyfaces like the NWA's Rock 'n' Roll Express in the eighties. I knew they appealed to the women and teenyboppers, selling tons of merchandise and receiving huge pops from their entrance to the finish. But once I performed with them, I was pleasantly surprised by their wealth of talent. They understood psychology and storytelling and knew the fluid timing and pacing of a well-balanced dance within the ropes.

Once I was out, Jeff Hardy went to the top and did his vaulted somersaulting Swanton Bomb for the pin. I didn't mind dropping the titles to The Hardys at all, because they represented themselves and the WWF perfectly.

Moving ahead to the No Mercy 2001 PPV in St. Louis on October 21, I lost a clean match to The Undertaker courtesy of the Last Ride. While The Undertaker was in the corner, I mounted the ropes and hovered over him, punching his face again and again. The Undertaker skimmed me off the top onto his shoulders for the big bump and the pin in the center of the ring. No complaints there, either. Working and talking with The Dead Man, who was working as his American Bad Ass character, was always a spotlight for me.

Another highlight came November 1 at *SD* in Cincinnati, when Test and I teamed up again to win my first WWF World Tag Team title from Jericho and The Rock. Test had the honor of covering The Rock for the three count after dodging Jericho's missile dropkick, which struck The

CHAMPIONSHIPS	
WCW World Tag Team Championship	11
WCW World Television Championship	6
WCW United States Championship	1
WCW World Heavyweight Championship	5
WWF World Tag Team Championship	1
Total	24

People's Champion down for the count.

In Boston on November 12, we again lost to Matt and Jeff, dropping the World Tag Team Championship. At that time, The Hardys were running with a female wrestler named Lita, who could work just like them. She focused on a lot of *lucha* moves like the *hurricanrana*, which she did off the top turnbuckle. It was impressive to see her hitting high-flying moves as if she were Rey Mysterio. That night I was the one to catch her act off the top, allowing Jeff to roll me up for the win.

With so many title switches, I felt like I had in WCW, not knowing whether I was coming or going. Now that The Invasion was finally dying off, creative came up with its final, fatal blow with a Winner Take All Match at the Survivor Series on November 18 in Greensboro, North Carolina. The main event Five-on-Five Elimination Match featured Team WWF, consisting of The Rock, Jericho, The Undertaker, Big Show, and Kane, versus Team Alliance, featuring Stone Cold, who had turned on the WWF side, Rob Van Dam, Angle, another ECWCW defector, Shane, and me.

When the action got going, Show was taken out by an Angle Slam, a scissor kick from myself, R.V.D.'s Five-Star Frog Splash, and finally Shane's flying elbow from the top. Immediately after, Shane was destroyed by the trifecta of a Kane chokeslam, The Undertaker's Tombstone, and Jericho's backward flying Lionsault from the second rope for the elimination.

Even though Shane wasn't a full-time wrestler, he took every bump like a pro and could perform with the best of them.

From there, Kane was eliminated by R.V.D. The Undertaker was pinned by Angle after Austin stunned him. Then I had the displeasure of getting rolled up by The Rock, and I was gone too. Eventually, The Rock would catch Angle in the sharpshooter, causing him to tap out.

It was now The Rock and Jericho against Austin. Jericho tried for the roll-up on Austin, who reversed it, pinning him and evening it up one-to-one. However, Jericho had enough of The Rock and double-crossed him by driving him to the mat with a front-facing full-nelson slam before leaving.

Not to be outdone, at the end of the match, Angle would make his way back down to ringside, and while the ref was knocked out, he would double-cross Austin by hitting him with the WWE title, allowing The Rock to hit Austin with the Rock Bottom for the win.

As a stipulation of being defeated, a select few of the WCW guys, including me, were fired according to the story line for being the enemy faction Shane brought in to destroy his father. Now that I was unemployed, I'd have to find some way into the WWF to get a job. They kept me off TV to sort out the plot while I sat in Houston.

The next night on *Raw* in Charlotte, Paul Heyman was the first to be fired straight from the commentary table, complete with security taking him out and hauling him away in dramatic protest. Jerry "The King" Lawler was his replacement.

My old respected nemesis-turned-ally from WCW, Steven Regal, had long before made his way to the WWF and was now William Regal. Regal got the worst of being associated with The Alliance when Vince allowed him to keep his job on one condition. In the middle of the ring, Vince declared he'd created the Kiss My Ass Club, and if Regal wanted to stay employed, he had to be the first honorary member.

Vince dropped his pants, and there it was: the boss's bare white butt wagging in Regal's direction.

I was in the back, cringing and thinking, *Aw, man. Is he serious with this?*

He was. I'll tell you right now, I'm not sure what I would have done if I had been put in that situation. I just know I'm glad I didn't have to make that decision.

He even gave Regal a ChapStick, which Regal used before getting down on his knees and applying his grimacing pucker to the boss's naked cheeks. It seemed he moved in on Vince's rear for a million years, but he did it, kept his job, and walked around with a sour look on his face for the rest of the night.

To this day, Regal still hasn't heard the end of the ribbing.

It was also announced that any Alliance member holding a championship was granted clemency and kept their jobs. That applied to Tag Team Champions The Dudley Boyz, Hardcore titleholder R.V.D., and WWF European Champion Christian.

With WCW being officially disbanded, some of the titles were merged. The Intercontinental took over the United States belt. The WWF World Tag Team Championships superseded and eliminated the WCW tag titles. The WCW World Heavyweight Championship was unbranded, having *WCW* removed from the name to make it simply known as the World Heavyweight Championship.

The dismantling of WCW was now complete, with all visible traces erased in a flash.

Later that night at *Raw* in the closing segment, the "Nature Boy" Ric Flair, the epitome of WCW, made his triumphant return to the WWF after nine years.

When his entrance theme hit, JR played it up dramatically. "Wait a second. What is that? It can't be what I think it could be."

Flair came styling and profiling down the ramp, and the place went insane with everyone on their feet in deafening chants of, "Woo!"

He stated to Vince in a classic promo that prior to his purchase of WCW, Shane and Stephanie McMahon had sold their majority stake of WWF stock to him, making him 50 percent owner of the company along with him. As he spoke, he took breaks to run into the ropes and hard strut toward a disbelieving Vince. Finally he said they were partners and gave him a big hug and a kiss.

It was perfect.

I was happy to see Ric backstage the following week, and we hugged like POWs finally finding each other in a war camp.

"Strange days, right?" I said.

He smiled. "The strangest."

Whenever I saw Ric, he brought the comfortable WCW feeling back. His presence was always good for business and everyone's morale.

I got the call to return for *Raw* on November 26 in Oklahoma City to curry favor with Regal, who was now Vince's stooge. Regal was booked into a match with Big Show. Since I was in the doghouse and needed an in with Vince to get my job back, Regal was my opportunity. As I'd done so many times since signing with the WWF, I ran down through the crowd and distracted the referee so Regal could knock out Show with a pair of brass knuckles and score the pin. Security officers chased me while I hightailed it out of there.

The next few weeks of TV saw me developing creative, funny material completely different from the WCW Harlem thug's. The closest thing to humor I'd done there was the concession stand fight with The Nasty Boys, and even that I'd done as seriously as possible.

On the December 3 *Raw*, my quest to gain Vince's acceptance continued. While Austin and Jericho were wrestling, the cameras caught me in the parking lot hot-wiring Stone

Cold's truck and taking off with it.

Six days later at Vengeance 2001, Vince and Flair declared that the WWF needed only one World title and decided to merge them into the WWF Undisputed Championship. The new champ would be decided by having WWF Champion Steve Austin defend against The Rock, with the victor squaring off against the winner of the World Heavyweight Title Match between Champion Chris Jericho and Kurt Angle.

Both Austin and Jericho won, setting up the immediate final match for the Undisputed title, where all kinds of shenanigans went down, including my climactic involvement.

Vince ordered Nick Patrick to ref the contest because he too was a WCW guy on the outside and needed to maintain his job. But Flair pulled Nick out and beat him down, prompting McMahon to toss Ric into the ring post.

All the outside action with no referee allowed Austin to hit a low blow on Jericho and put in his own finisher, the Walls of Jericho, a modified Boston crab. With no official available to see Jericho tap out, I ran into the ring and cold-cocked Austin's head with the WWF Championship belt. Chris made the cover and became the first WWF Undisputed Champion in the history of the company.

It was a really easy night of work for me, and I knew at that point I was on a collision course with Austin, one of the all-time biggest names in professional wrestling. Business was about to start booming.

The next night on *Raw* in Anaheim, I really started to relax and have some fun in the spotlight without even stepping into the ring. I had a dramatic backstage entrance with Vince, Flair, and a crew of security guards with dogs to prevent a possible Austin attack. It was such an empowering feeling to be walking in front of the cameras with the two bosses and those dogs, as if we were some militant force controlling the WWF. Because Vince was so pleased with my assisting Regal against Show, he invited me to his luxury box to enjoy the evening's entertainment with him.

While there, we watched all the matches. Vince got on the microphone and started saying hi to the people. They waved, and we waved back. Vince said the Kiss My Ass Club was officially closed and announced he was now opening the Get My Ass Kicked Club. All you had to do was cross the boss to get in. He even referred to me as the biggest star of them all.

Man, I was having the time of my life doing this kind of character performance, and it got even funnier when the catering girl showed up with a platter of sandwiches. I acted suspicious and asked her who made them and to be my royal taste tester in case Austin poisoned them.

The big payoff was during the main event Steel Cage Match for the World Heavyweight Championship between Austin and Jericho. Just as Stone Cold was making his exit to win the title, I ran down and slammed the door in his face.

Jericho, looking badly beaten, scurried out to retain the gold.

It was a great night of assimilating to the WWF's method of operations. The mischief to come would take me to a level of ridiculousness and popularity I never imagined in my wildest dreams.

After costing Austin the victory against Jericho for the Undisputed title, Vince and I were on high alert the next night on *SD* in Bakersfield. Flair greeted us in the back and invited Vince and me to partake in the luxury box at the Centennial Garden Arena just as the three of us had in Milwaukee. Of course, we suspected the obvious setup by The Nature Boy for Stone Cold to get his hands on us, and we proceeded with caution. When we arrived, the coast was clear and Flair professed, "Vince is the boss, and it's his show!"

A few matches later, while Vince and I watched like Roman emperors at the Colosseum, a mysterious tray of food arrived. We concluded it was misdirected to us from Austin's dressing room and didn't hesitate to dig right in.

A couple of segments later, Vince had the waiter cook a burger on a little hibachi grill, which caught on fire. McMahon doused it with a beer, and we settled on fries instead. When the fire brigade showed up to check on the remnants of the fire, it turned out one of them was Austin dressed in full gear, and he knocked Vince out while I ran for the hills.

Flair had led us into the trap we'd expected all along.

I made it out to the parking lot, hopped in my rental car, and raced out of there with Austin right behind me in the big Stone Cold skull-themed pickup truck. I made it to a local grocery store, where the greatest produce and dairy showdown ever filmed was about to ensue.

It was all mapped out, and Steve and I did some basic rehearsals as if it were a movie set to make it as flawless as possible—without laughing.

The attention to detail and professionalism surrounding me by the expansive crew made it clear why WCW had collapsed. There was no comparison to the production infrastructure Vince had perfected since the eighties.

The grocery store script was pure gold. Thinking I was safe from Austin in the store, I was in the cereal aisle eating out of a box and checking the stamped date for freshness. Just then a distorted voice came over the PA system asking for "a can of whup-ass in aisle two—that's aisle two!"

I bugged out, ran to the first bald guy I saw, and beat him while yelling, "Get your ass up!"

It turned out to be an innocent customer. Just as I realized my mistake, Austin came up slowly behind me.

As soon as I felt his presence and spun around, Stone Cold lit me up all over the grocery store with relentless stomps, punches, and throws, leaving no milk jug or egg intact. He smashed me with oranges and squirted me with ketchup, which I'd sworn would never happen to me again. He even said, "Excuse me, sir, do you have any Grey Poupon?" and sprayed mustard all over me before emptying an entire bag of flour over my head. He grabbed a big salami and sang, "That's *amore*," before cracking me with a frozen pizza. It was over-the-top and undeniably hysterical as they kept cutting to Flair and Vince watching from the luxury box with Ric laughing and Vince staring, openmouthed.

From that point on, it was a complete shoot with Austin in control. The ruckus finally ended when I was dumped into a shopping cart and then onto the cashier's conveyor belt. Police sirens wailed in the background.

"It's been fun shopping with you, Book!" Austin said.

I lay there moaning and clutching my stomach, muttering, "I'm gonna get you!"

In the history of *Raw*, I'm not sure there was ever a segment before or after my time there where the live audience sat spellbound for almost nine full minutes of pure action and entertainment while watching the Jumbotron alone. It was a five-star payoff for the many weeks of buildup by both Austin and me, but more importantly, it was my golden ticket to unimaginable new heights in the WWF. That sequence follows me wherever I go.

It was a lot of fun for everyone except the production crew, who had to go back and clean up the disaster area we left in our wake.

Everybody backstage felt the grocery store angle was so impressive they wanted to follow it up with something similar. For the next *Raw* in Lafayette, Louisiana, Vince had Austin in the ring and demanded an apology for what he did to me. The image cut to the parking lot, where I smashed out all the windows on his truck with a pipe. I jumped into a limo and took off, with Austin giving chase once again.

As Steve stalked me, I hid in a church doing everything from cheating at bingo against old ladies to hiding in a confessional. While in the booth, I listened as the woman on the other side confessed to videotaping an affair with her boyfriend's brother, and as penance, I told her to say a bunch of Hail Marys and send me the tape and all would be forgiven. Finally, after Austin found me, I escaped to safety with a group of nuns, asking if they would drive me to an orphanage.

In the ring, all my efforts against The Texas Rattlesnake paid off as Flair offered me a contract on behalf of Vince for a couple hundred grand more than he would've given me, saying he was on the Booker T bandwagon and wanted in on McMahon's good graces. I was overjoyed and signed the contract, letting Flair know he was getting more than his money's worth.

He said, "I can dig it!"

I didn't realize it was Flair who drew up the contract, stipulating I'd have to face Austin in a first-blood match that very night in New Orleans. *Great.*

BOOKER T. HUFFMAN

Shortly after, Vince showed up in the parking lot where I was dancing around, happy to be back with the company, and I gave him a big hug. McMahon explained he had nothing to do with it and I'd just been had.

When we met with Flair, I found out about the match and wasn't happy about it. In a fit of desperation, I asked Kane if I could borrow one of his masks.

He denied me and offered only advice. "Don't bleed."

Then a messenger delivered a package: a first-aid kit from Stone Cold.

When it was go time, the showdown was less of a wrestling match and more of an unsanctioned murder scene. We were all over the place outside and inside the ring, where Austin exposed one of the turnbuckles, which I reversed and threw him into, failing to draw first blood. When Steve gave me his spinebuster, we were both knocked out.

During the match, the Big Boss Man made a surprise return to the WWF and made his intentions known by throwing me a chair, which I promptly smashed Steve in the face with, busting him wide open. He recovered and gave me a Stunner, but the ref, who'd been knocked out until then, saw Austin bleeding and declared me the victor. Vince appeared with an evil grin and started laughing to close out the show on the Jumbotron.

In the final show of the year, hating the cold cities as I do,

I was happy to end 2001 with *SD* in Orlando, WCW's old MGM Studios stomping grounds. Boss Man and I took on Stone Cold in a Handicap Match. Although Austin got some revenge on Boss Man with a stiff low blow to the groin, I knocked Austin into 2002 with a huge Houston Sidekick and pinned him for the win.

With my first year in WWF tucked into my back pocket, I went back to Houston to enjoy some rest and recuperation at home. On the Gulf of Mexico in my boat with my trusty fishing rod, I drifted with the currents, lulled into a nap where no dream could compare to what my life had become.

16

THE GRAND STAGE OF WRESTLEMANIA X8

At the beginning of 2002, I returned to New York City for *Raw* on January 7 at Madison Square Garden, where Boss Man and I lost a tag match to Austin and The Rock.

On January 10 on *SD*, also at the Garden, Rikishi introduced me to his horrendous trademark Stinkface. The dreaded finisher came as an opponent was downed in one of the corners in a seated position and the big man would pull his tights way up until they were wedged into his butt crack, turn around, and bury his giant backside into his opponent's face. It wasn't a pretty sight from a distance, much less when you were the victim.

That night I brawled with the four hundred pounder and took the Stinkface for the first and only time. As Rikishi was just about to sit on me, I exaggerated a look of panic. I held my breath and tried to keep my eyes closed and head turned. It was brutal, but I took one for the team in the rite of passage, then bailed, holding my stomach and dry heaving.

I barreled over to Michael Cole across the table and

vomited all over him and his white shirt. The Stinkface was so awful I probably could've managed to vomit without the special effects.

His commentary partner, Jerry "The King" Lawler, jumped, pointing and laughing. The segment came off great.

After the match, Rikishi was pretty hot at me in the back. "What's up with all those stiff shots? You were way too aggressive."

I wasn't even aware of it while we were in there, but when performing on TV, you go the extra mile. Red light fever is what they call it. In those early days, fresh from WCW, I was pretty intense and didn't hold back.

I let Rikishi know it wasn't purposeful, and we shook hands. But he was pretty pissed about it for a while.

On January 20, I entered the Philips Arena in Atlanta for my first Royal Rumble in WCW country. It felt a little odd stepping into a WWF ring on those once-hallowed grounds of my former company.

When my number was called, I ran into the chaotic turbulence of WWF Superstars and tried to make the best of it. R.V.D. became my target, and I tossed him over the top and followed up with a celebratory Spinarooni only to be greeted by Austin and a Stone Cold Stunner, which vaulted me out of there. My night was already over.

Continuing their power struggle over the fifty-fifty ownership of the WWF, Vince and Flair met each other in a Street

Fight Match. Flair scored the victory in classic style with the figure four.

Another highlight for me was to see my friend Curt Hennig make his WWF return in the Rumble as Mr. Perfect. He made it to the final four in the match before Triple H eliminated him. It was great to have the jokester back around.

Four days later on *SD*, Austin and I squared off again in my losing effort for the WWF Undisputed Championship. That pretty much put an end to our feud, as he'd now focus on Jericho's title.

The big news that night came at the end of the broadcast when Vince cut a promo. He stared into a mirror and ranted about how he never intended for the company he built into an empire to be ruined by someone like Ric Flair. With his hands together, as if in a deranged prayer, he said the WWF was dying and had cancer. Since he was the one who created it, he said it was up to him to inject the Federation with "a lethal dose of poison. If anyone's going to destroy my creation, I'm going to do it!" He hammed it up brilliantly, weeping, grimacing, gripping his fists, and raging.

As he finished, Vince swiveled his black leather chair around to stare at the camera, which pulled out in a long shot. McMahon thrust a thumb back toward the mirror, revealing the infamous nWo logo painted in white shoe polish on the back of his chair. "The nWo!"

Hollywood Hulk Hogan, Scott Hall, and Kevin Nash were on their way back to the WWF.

At the January 31 *SD*, the WWF was doing a promotional angle with a new movie called *Rollerball*, starring LL Cool J, Rebecca Romijn-Stamos, and Chris Klein. I'd been a fan of LL's during the eighties, and since the creative guys knew that, they produced a backstage segment between the two of us.

In the spot, I confronted him and asked why he didn't invite me to the film premiere. He shot back that it was no place for a guy who got beaten up in a grocery store and left me hanging.

Meeting LL was funny because we were both street-savvy tough guys. He was my size, and I could tell he'd been in some fights just by the way he carried himself, but he was down-to-earth and cool.

That night, I teamed up with Test again versus The Acolytes. We lost after Bradshaw knocked Test out with his Clothesline from Hell, which was a big shooting draw back and swing from the right arm of a guy who was about six feet five, three hundred pounds. I was glad it was Test and not me; that's for sure.

At No Way Out in Milwaukee on February 17, Hogan, Hall, and Nash made their in-ring debut.

When the three first started showing up backstage, they

came in without any attitude. It was like seeing old pals. Many of the boys, like The Undertaker and Hunter, were nothing but gracious with the infamous trio. The only questions remaining were how they'd perform, how the crowd would react, and how they'd conduct themselves behind the curtain.

At No Way Out, the three walked out to the old nWo theme song and cut a promo about how they were back in the WWF not to kill it off but to make it better. They were met with a mixed reaction of cheers and boos, yet there was still something electric about Hogan being in the ring after nine years.

In general, the guys were quiet and kept off to the side, not stirring up any kind of trouble and arriving on time. Their vibe was totally different than it had been in the WCW. They didn't have the same carefree disposition.

Hogan was on another plane and was almost untouchable. He even had his own dressing room. He was simply coming to work to reestablish himself with the company that had put him permanently on the professional wrestling map.

I quietly wondered if the rumors were true that Vince had sent them all to WCW. During the original nWo invasion beginning in 1996, people said Hogan, Hall, and Nash were in the company as legitimate saboteurs in a secret pact and when the master plan had been carried out, they'd come back home to Vince.

However, those guys had almost literally put Vince out of business. Through it all, he was willing to bury the hatchet for business with no personal resentment attached. It didn't add up. It reminded me of a story Vince once told me backstage.

It was about his father, Vince Sr., who'd run the World Wide Wrestling Federation since before Vince Jr. was conceived. When Vince Jr. was growing up in the business, his dad was embroiled in a bitter feud with another territorial promoter with a bad reputation. The guy was trying to drive him out of business, and one day Vince Jr. walked into the TV studio in Stamford and was shocked to find his father sitting with the very promoter they were at war with.

Later on when they were alone, Vince said, "Dad, what's going on? You hate that guy. Everyone says he's an asshole."

His father leaned back and said, "Son, I bought him out, and now he's *my* asshole."

And that is probably the only way to explain Vince's philosophy in the world of sports entertainment. No matter what you hear, if a performer leaves the WWF, if it's good for Vince's business, you'll see them on the next *Raw*.

At the actual No Way Out 2002 PPV, Test and I were at the end of a losing effort at the hands of the WWF Tag Team Champions Tazz and Spike Dudley. Test ate the finisher when he lost his cool and shoved referee Jack Doan, who then shoved him right into Tazz's Tazzmission for the tap out.

For the next few weeks, I separated from Test and went on the road wrestling R.V.D. in singles matches, usually getting the clean win with the Houston Sidekick or a Book End. I liked working with Rob, and he became a true friend. He's a hard-working performer who clicked with me in the ring due to our acrobatic repertoire. We'd both try to steal the show, which made our matches even more explosive. I could always count on a ton of stiff kicks and shins to my mouth and face, and I'd respond in kind.

The first time we ever saw each other outside of the business, we met up in Venice Beach, California, and he showed me all the sights and sounds: street performers, artists, old beatniks and hippies, people rollerblading by. He also took me to one of his favorite smoke shops and showed me the digs around there.

R.V.D. is all about intensity and innovation in the ring, but once he's out of it, wrestling's the last thing on his mind. We'd talk about creative ventures both of us saw ourselves getting into. He was interested in getting into action movies, opening up his own comic bookstore, and even producing his own brand of comics.

I'd contemplate opening a wrestling school one day and maybe getting behind the camera and producing TV shows or movies and getting involved in charitable causes.

R.V.D. and I both knew there'd be a day beyond wrestling, and it was all about planning and setting those ideas in motion. Since day one, Rob and I have remained confidants in a world where trust is a rare gift.

On March 4 in Austin, Texas, on *Raw*, Stone Cold and I had yet another rematch early in the show. Just a couple of minutes in, Hogan, Hall, and Nash, in old-school nWo form, ran down and attacked The Texas Rattlesnake. Hall went after Austin with a wrench and beat him into a bloody mess before they all started laying in with the boots. After they left the ring, Scott turned around and went back to give Stone Cold his own Stunner. It made me remember my match with Bagwell when Austin interfered and physically threw me out of the building.

Backstage, Vince was pleased with the reaction. I'm sure he saw dollar signs for the foreseeable future. The only problem with the nWo was that once they got going and felt the popularity soaring as it once had, the guys could be hard to control. Each of them wanted to take his role further, and it was evident the ego factor could build until it ruined the whole arrangement. Vince was obviously willing to make it work, but everyone knew if needed he'd pull the plug without thinking twice. I also thought if any single member would blow it up for the trio, it would be Hall, whose personal demons, which had resulted in his firing from WCW less than a year before, clearly still tormented him.

Finally that month, I completed my first Road to WrestleMania when the WWF took the Super Bowl of professional wrestling back to the Toronto SkyDome, the site of WrestleMania VI in 1990, where The Ultimate Warrior had unified his Intercontinental title with Hogan's WWF Championship. Now it was WrestleMania X8, and I was booked for the sixth match on the card against Edge in front of nearly seventy thousand of his fellow Canadians and fans from across the globe.

This was it—the big stage every wrestler dreams of performing on at least once. It was the most mainstream event I'd ever been a part of. There were festivities for days in Toronto before WrestleMania even happened, including the WWF Fan Axxess at the Canadian National Exhibition's Automotive Building, where fans could meet performers and see WWF memorabilia and staging. It was pretty easy to get caught up in the hype, and I found myself again fighting nervous energy.

When they put the undercard together and decided to pair me with Edge for the show, one of the WWF agents initially wanted a Hair vs. Hair Match, which would've resulted in me losing my prized locks.

"No way," I said. I was in the early stages of growing out braids and wasn't about to let anyone take liberties with my hair. However, hair would end up playing a big part in our feud.

In the few weeks before WrestleMania, Edge cut promos questioning my intelligence. As part of the story line, he stole my role in a Japanese shampoo endorsement deal I'd been working hard to secure.

The shampoo angle gave me yet another great opportunity to flex my comedic muscles, and as with everything in this business, I threw myself into it 100 percent.

In one segment I was backstage in front of a blue backdrop, doing a run-through to a small off-camera audience of how my shampoo commercial would go.

"Yo! Japanese people. What's the deal which yo' nasty hair? Just because you know kung fu doesn't mean you know shaum-poo."

I mimed my best kung fu moves as I smiled and continued, "But that's all about to change thanks to *new* Yak-ah-moe-she Shaum-poo." Again, I paused to grin from ear to ear.

"It won't make your hair look as good as mine"—I shook my hair like a head banger at a metal concert—"but you gotta start somewhere!"

Standing there in my pride, I looked off camera and said, "Whatchu think of that?"

As the camera panned around, it revealed Japanese wrestler Taijiri sitting in a director's chair, along with the beautiful Torrie Wilson at his side.

Taijiri said something in Japanese, which Torrie translated, "He said, 'Huh . . . it's very offensive.'"

I was shocked and hurt. My eyes got wide with anger as I replied, "Very offensive? Hey, I wrote this myself! You ask that sucka what's wrong with it."

Taijiri replied again in Japanese, which Torrie translated,

"He said he wants to know why you make fun of his people's hair when your hair looks like . . ."

"Bad weave on crack," Taijiri finished in English.

I stared him down and said, "You didn't say that . . . Tell me you didn't just say *that*! You know what? I don't know why I asked for your advice anyway, sucka!"

And I stormed off set, fuming.

Although it was humorous, it also added another level of entertainment to our story line.

On the night of WrestleMania, just before going out to my match, I wore a pair of glasses to cut a promo with Michael Cole. When Cole mentioned Edge's insults about my intelligence, I retorted about how smart I was because I wore glasses, aced my SATs, and won an award for my thesis on Einstein's theory of relatives. My eyes were bulging with seriousness.

Cole said, "You mean the theory of relativity, right?"

I snatched the glasses off my face and barked, "Shut up, sucka! He had two theories."

That night, while I waited for Edge to make his way down to the ring, I looked at the ground section of fans that stretched for a mile before even hitting the upper sections. "Damn," I muttered, "this definitely *is* WrestleMania."

When Edge got there, as always, we matched up well due to his height and speed. Looking around at the packed stadium, I thought it was funny to see a sign in the crowd that said,

They Are Fighting Over Shampoo. We ran the ropes, took it outside, and hit plenty of high-impact moves, including Edge flipping me in a nasty *hurricanrana* from the top.

In just under seven minutes, we'd hit each other with every crowd-pleasing maneuver in our repertoires. When it was time for the finish, I whacked him with a Houston Sidekick, gave a dramatic WrestleMania Spinarooni to a flood of camera flashes, and hit him with the scissor kick. But Edge made a comeback, mocked me with an Edgearooni, kicked me in the stomach, delivered his Edgecution DDT, and covered me for the win.

I was happy with the entire performance, and afterward we hugged each other.

"That's how it's done at WrestleMania," Vince said. "Well done, boys."

At WrestleMania, Vince is Santa Claus on Christmas morning watching everybody around the world open their presents to see if he pulled it off successfully for another consecutive year. There was no coal in my stocking for my first WrestleMania. I kept thinking, *I can't wait until next year! I'll do it even bigger and better!*

Also at WrestleMania X8, Hollywood Hulk Hogan would contend with The Rock. They'd been building up to it ever since the nWo returned to the company with The Rock confronting Hogan, Hall, and Nash, posing with Hulk for a picture, and then verbally destroying all three of them.

I'm sure Vince saw huge revenue potential in placing two kings on opposite sides of the WrestleMania chessboard. It was to be Hogan as the dreaded heel versus the biggest babyface in the company. What transpired in the SkyDome was a perfect storm that developed without warning: Hulkamania.

Hogan, probably assuming he'd be on the receiving end of the entire crowd's wrath for leaving the WWF so long before, was instead greeted with a standing ovation, the loudest pop I've ever heard in the business. Huge signs were emblazoned with Hulk's face. He was visibly stunned and stopped dead in his tracks, frozen by emotion. The bad-guy scowl turned into an ear-to-ear smile as nostalgia turned longtime fans back into ten-year-old kids and brought The Hulkster home where he belonged on a red-carpeted time machine in Toronto.

When The Rock came out, he too was completely taken aback by the reaction of boos and jeers. The People's Champion was overtaken by Hulkamania, a crowd reaction unparalleled in the business.

I sat in the back, thinking, *For one night, the prayers, vitamins, and vintage Hulk Hogan are back!*

It was an unforgettable moment in our industry.

Pandemonium ensued as the two squared off, Hogan circling the ring, stalking The Rock, even saying, "Come on, meatball," his classic line from *Rocky III*.

When they locked up, Hogan kept throwing The Rock,

who'd stumble backward into the corner as Hulk hit his famous muscular poses as if he'd stepped out of 1985. He even started twirling his right hand before cupping it to his ear, his cue for the people to give him some noise, and they couldn't have been happier to indulge him.

The SkyDome was about to shake itself to the foundations from the thunder of the audience. Even JR on the microphone was having difficulty explaining what was transpiring in Toronto as the crowd booed everything The Rock did.

Hogan played all his Hollywood Hogan tactics—poking the eyes, raking the back, and whipping with his leather Hollywood weight lifting belt—but he could do no wrong. The nastier he was, the more people ate it up, but he knew he had a job to do, and that was to lie down for The Rock.

After The Rock took Hogan's trademark three punches to the face, the big boot, and the iconic leg drop, The Rock kicked out and Rock Bottomed Hogan twice before pinning him after The People's Elbow.

Hogan, defeated, really sold his dejection and started to leave the ring only to be beckoned back by The Rock, who shook his hand.

The torch was passed, and The Rock demanded The Hulkster give the people what they wanted. Hogan spent the next few minutes hitting every single one of his Mr. Olympia bodybuilding poses: the double biceps, the arms to the side, and the double-most muscular.

I'm positive both Hogan and The Rock consider that night one of the highlights of their careers. It was a great event for the WWF and the world of professional wrestling.

After that night, there was no returning to heel status for Hogan. The fans wouldn't allow it. The nWo reunion didn't stand a chance. Hogan, Hall, and Nash were destined to part ways.

Hogan went into business for himself, understanding the power of Hulkamania, which the fans and Vince couldn't deny. Not long after that, Hogan returned to a Hollywood Hogan version of the yellow and red, with tie-dyed leggings and a feather boa, looking like a combination of vintage "Superstar" Billy Graham and Jesse "The Body" Ventura.

The nWo moved on without Hogan. Hall and Nash came out and cut a promo on him, asking who he thought he was and what was he was doing. The nWo soon became just the old faction in WCW, with new members like X-Pac, Big Show, and even the returning Shawn Michaels. However, without Hogan, it lost steam.

If Hall and Nash could've abandoned the nWo altogether and returned to their original Razor Ramon and Diesel characters to relive their own nostalgic golden days, maybe things would've been better for them, but it never happened.

Sadly, Hall would be around only a couple more months. His demons kept their chains around him, and he would lose the biggest comeback opportunity he would ever have for the rest of his career.

Two weeks later at the *SD* taping in Philly on March 26, I was in a match with DDP when only a couple of minutes in, new-comer monster Brock Lesnar came out of the crowd. Brock was the latest powerhouse to be called up from the WWF's developmental promotion in Louisville: Ohio Valley Wrestling (OVW). He was a former NCAA Division I Heavyweight Champion. Clocking in at six feet three and around 290 pounds, he was an unstoppable force of lightning-fast power.

Much like Kurt Angle, the former Olympic wrestling gold medalist, Brock had all the tools to make it. He perfectly transitioned into professional wrestling, being billed as The Next Big Thing by his manager Paul Heyman.

For the previous few months, beginning in late 2001, Lesnar had been wrestling dark matches before *Raw* and *SD*. During the beginning months of 2002, he routinely came down to the ring, impressively interrupting the action and obliterating whoever was in his way. One night he ran in on The Hardy Boyz and destroyed both of them with ease, even triple powerbombing Jeff. It was a mind-boggling feat.

Due to his style, size, and all-black gear, the crowd started chanting Goldberg's name from Lesnar's first day in the ring. Soon he'd gain his own identity and leave that comparison in the dust.

That night at *SD*, he chose DDP as his victim, picking him

up for a brutal spinebuster followed up by the F5, a finisher no one had seen before, where he tossed Dallas up and across his back, as if he were a lumberjack squatting a giant log. Then in one swift, graceful move, Brock put a hand on DDP's right leg, helicopter spun him around ninety degrees over his head, and pancaked his face and sternum onto the mat.

The demolition was awesome, and I stood there, unsure what to make of the interference but mostly happy it wasn't me. I was smart enough to take a powder and rolled out of the ring to watch with a smile from the ground position.

Having seen Vince pushing Brock since his arrival, I anticipated standing across the ring from Brock one-on-one.

17

JOINING THE NWO

On April Fools' Day, it was announced the WWF was going to divide the entire roster of performers between Flair's *Raw* and Vince's *SD*. In order for both brands to have a World title, the Big Gold World Heavyweight Championship was brought back as *SD*'s greatest prize, while the WWF Championship remained on *Raw*. Eventually, to have their own title parallel to the WWF Intercontinental Championship, *SD* would also bring back the decommissioned United States Championship.

A lottery was held to decide where each performer went. My name was selected to stay on *Raw* for the time being. I went on the road for a while, being slightly edged out by R.V.D. in a series of matches for his Intercontinental belt.

In the midst of my house show schedule against Rob, I performed on a *Raw* with WWF Hardcore Champion Bubba Ray Dudley. My bid for the win was disrupted by Goldust, Dustin Rhodes' over-the-top, androgynous character, complete with a black-and-gold bodysuit and matching face paint. I was Bubba Bombed through a table, costing me the match.

On *Raw* in College Station, Texas, on April 15, I sought out Goldust and cut a promo on him for costing me my opportunity. Instead of getting into an altercation, he suggested that teaming up would be box office gold. Thus, the team of BookDust was born.

Goldie and I went back almost ten years to the early WCW days, when he wrestled as Dusty Rhodes' son Dustin. I'd found him to be a really good guy with a great sense of humor. When we reunited, he'd already gone through a fairly successful run as Goldust with the WWF during the mid-nineties after leaving WCW.

Prichard and the creative guys thought the sharp contrast between the two of us might be an entertaining formula for TV, so they paired us as the oddest couple in the WWF. At the time, I was a little disappointed because it was apparent the company was steering me away from the major title picture. I went with the flow, but I craved a bigger, more substantial test, feeling that my physical and character capabilities were the strongest they'd been in my career.

I look back now and see how much good it did me to be pushed out of my comfort zone. Thankfully, I stayed focused on the positives and looked at working with someone like Goldie as another challenge that would heighten my comedic value and acting skills.

Right from the start, for the April 22 *Raw* in St. Louis, we shot a parody of *Ebert & Roeper* as we reviewed The Rock's movie *The Scorpion King*. The production guys were cracking up the whole time, and so were we, which meant dozens of takes. The end result showcased what a great contrast Goldust and I were to one another, just in the way we talked about the movie.

Goldust in his breathy tone would say, "Note the felonious way in which our protagonist must engage in his goal, in his quest for salvation. The pathos we feel is only underscored by the magnanimous . . ."

"Yo, man, what the hell are you talking about? Just roll the damn footage!" I would yell.

After watching footage, I would argue that it was a great movie except for one problem. It didn't have me in it. And if it did, it would have been over the top, a bigger smash then it was. Goldust thought that sounded delicious, to which I replied, "You're damn right it sounds delicious!"

I then had them roll footage of me in The Rock's place in *The Scorpion King*.

As the trailer played, fans watching *Raw* were treated to me busting onto the big screen, swinging a sword. "That's right. You suckas better run! 'Cause it's me, Booker T! Not only am I the Scorpion King, but I'm the five-time WCW Champion, and I got a sword too! Now can you dig that, suckas?"

It was a great skit, and both Goldust and I had a blast filming it.

Before Goldie and I really took off on our tag team

comedy quest, though, some singles hurdles were set in front of me.

On May 1 in Cologne, Germany, a city I was very familiar with because of WCW, I stepped into another showdown with The Nature Boy. Times had changed since our first encounter in 1993, and the roles were reversed. Without a drop of nervous energy this time, I took charge and made Flair look as good as ever.

By that point, I knew all his tricks of the trade, and our match moved like clockwork. It was an absolute pleasure to guide Flair through the match and watch him entertain as only he could. It was a privilege to take a loss to him once again, just like the first time, with a figure-four submission in the middle of the ring.

After the show, Ric and I met up at a bar and talked about the WCW days and his passing the torch to me when I won the Big Gold from Jarrett in 2001. It was great to reminisce together.

From Cologne we headed to the Insurrextion 2002 PPV from Wembley Stadium in London. I won and lost the Hardcore title twice that night.

The rule of the WWF Hardcore Championship back then was that the champ was subject to being attacked and pinned for the belt at any time. I pinned Stevie Richards with the Book End. Hardcore Holly's lookalike sidekick, Crash Holly, flew into the ring behind me for the roll-up and pin. I didn't have the title for more than a hot minute before dropping it.

Within seconds, I scissor kicked Richards and took my belt back. Suddenly I was a two-time Hardcore Champion.

The comedy went even further as Tommy Dreamer and Justin Credible wanted some, so I gave them a solid beatdown before Jazz, a new WWF Diva, gave me a surprise low blow to the groin, allowing Stevie to recover and put me through a table.

That was the first time I won and lost a championship twice in one match, and thankfully it was the last. The Hardcore playground was not my scene at all.

As eventful as that European tour was, the most memorable moments happened on the way home. A plane ride from London to Newark International in New Jersey takes a little over seven hours, but this flight felt like it lasted an eternity. We were on our private WWF charter, and I was trying to relax and maybe get some sleep. Hall was near me, fast asleep after having a few too many. He'd been a wreck during the tour, and management took notice.

Sometime in the middle of the flight, I started hearing a commotion coming from the front and took my earphones off to see what was going on. It was Brock and Curt trying to take each other down in the middle of the aisle with everybody standing up, watching.

Lesnar and Hennig weren't fighting. They were just tussling like little kids, but in such cramped confines, I kept thinking, *These two might throw the plane off-balance or something! We're going to be in a tragic news story.*

The bedlam spread in all directions. Flair was prancing around the aisles wearing only a robe, laughing.

But even funnier was what happened to the sleeping Michael Hayes. When he eventually woke up as we landed in Newark, he found his famous mullet had been lopped off. He stormed off the plane in the freezing temperatures, yelling and screaming. "Somebody tell me who did this! Nobody messes with a Freebird! Let's go. Now!"

Jerry Brisco strolled over and said, "Michael, shut up. You're not going to do anything."

Hayes was fuming, and the rest of us were trying to keep the laughter in, hiding our faces or looking down.

I'd never gotten involved. There are guys who can and guys who can't get away with that kind of behavior. For me, the best philosophy was to never find out which of those types of guys I was.

It turns out I'd just observed situations that would result

in a couple of terminations from the company. The next day, the WWF released Curt Hennig. Scott Hall was let go not long after for his continued personal issues, which had surfaced during the tour.

For me, it was back to work in another humorous vignette. The film crew followed me into a 7-11, where I looked for a Booker T cup for a Slurpee. Since they didn't have one, I assumed they were sold out, then turned around as Goldust caught me by surprise and started begging me to join him as a team. I declined.

Later that night, I joined Eddie Guerrero against R.V.D. and Jeff Hardy, but thanks to Goldie getting involved and clumsily messing it all up, we took the loss.

In the remainder of the month, I was forced into the nWo, consisting of Nash, Show, and X-Pac. It didn't make a lot of sense to me because I thought they were gearing me up for a run with Goldie in the tag division. To resolve the confusion, they incorporated Goldie by having him follow me around, trying to join the nWo, which they did not allow.

On the road for house shows, which usually never related to the story lines on TV, I was wrestling and scoring victories over Matt Hardy in some strong matches.

On May 18, twelve days after the company publicly announced its name change to World Wrestling Entertainment

(WWE), we received sad news about one of our veterans. "The British Bulldog" Davey Boy Smith died of a heart attack at the age of thirty-nine while on vacation with his girlfriend. He left behind a son, Harry, now a professional wrestler himself. While I was never close to Davey Boy during his time in WCW, he was always friendly.

Unfortunately, within the next few years the wrestling world would experience more tragic losses.

However, one thing was certain. Knowing where I'd come from gave me all the motivation I needed to make sure I didn't end up down the same road.

On June 3 in Dallas, The Heartbreak Kid (HBK) Shawn Michaels made his return to the WWE on *Raw* and joined the nWo. That night I beat William Regal in a KOTR qualifying match in just over three minutes by smashing him upside the head with his European title belt when the ref wasn't paying attention.

On *Raw* on June 10, during his first in-ring promo on the mic, with all the members of the nWo, HBK said the group was losing focus. He then sucker punched me out with the microphone. While I was down, he said he didn't like my kind and complained I'd been showboating too much with the Spinarooni. They left the ring as I was still lying on the mat, which meant the merciful end of my tenure in the nWo.

Also that night, there was a big showdown between Flair and Vince as they agreed to a no-holds-barred match for 100 percent ownership of the WWE to finally settle the seemingly endless quagmire over who had more control over the company. Flair naturally assumed he had the upper hand, being a former World Heavyweight Champion and a master ring general, but he didn't count on the ace Vince had up his sleeve: Brock Lesnar.

When the bell rang, those two went at in a vicious, clawing, slapping, punching free-for-all in and out of the ring, with Flair bodyslamming Vince out onto the concrete. Predictably, Flair got busted open and bled into his face and bleached hair but kept on the offensive in one of the most action-packed matches I'd seen all year.

All the boys in the back were huddled around the monitors for this one.

Finally, Flair locked in the figure four, and Vince writhed as if his legs were in a car compactor.

Arn Anderson, who was working with the company as an agent, was in the ring screaming for Vince to submit, but then Brock Lesnar hopped into the ring. Arn dove out as if a grenade had been thrown in there. Brock broke the hold and delivered a devastating F5 finisher to Flair, so Vince stole the victory and regained full control of the WWE.

The next week in Oakland, to get revenge on those nWo

clowns for the microphone cheap shot, I jumped into the ring during X-Pac's KOTR qualifier and Book Ended him to the canvas, helping R.V.D. score the victory. When it was time for my own KOTR follow-up match after having already beaten Regal, it was against the beast Brock Lesnar in my first-ever matchup with The Next Big Thing.

But beforehand, in a total shoot in front of the world, Vince walked out and announced Stone Cold had walked away from the company as of the previous week.

Apparently Austin hadn't been happy for a while, beginning around WrestleMania, about the creative direction of his character. He and the company had come to an impasse, and he'd simply gone home. Just like that, The Texas Rattlesnake was gone from the WWE.

McMahon sincerely thanked him for helping build the company to where it was and ceremoniously cracked a beer in his honor, took a drink, and left it in the ring.

I thought of the great TV we'd done together not long before, which was instrumental in helping me establish the new WWE version of Booker T, and I wondered if I'd ever see Austin with us again.

When it was time for my match, Nash, HBK, Show, and X-Pac walked down to the announcers' table. Nash and Shawn provided guest commentary while Show and Pac stood around ringside to intimidate me. In the ring, my hands were more than full with Brock the monster. The match lasted only about three and a half minutes, with me on the receiving end of his clothesline, overhead belly-to-belly suplex, and over-the-shoulder powerslam.

Brock was adapting perfectly to the ring. Backstage he was a humble guy who was eager to learn. He was easy to admire, and I knew Vince would catapult him to the limits of the WWE as yet another bankable megastar.

When Goldust came down and confronted Lesnar's manager, Paul Heyman, I took the upper hand on Brock with a thrust kick, Houston Sidekick, scissor kick, and the Spinarooni. I corkscrewed up to my feet to find X-Pac on the apron antagonizing me. When I went to nail him, Brock got me from behind, hoisted me onto his shoulders, and swung me around for the F5 and the win.

As soon as it was over, the entire nWo ran in. Show gave both Goldust and me chokeslams, concluding our night's work.

Our beat-down at the hands of the nWo set up a series of tag matches on the road, with Goldie and me taking on Big Show and X-Pac, defeating them every time.

At the Philly *Raw* on July 8, we faced them again in a huge Ten-Man Tag Team Match with the combined efforts of Nash, Pac, Show, Benoit, and Guerrero, taking on Goldie, R.V.D., Bubba Ray, Spike Dudley, and me. HBK, who was at ringside, got into the mix and gave me his Sweet Chin Music superkick, allowing Show to throttle me with a chokeslam and the pin.

When R.V.D. chased HBK out of the ring and up the ramp to the Jumbotron area, Brock appeared, clotheslined R.V.D., and then picked him up and dropped him onto the ramp with a devastating F5.

The most notable aspect of the event wasn't the beginning or the conclusion to the match. It was Kevin Nash's nasty mishap.

At one point, Nash ran up and tagged me with a big boot to the face, but when he ran across to attack Bubba in our corner, Nash took an awkward step and tore his right quadriceps right off the tendon. He fell like a fifty-foot pine tree, yelling in excruciating pain.

While I was down, I saw Nash neutralized in our corner. It was pretty ugly. He was holding his right leg, making me flash back to Sid when his left leg collapsed sideways.

Nash was gone for months after that, undergoing surgery and rehabilitation.

With Nash out of the picture and not a single original member of the dwindling stable, Vince personally disbanded the nWo on the July 15 *Raw,* saying it was the end of an era. He also announced he'd be hiring two new General Managers to be in charge of the *Raw* and *SD* brands.

Meanwhile, still feeling the effects of Show's repeated chokeslams over the weeks, I was ready to give Show an old-fashioned whuppin'. I was in the middle of cutting a promo about Show backstage when former WCW head Eric Bischoff walked into the frame.

"Tell me I didn't just see that," I exclaimed.

Vince went on to name Bischoff General Manager in charge of *Raw,* with Vince's daughter Stephanie being placed in charge of *SD.*

I thought I'd seen everything. Eric in the WWE was the unlikeliest of scenarios. A lot of guys in the company, such as Flair and JR, had issues with the guy. It was going to be interesting to see how everyone would receive Bischoff and how he would handle being on-air talent instead of the boss. One thing's for sure: Vince must've enjoyed negotiations to bring him into the WWE. I wonder if he remembered Vince Sr.'s words from decades before: *Now he's* my *asshole.*

When my match with Big Show started, I tried to be as aggressive as possible with the seven footer. I clotheslined him over the top rope, but from there it was a massacre. I jumped out and grabbed a chair, looking to do some damage, but he dumped low as I swung into the post. Show grabbed the chair and came at me in a fury, smashing all over my body before picking me up for yet another chokeslam and leveling me through the commentary table. I was out for the count but took the DQ win.

I loved working with Paul Wight, who'd come such a long way since those early days as The Giant in WCW. His character performance had been enhanced tremendously, which was the WWE formula. But most of all, he'd matured into a fun, laid-back guy who was easily one of my favorites backstage.

At Vengeance 2002 in the Joe Louis Arena in Detroit, it was time for a final confrontation with Show. We went at it hard, and Show really put me over to solidify our story in the remaining chapter of our feud. When it was time, I gave him the low blow to double him over before springing off my ropes with extra height to scissor kick him to the mat. The match called for an extraordinary finish, so I went up for the Houston Hangover, a rare move at that point in my career. I flipped over for the leg drop from the top for a clean victory.

After the singles feud was over, The Undertaker and I teamed up for a series of *Raw* house shows throughout Texas and Florida against Show and Brock Lesnar, with us Texans claiming victory each time. Working with The Undertaker was always a unique privilege, and the crowds were hot for the odd but explosive pairing of his size and legendary presence with my speed and athleticism.

By August 12 at *Raw* in Seattle, Goldust was at it again, adamantly trying to join up with me as a tag team partner, only it seemed more like he was looking for a life partner. Backstage, he suggested to Bischoff we should get a shot at the WWE Tag Team Championships at SummerSlam after I beat Lance Storm that night. Bischoff agreed. In the match, Goldie punched Storm in the face behind the ref's back. I took advantage with the scissor kick, and our stage was set for a shot at the belts on August 25 in Long Island.

SummerSlam was my opportunity to claim my second WWE tag title, only this time it would be us together once again as BookDust. It was a funny angle, and they kept it rolling with Goldie's persistent comedy routines. We wouldn't take the titles that night, however. I was pinned by Christian after my old partner Test climbed in and hit me with a boot to the face before taking off through the crowd.

Goldie and I continued with matches, usually exiting pulverized, and we enjoyed ourselves the entire time.

At Unforgiven 2002 on September 22 in Los Angeles, Bischoff pitted Christian, Lance Storm, Test, and William Regal against Goldie, Kane, Bubba Ray, and me in one of the most action-packed matches I'd ever been involved with. Every single guy hit his finisher in spectacular fashion, with Kane getting the pin on Storm after a huge chokeslam. It was a hell of an opener to the PPV, and we knew the tone was set after we brought the house down.

Also that night, Bischoff took a Stinkface from Rikishi, allowing Goldie and me to have some fun the next night on *Raw* in Anaheim.

We put together another *Ebert & Roeper* parody bit analyzing Bischoff taking Rikishi's Stinkface. When Goldie and I went to the locker room to show it to the boys, one of

BOOKER T. HUFFMAN

Bischoff's stooges, Rico Constantino, peeked in, scolded us for having some laughs at the GM's expense, and said he was going to rat us out. Later in the show, Bischoff was in the ring and screamed for me to come down. While in there, Bischoff asked me if I thought his eating a Stinkface was amusing.

"Damn skippy, hippie!"

He brought out his enforcement tag team of Rosey and Jamal, known as 3-Minute Warning, to take me out, with Goldust failing to make the save. In a match shortly after, I got my hands on that little weasel Rico Constantino, who'd ratted us out, and squashed him in record time.

18

LOCKED IN THE ELIMINATION CHAMBER

On the October 7 *Raw* in Vegas, not only did Jericho cut a promo calling me a loser, but Bischoff was still out to get me. I confronted Jericho about his rant and then ran into a smiling Bischoff and his random match selector known as the Roulette Wheel, which was filled with different match stipulations, like a TLC match, a Las Vegas Street Fight, and even a Capture the Midget match. He gave it a *Price Is Right* spin, and it landed on me getting a Steel Cage Match with Show. Show and I ended up on the top rope, vying to get out of the cage. When the time was right, I gave him a swift kick to the family jewels, causing him to come crashing onto the mat. With the giant down, I scurried up and over the cage for the win.

Just as I started to celebrate and my music hit, Jericho attacked from behind and busted me open, one of the very few times I've ever bled in the business. It was funny: I was in a cage where the most damage could've been inflicted, but it was outside of it that the blood started flowing.

Jericho's Pearl Harboring of me established a tag team

showdown with him and Christian, the champs at the time, against Goldie and me at No Mercy 2002 in Little Rock, Arkansas. Again, BookDust lost as Jericho pinned Goldie after a face-first bulldog onto one of the belts followed by a big moonsault from the top. When he attempted a Lionsault from the second rope, it snapped on him in a complete shoot of a ring malfunction, just like in that match with The Steiners back in WCW, and he fell on his ass.

Following yet another loss in our pursuit of the tag belts, BookDust fell apart for a little while as I was paired with various combinations of Bubba Ray and Kane on the road.

On October 26, I replaced The Undertaker, for whatever reason, and wrestled against Matt Hardy at the Rebellion 2002 PPV in Manchester, England. Our chemistry in the ring had increased over the last full year of facing each other individually and in tag matches.

That night Matt almost caught me in his Twist of Fate finisher, but I pushed him off and hit the scissor kick and gave those screaming English fans a dazzling Spinarooni.

After I was booked in and out of a lot of tag teams, it looked like I was finally being scheduled in the title picture again as Bischoff announced I'd be one of six to compete in the first Elimination Chamber Match ever at the Survivor Series 2002 PPV on November 17. In the couple of weeks before the big event, I teamed up with Kane against Jericho and Hunter, the World Heavyweight Champion at the time. HBK, who would also be in the Elimination Chamber with us, managed to meddle his way into the performance, allowing me to score the pin on Hunter. Hunter was so pissed he demanded a singles match with me the following week in a non-title match on *Raw*.

At the Survivor Series 2002 at Madison Square Garden in New York City, the inaugural Elimination Chamber Match was dangerously similar to WCW's defunct War Games concept.

I got to the building early because the six of us—HBK, Hunter, R.V.D., Jericho, Kane, and I—needed to see the steel-and-iron structure for the first time to feel it out and go over some sequences.

When I walked onto the main floor and saw the chamber, I immediately thought, *How am I going to make it through tonight in this thing?* It was the most ominous and unforgiving contraption I'd ever seen: a big, domed iron cage sitting on top of the ring with about four or five feet of metal grating, like a cheese grater, between the edge of the ring apron connecting to the chamber. One spill over the top rope onto that surface and you'd not only take a dangerous bump but you could cut yourself up into pieces.

At the edge of that surrounding platform around the ring were the outer walls of the chamber itself, a spiderweb of metal linked together from top to bottom. It was kind of like those ropes you'd see soldiers climbing at boot camp, only this was comprised of linked chains designed for one purpose: pain. In each of the four corners stood tall Plexiglas closets that competitors would be stationed in until our time counted down and they opened to release us into the abyss of the action in the chamber.

Just like War Games, the key to victory or loss was submission or pin fall. In this event, however, it was every wrestler for himself. The last man standing would win the World Heavyweight Championship.

First and foremost, I'm a wrestler, not a daredevil or a stuntman. I knew from the very beginning this match was going to need a special approach if I wanted to avoid as many risks as possible, which was always paramount in my mind when stepping into the ring.

The other five guys in there with me must've been thinking the complete opposite, especially R.V.D., a death-defying risk taker. I don't think even he was sure what he'd do next. Jericho was another guy I knew would pull out all the stops for this night.

When it began, R.V.D. and Hunter were in the ring while Kane, HBK, Jericho, and I were stationed in the glass closets, which looked like clear vertical coffins. Every five minutes, one of us would be released into the chamber.

As Rob and Hunter battled it out, I watched from my casket, as anxious as I'd ever been, realizing this could be one of those events that took a year off my life, literally. The adrenaline was pumping.

Within the first five minutes, as Jericho made his way into the match, R.V.D. and Hunter, who was already busted wide open, were lying on the grates, writhing around, almost immobilized. Jericho and Hunter double-teamed R.V.D., taking liberties into the chain links and beating him senseless.

The time was up, and I was the next one in. I destroyed Jericho and Hunter with Harlem Sidekicks and clotheslines over the top. With the ring cleared out, I got down on one knee and gave the raucous crowd in Madison Square Garden one of the most dramatic Spinaroonis of my career.

I turned around to find R.V.D. right in my face, just the two of us. We slugged it out, and I took him down with a spin kick to the face and tried for the pin.

After that, everything was a total blur. The next thing I remember was seeing Rob in the middle of the ring, so I went to the top for the missile dropkick, pinned him, and sent him packing.

Kane came in next and smashed Jericho face-first through one of the glass corners, leaving him lying there broken before chokeslamming me. I didn't last much longer. Jericho recovered and took advantage of my position and pinned me with the Lionsault. In the end, I went safely behind the curtain.

HBK, beaten to a Flair-like bloody pulp, pinned the only other man standing, Triple H, for the win and the Big Gold.

Backstage, we all congratulated each other for the history-making war we just went through. We'd set the bar high for every version of the Elimination Chamber to come. As we stood there taking it all in, we got a standing ovation from the rest of the boys, with Vince right out in front with an ear-to-ear smile. The six of us had delivered the spectacle he envisioned for fans in Madison Square Garden and at home.

I was glad I'd put on a good show while sticking to my game plan of staying safe. Now I was ready for the next challenge.

That night, there was another commotion at the PPV that caused quite the uprising at Madison Square Garden. While Chris Nowinski and Matt Hardy were in the ring cutting heel promos on the crowd, calling them stupid losers, they got massive heat from the sold-out audience. No sooner had they gotten the words out of their mouths than police sirens blared and the familiar music filled Madison Square Garden for none other than my buddy "Big Poppa Pump" Scott Steiner.

JR on commentary said, "I think business just picked up here, King."

Lawler carried on like a kid on Christmas morning. "It's him, JR! He's here! It's Big Poppa Pump!"

It was one of the loudest ovations I've ever heard at Madison Square Garden. I know it blew Scotty away. Backstage beforehand, he hadn't known what to expect. "What do you think I'll get out there, man?"

I said, "You're Scott Steiner. They'll be all over it."

He came out slowly walking to the ring, hitting his classic

big right-biceps pose, kissing his arm. Scotty entered the ring and destroyed both Nowinski and Hardy with a series of his famous overhead and belly-to-belly suplexes before dumping Chris over the top rope by the back of his neck.

The crowd chanted in a unified chorus, "Steiner! Steiner!"

He yelled back, "Who's the man?" Then he gorilla pressed Hardy and threw him out of the ring to collide with Nowinski. Scotty started doing push-ups before grabbing the mic. Before he spoke, Steiner stood there absorbing the energy of The World's Most Famous Arena, then declared, "This goes out to all my freaks in New York City. Big Poppa Pump is your hookup. Holler if you hear me!"

Just like Hogan, Hall, and Nash, Scotty brought huge nostalgia with him. It was an incredible return moment I know he'll never forget.

Much like his character Poppa Pump, Steiner liked to be in control of everything, especially the creative direction of his role. After learning the WWE system myself and understanding the delicate nature of listening and being patient while waiting for the big push, I was curious if Scotty would be as tolerant. He'd been running hard, full steam, for about fifteen years as a major player by then, and if or when Scotty wanted something, he'd usually get it—or simply take it.

I was happy to have Steiner in the company and welcomed him with open arms. I knew he'd mix it up one way or the other, and I looked forward to seeing him terrorize the roster and chase after all the Divas.

We went out after the PPV was over, even though we're not big partiers, especially Scotty, who's a loner. We laughed about old times and discussed our parallel careers. After sweating it out to the very top of the old regime, both of us broke away from teams with our brothers and emerged as WCW World Heavyweight Champions. Now we were in New York City together with the WWE. It was an unforgettable night.

In late November, we took our show overseas again, this time for my first trip to India. We kicked off in New Delhi, Mumbai, and Bangalore, where I gained victories over Lance Storm and Christian in singles competition.

The BookDust curse carried over internationally as we suffered a loss yet again to Jericho and Christian. My worst suffering while in India, though, didn't happen in the ring.

I knew I needed to avoid the unsanitary water at all costs. Even while washing in the hotel, I'd make sure nothing went in my mouth, eyes, or other orifices. When I'd get out of the shower, I'd wipe myself down with a towel doused in bottled water.

I successfully avoided consuming the tap water—until the very last day.

To celebrate our successful tour, I had a few cocktails and realized only afterward that there'd been ice cubes in my drinks. All of a sudden, I felt like I'd just drunk poison, worrying about what insidious sickness might catch up with me.

It wasn't until the flight home on Sunday that I started feeling a little ill. I tried to sleep it off.

By the time we were at *Raw* the next night, November 26, in Raleigh, I was on the floor, unable to move. The trainers said it was dehydration and gave me an IV of fluid right then and there. I lay there in cold sweats, completely immobilized.

Jericho casually came over to discuss what we'd do in our tag match. "What I really need you to do tonight is come in and—"

Next thing I remember was waking up in the ambulance. I was in recovery in the nearest hospital for an entire week that almost completely escapes my memory, although I do remember Sharmell being by my side.

By that time, she'd retired from the WWE and left the business altogether because, over the summer, while training in the ring with the Suicide Blondes, she'd torn the ACL in her right knee. As a result, Sharmell and I had found ourselves at a crossroads in our relationship. I didn't want her to have to move home with her mother in Gary, Indiana. The experience of the divorce from Levestia still played with my mind, but I couldn't bear Sharmell living so far away. She was important to me, so I made a serious decision. We agreed she should move into my home in Houston, and she's been with me there ever since.

With her by my side in the hospital in Raleigh, the doctors told me I'd contracted dysentery. I could still kick myself for drinking that cocktail!

When I was good and recovered, it was back to business. At Armageddon 2002 in Fort Lauderdale, a nice warm city to be in on December 15, Goldie and I took on The Dudley Boyz, Lance Storm and William Regal, and WWE Tag Team Champions Jericho and Christian in a Fatal 4-Way Match. It all went down as Regal got the pin on Bubba Ray by pulling his pants for leverage, removing him and Devon from the equation. That was followed by Goldie pinning Regal after his trademark powerslam, and then I did the honors of Book Ending Jericho when he attempted to hit me with one of the belts. I covered him for the count, and Goldie and I became the new champs, making it my second run with the WWF Tag Team Championships, which was now under the WWE banner. It was validating for all of Goldust's and my efforts to be recognized by the company on the last PPV of the year.

The next night on *Raw*, Goldie dressed like Santa and cheerfully handed me my championship title.

BookDust closed out the remaining dates of 2002 proudly defending the title against Jericho and Christian.

CHAMPIONSHIPS	
WCW World Tag Team Championship	11
WCW World Television Championship	6
WCW United States Championship	1
WCW World Heavyweight Championship	5
WWF World Tag Team Championship	1
WWF Hardcore Championship	2
WWE World Tag Team Championship	1
Total	27

No matter where I was or what I was doing, Brandon was on my mind. He'd just turned nineteen and still lived with Billie in Dallas. We hadn't reconciled since he'd taken me up on my ultimatum over a year earlier.

I saw him on occasion at family functions at my sister Carolyn's not far from my house, and I even ran into him at the movies one night. We were always cordial toward each other, but we interacted like strangers.

My sister kept me informed of what he was up to. School had faded out of the picture long before, he didn't want to work, and he'd fathered a son, my grandson. He had no further contact with the mother or his son, so I never met my grandson, even to this day. I wasn't content at all with the way things stood between us after our falling out, and I was determined to try to reconcile. I just didn't know how yet.

Back in Houston, it was nice to come home to a peaceful environment with Sharmell, who was still recovering from her ACL tear, working, and had signed up for local college courses. She also continued working out as much as she safely could.

In Sharmell I'd found the person who complemented me in every part of life, especially my career because she had firsthand experience in the business. I realized she'd been the missing piece in my life, and I started to dream of building a life with her.

Back on the road only six days into 2003, Goldie and I immediately dropped the WWE Tag Team Championship belts to Storm and Regal at *Raw* in Phoenix.

On January 19, 2003, in the Royal Rumble match in Boston, I scissor kicked Kane, then Flapjacked Matt Hardy before eliminating Eddie Guerrero over the top with a backdrop. I wasn't in there even five minutes before Team Angle, comprised of Charlie Haas and Shelton Benjamin, dumped me over the top for the end of another solid though brief night of work. I came in at number twenty-four.

On February 3 in D.C., Goldie and I gave it one more effort to win the WWE Tag Team Championship. During a backstage segment, Goldie told me he was holding me back. If we didn't win, he said he'd walk away and let me go on my own. Suffice it to say, the WWE invented this tragedy to play out with Storm shoving Goldie into me, causing the pin fall.

As if he'd plunged a dagger into his own brother's chest by mistake, Goldust left the ring dejected.

But I called for him to come back. "If we're going that way, let's do it right!"

As the audience stood and cheered, in another character breakthrough for each of us, we hugged in a legitimate show of gratitude and respect. After a long, arduous road filled with mostly roadblocks but a few successes, comedy blockbuster segments, and a taste of championship gold, BookDust was no more.

I still consider that period of time one of the most important in my entire career in respect to the constant personal challenge of my character development—a breakthrough after the static character of my WCW days.

That night, they wrote Goldie off by having Randy Orton, the third-generation wrestler fresh from Ohio Valley Wrestling, along with fellow graduate Dave Batista throw Goldie into a power box, where he was electrocuted. Orton and Batista along with Flair and Hunter formed a Four Horsemen–like stable called Evolution, which I knew I'd have to contend with sooner than later.

A week later, we took *Raw* to Los Angeles. Hours before the event, there was a funny encounter with D'Lo Brown and Michael Hayes. Since my later days in WCW, I'd frequently traveled with a Sony PlayStation and big-screen TV, which the company took with us in the production crew trucks. When I came to the WWE, the tradition carried on. At the arenas, I'd sit and relax before the events, playing the latest edition of Madden NFL. It became my ritual. Once in a while, Nick Patrick or one of the other boys would come in for a video game whuppin'.

Before *Raw* that night in Los Angeles, I was scoring touchdowns and getting into my comfort zone backstage when D'Lo walked by, stuck his head in, and said, "You're playing Madden at the arena?"

"Yeah, bro. Come on in and grab a controller. Let's go!"

He stepped in for a hot minute to check it out.

Just then, Michael Hayes walked by the open door and immediately turned around to stand in the doorway. "So, D'Lo, what you're telling me is you're not too busy to be playing video games?"

D'Lo was rattled. "No, Michael, not at all. I was just saying hi to Booker."

He looked at me with fear in his eyes as Hayes walked off. "I can't play anymore, man." And he hightailed it out of there.

The scene was a prime example of the eat-or-be-eaten theory most of the talent walked around with back there. It was expected they should be going over their match down in the ring or rehearsing promos and vignettes with creative. I was over all that long before my WWE days. Everyone knew when it was time to go, nobody went as hard as me. At that point, I was a ten-year veteran and five-time WCW Champion and had proven myself with the two major wrestling companies in the world.

If I felt sleepy back there, I'd close my eyes and nap. If I wanted to decompress for an hour before activity started picking up for the show, I was going to sit down, turn on the PlayStation, and pick up a controller. I had touchdown records to break.

Later that same night, I ran down to the ring and defeated

Batista, the six-feet-three, 290-pound rookie, after his match with Tommy Dreamer. Predictably, it didn't last long as the rest of Evolution came down to outnumber and take me out. Suddenly, of all people, my old WCW brother Big Poppa Pump came to the rescue and we cleared the ring. It was a memorable moment to finally be standing in there *with* Scotty and not against him for a change. It was a good, action-packed night, and I looked forward to getting some rest.

But when I woke up the next morning, I received devastating news: "Mr. Perfect" Curt Hennig, my good friend since his debut in WCW years before, had been found dead at age forty-four. My smiling, carefree friend was gone. It knocked the wind and feeling right out of me, and I was in a daze throughout that Tuesday, flooded by memories. I wept for the loss of Curt and poured a drink to the ground for him that night. My dear buddy, one of the best performers I ever witnessed in the ring, was gone, and it hurt too much for words.

Curt left behind a wife and four children. One son, Joe Hennig, is proudly carrying on the excellence of his father's performances in the WWE under the name of Curtis Axel, an homage to his grandfather Larry "The Axe" Hennig and his dad, Curt.

In 2007, Curt would receive a posthumous induction into the WWE Hall of Fame, where he belonged.

Still grieving, I knew the show had to go on.

19

GOING FOR GOLD

In the early days in WCW, Harlem Heat frequently faced The Steiners, and Scotty and I met as singles contenders in the WCW title scene. I'd never envisioned working alongside Scotty, but soon we were booked for a week of house shows. In Huntington, West Virginia, we formed a tag team for the first time in our storied history and faced "The Game" Triple H and Batista.

Much as I had reduced the strain on my body by limiting my use of certain maneuvers like the Hangover, Scotty also no longer powered through his vast arsenal of destructive and acrobatic moves unless he felt the need at a big show. To his credit, Steiner worked harder and with more heart and intensity than I'd ever seen, and I was proud to be in there with him as he took the victory.

We took our tag performance through a couple more towns over that weekend before putting it on the big stage at *Raw* in Columbus, Ohio. Once again, we took on and defeated The Game and Batista.

My next big moment, which surprised even me when I was told about it, was on *Raw* in Toronto on February 24. I was scheduled to win a Twenty-Man Battle Royal that included every major WWE Superstar on the roster, even The Rock, where the winner would get a shot at the World Heavyweight Championship at WrestleMania XIX on March 30 in Seattle.

For the first and only time in my career, I won a battle royal, one of my least favorite varieties of matches, by taking part in eliminating WWE Superstar after Superstar until the dust cleared in the end to reveal only The Rock and me standing in the center of the ring one more time. We wasted no time in aggressively going after each other. I got the upper hand with slaps and Flair chops to the chest before finally flinging him over the top for the win and my ticket to the grand stage.

Now not only was I going to WrestleMania, but I was entering with the rare honor of a grand marquee slot on the card, going for the Big Gold one more time against one of the company's biggest homegrown stars, Triple H.

It reminds me of what Paul Heyman once said to me: "You know why you outlasted everyone else who came over from WCW, don't you? Because you never took Turner money when you had the option to sit out and collect. Vince respected that, and he respects you."

I was so excited I could taste it, and I felt truly honored by Vince and the WWE.

Building up to our big championship showdown at Wrestle-Mania, the next few weeks of *Raw* saw Hunter and Flair bringing my character down in every way possible, including implied racial slurs.

Hunter said, "You're nothing but a common street thug. Somebody *like you* . . . I laugh my ass off thinking about you challenging me for the World Heavyweight Championship."

Flair even suggested I become their chauffeur, which resulted in my instant beat-down on The Nature Boy.

When I caught Hunter washing his face in the bathroom, he threw a dollar bill at my face and said, "Get me a towel." I left him lying on the tiles.

They continued comparing my five-time title run with the wins of David Arquette and Vince Russo and even brought up my criminal past. JR felt I should publicize my prison history and let fans know it wasn't just an angle. Naturally, I was resistant at first, being insecure about the WWE exploiting something I'd been trying to hide for years, but taking JR's advice and embracing it inspired a lot of kids to stay on the straight path, even then, and I dreamed of one day sharing the whole story to help even more people.

On one *Raw* leading up to WrestleMania, Goldie came back with a stutter and Tourette's syndrome due to the electrical shock at Evolution's hands. He said he wanted to team up with me one more time and remind me of my old catchphrase,

"Don't hate the playa; hate the *game!*"

After a long and grueling match, Goldie and I defeated Flair and Hunter, with me getting the pin on The Game, who was busted open and bleeding. With my psychological advantage over having pinned the champ, it seemed like the stars were aligning and I might leave Safeco Field in Seattle as the six-time World Heavyweight Champion.

On Sunday, March 30, 2003, at WrestleMania XIX in Safeco Field, in Seattle, I faced "The Game" Triple H for the biggest prize of the *Raw* brand. I was more than ready, skipping rope in the back to limber up and get the adrenaline flowing. Even deep in the cavernous hallways of Safeco, far from The Gorilla Position, the staging area just behind the curtain, I could hear it, the sound of fifty-five thousand people stomping. It felt like an earthquake that I was only too eager to jump right into.

I set my focus on what it would take to ensure we stole the show. I'd do anything and everything for Hunter and myself to shine brighter than we ever had before, and knowing The Game, he was preparing with the same mentality. The two of us met up in the back and briefly went over our match, but we both knew once we were out there under those lights and hearing the roar of the crowd, we'd be completely without a net and calling it on the fly like veterans should.

After we made our long, winding entrances to the ring, I stared him down, put a finger on his chest, and yelled, "Yo' punk ass in trouble!"

We went at it hard like two consummate professionals for just under nineteen minutes. They don't put just anybody in a World Title Match at WrestleMania. I felt honored Vince and the creative team felt I would have the most credible and entertaining synergy with Hunter, which was a victory in itself.

After nearly twenty minutes, it was time to close it out. After a failed Pedigree attempt on me, Hunter sprang off the ropes and I countered with a flying reverse elbow followed up with the scissor kick. I covered him for only a two count.

Then I slowly got up and looked to the top turnbuckle and made my way up. The people knew what I might be trying for and rose to their feet in anticipation, but Hunter recovered and climbed the second rope, knocking me to a seated position, and tried for a superplex. I got him back down and repositioned myself on the top when Flair, who'd been at the side of the ring the whole match in support of The Game, tried to crush me. I caught him with a stiff right, sending him crumpling to the floor. I steadied myself and hit my first WrestleMania Houston Hangover a bit wildly and off-center, smashing Hunter right across the face with my right leg. The sad truth was that at such a late point in my career, I wasn't as pinpoint accurate with the Hangover as I had been in the early days.

We both lay there for a dramatic fifteen seconds before I went for the cover. Right as the ref's hand went for number three, Flair placed Hunter's leg on the rope, breaking the pin. As we both got up, Hunter gave me a thunderous face-first Pedigree and stole a sixth World Championship from my grasp in a three-second count.

I stayed in the ring, still feeling the effects of the grueling performance for quite a while, talking to the ref as The Nature Boy helped Hunter exit. When I finally limped the couple hundred yards out, the people chanted my name and gave me a standing ovation.

Triple H was waiting for me, and we smiled in congratulations. Flair gave me a pat on the back. I felt like I'd been in a real battle. I went to the dressing room and just sat for a while, physically and emotionally exhausted.

That night also featured the return of Stone Cold, who'd walked out of the company exactly a year earlier. In addition, Brock Lesnar defeated Kurt Angle for the WWE Championship, though he nearly broke his neck after landing on his face following a botched shooting star press.

I managed to make it to the traditional after party, but I found it next to impossible to really enjoy myself. While everyone else seemed enthralled by the success of the show, it felt anticlimactic to me and I knew the whole process would start over the next day on *Raw*.

After an entire year of planning, developing, and then finally executing the biggest event of the calendar year, the

BOOKER T. HUFFMAN

Road to WrestleMania began again the second that clock struck midnight. That's the heartbeat of the WWE: a constant pulse of planning, evaluating, and increasing excitement until the big day is around the corner again.

We all moved over to the Key Arena for the next night's *Raw*, which featured Jericho congratulating HBK in a heartfelt address in the ring for being the better man after defeating him at WrestleMania. Then he brought me into the equation, saying he was going to take his frustrations out on me. My music hit, and I was on my way out. Just when we really got going, predictably, Hunter and Flair got involved and I received a triple-team beating. The Game hit me with the Pedigree, and Flair figure-four leg locked me. HBK tried to be the savior with an assist, but they stomped him into the canvas too.

At the end of the show, The Rock was giving himself a Rock Appreciation Ceremony, putting Stone Cold and himself over for their performance the night before, until the familiar sound of Bill Goldberg's gladiator, UFC-style music hit.

His entry was a huge surprise to me. Yeah, there were rumors and such. And the crowd, tipped off by the Internet, had been chanting his name all night, just as in the WCW days. But Vince did a really good job of keeping him hidden just until it was time for his cue, as they'd hidden me for KOTR 2001.

All of a sudden, Goldberg was standing on the ramp of the set of *Raw* as sparks and pyro set him in a blazing silhouette.

He made his way to the ring, told The Rock, "You're next," and then speared him in classic brutal form. Take it from me, nobody speared like Goldberg. It's a solid shot from a speeding locomotive.

Just as when Steiner came in, I was curious how Goldberg would fare in the WWE, but I was definitely happy to see another WCW brother. That night we met each other afterward in the hall and shook hands. He told me I'd been one of the few he could talk to in WCW. It was evident from the very beginning, Goldberg felt out of his element here. There was no backstage fanfare, and nothing was handed to him on a silver platter as it had been in WCW.

Goldberg had never shown a true passion for the business. He'd played for the Atlanta Falcons and, during rehabilitation after a severe abdominal injury, Sting and Luger had recruited him at their gym. He turned out to be the right guy, and the rest of the story was a monstrous winning streak that made him a legend in the business.

But now he was in the WWE, where everyone on the roster lived, breathed, and bled professional wrestling. Bill had everything to prove while being scrutinized from every angle. He had a broken path of obstacles ahead of him to stomp through, but he could count on me for a friendly face along the way.

The biggest action of the night for the fans and for us came after the cameras were off and the broadcast was over.

My music hit and stayed on a continuous loop as I came out to the ovation of the audience who were on their way up and out but immediately went running back to their seats.

With a giant smile on my face, I went straight for the ring and hit a Spinarooni as the crowd went crazy. It was only the beginning of a monumental occasion.

One after another, like a limbo dance contest, each WWE Superstar, heel and face alike, came down the ramp to join in on the fun. Christian got in and did the Peeparooni, Kane stomped down and hit a Kanearooni, Stacie Keebler hit a sexy Legarooni. Everyone came out, even Stephanie and Shane McMahon and Vince himself, who did an executive Vincearooni. Finally, The Undertaker came into the ring to see what was going on, but he refused to join in. Big Show came down and hit a hilarious Showarooni. Eddie Guerrero and R.V.D. got in on the fun and did their versions. Finally, Show chokeslammed The Undertaker for not participating, ending the Spinarooni parade.

Over all the years and memories in the business, that night of the Spinarooni dance-off is always at the forefront of my mind.

The next few weeks, I was involved in continued angles of Hunter, Flair, and Jericho against me, HBK, and the returning babyface version of Kevin Nash.

On the final *Raw* before the Backlash PPV on April 21,

deep in WCW country in Atlanta, I demanded and received from Bischoff a WrestleMania rematch with The Game, with Michaels as the special guest referee. When I was closing in for the kill, Jericho interfered, causing Michaels and Flair to get involved as well. Nash came down and took a shot to the crotch from Hunter.

The quest for my sixth World title disintegrated. However, if I wasn't going to be the top guy, the next best thing was to be working with the top guy. I had no complaints.

Six days later on Sunday, April 27, at Backlash 2003 in Worcester, Massachusetts, our trio took on Hunter, Flair, and Jericho in a Six-Man Tag Team Match that I knew was only filler until creative came up with a new direction for each of us. We turned it on for the ten thousand in attendance with a display of aggressive action, high-flying offensive, reversals, and near falls. We lost when Hunter leveled Nash with his trusty sledgehammer while the ref was distracted.

Also that night, Goldberg emerged victorious in his debut dream match with The Rock, who needed to be written off TV to film his newest movie, *Walking Tall*. With the crowd strongly behind him, Goldberg destroyed The Rock by giving him two spears and the Jackhammer for a convincing win. I was proud to see him deliver a commanding performance for the company.

Although Goldberg was officially introduced to the WWE

BOOKER T. HUFFMAN

with a landmark first match, the next night at *Raw* in the locker room proved to be an even more important initiation at the hands of an unlikely old acquaintance from WCW.

We were at the FleetCenter in Boston a little while before the show started. Most of us milled around in the dressing area, gearing up and going through our individual pre-show rituals. I don't know what started it, but Goldberg and Jericho were loudly arguing about something, which wasn't surprising. Those two had legitimate heat since the WCW days, and now they were in the process of being booked into a WWE story line together that was supposed to start that very night. I don't know if they were upset about the past, the present, or both, but the clash was erupting.

All I remember is that Goldberg made first contact. As he went after Jericho, Chris took him to the floor with a double-leg takedown.

I was standing there with all the boys, saying, "Oh, shit!"

But, as soon as it began, it was over. The fight got broken up and they both got to their feet before anything really got going.

They kind of just stood there looking at each other, and that was it. There weren't any punches or kicks or broken noses. They simply went their separate ways.

Who knows what would have happened had it been allowed to continue. The funny thing is, the story will always remain that Jericho got the best of Goldberg.

Afterward, those two still had to go out on *Raw* and

perform a long and crucial first confrontational segment to establish their impending feud. Jericho called Goldberg down to the ring and asked him why he walked around like a big shot and told him he should've stayed home. I knew Jericho was relishing every second of playing off what had happened earlier, while Goldberg had to stand there and take it in front of an oblivious audience.

I also had a segment filmed with Goldberg that night. The cameras followed him through the halls, and as he rounded the corner, he discovered me in the middle of my pre-match jump rope ritual. We greeted each other warmly, and I told him, "It wasn't too long ago I was the new kid on the block. Now *everybody* knows I'm the five-time, five-time, five-time, five-time, *five-time* WCW Champion!"

Goldberg had a huge grin on his face.

"Can you dig it?"

He said he could.

I thought it was a phenomenal way for the WWE to have me formally welcome Goldberg into the company, showing the fans and him that he wasn't entirely alone.

It also served as a setup for him to save me from a Bischoff-sent beating at the hands of 3-Minute Warning and Rico. Just as I was in the middle of a match with Christian, the trio came to lay in the boots on me. Goldberg jogged down the ramp like a poised rhino. He punched, kicked, and clothes-lined everyone in his path and followed up with a perfect vertical Jackhammer on the three-hundred-pound Jamal. Then Christian knocked him to the outside. Goldberg landed on his feet, recovered, and speared Rosey through the barricade into the front row in an awesome display of power. Goldberg walked out through the audience up the steps, leaving everybody stunned, chanting his name.

It felt like 1998 all over again. In light of the events that had unfolded before the show with Jericho, I bet Goldberg wished it still was.

On May 1, 2003, I received news that seriously caught me off guard. Elizabeth Hulette, better known to the world as Miss Elizabeth, Randy Savage's on-screen valet during the eighties and the first lady of professional wrestling, died at the age of forty-two. I never got to know Elizabeth well. She was a shy and private person who never mingled with the boys. I knew she was married to Randy Savage for eight years. Toward the end of WCW, she'd started dating Lex Luger and they'd moved in together. Whatever had transpired, Elizabeth found herself in a despairing situation and didn't make it out alive.

After her death, Luger was devastated. He went through some tough times and wound up having a stroke. Partially paralyzed even today, The Total Package, one of the most intelligent and successful performers of my generation, fell from grace but picked himself up and turned his life over to faith. He keeps active in the speaking circuits, and I can tell you from experience, Lex hasn't lost his smile at all.

With Elizabeth's death, I was on alert more than ever around all the performers in the business, past and present, who might've been struggling. I wanted the heartbreaking pattern to end.

20

BRANDON COMES HOME

I wasn't in the May 12 *Raw* in Philly, but Teddy Long and Stone Cold, the new Co–General Manager, announced I'd be in another battle royal, the newly reinstated WWE Intercontinental Championship at Judgment Day that Sunday in Charlotte. I was optimistic the belt might be coming my way until I saw the promotional poster for the PPV. It was a magnificent work of art featuring only me in a creative double image standing in my entrance pose in color within a larger, blacked-out silhouetted version. I felt honored to be immortalized in such a way to promote the event, but being featured in a PPV poster is usually a kiss of death indicating it won't be your night.

When it was show time, I buckled up my boots, drank my two trusty Red Bulls, jumped rope, and was ready to perform as if the belt were coming home with me. As the match began, it was Jericho, R.V.D., Val Venis, Lance Storm, Christian, Test, Goldust, Kane, and I going strong for the second richest prize in the WWE.

Kane was the biggest threat, so the rest of us tossed him over in a group effort. Then Goldie came after me with an attempt, but I reversed and took him for a ride out of the match. I eliminated Test and smacked Christian in the face with a Houston Sidekick to the mat.

They hit my music, and Pat Patterson was handing me the belt until the ref, who'd been knocked out, came back to life just as Christian sneaked back in and hit me with the belt, sending me over the top to the floor.

Although Christian had clearly cheated in front of everyone, this performance was a definite move back up the ladder for me and escalated the conflict between the two of us.

Christian and I would continue feuding on *Raw,* weekend house shows on the road, and subsequent PPVs into July.

At Insurrextion 2003 on June 7, in Newcastle, England, the WWE's fourth and final exclusively British PPV, Christian rolled me up and used my trunks for leverage to score the pin fall.

Eight days later at Bad Blood 2003 in Houston, the hometown hex came upon me. I had all the momentum rushing forward to eclipse Christian as he rolled out of the ring and allowed himself to be counted out, keeping the title. Or so he thought. The ref made it clear that if he didn't get back in the ring he would actually forfeit his title. Reluctantly, Christian came back to the ring and hit me with the belt, taking the DQ but retaining his championship.

Every single time, everywhere we met, he managed to squeeze away by either cheating to win, receiving interference from Jericho, losing by DQ, being counted out, or even being assisted by Eric Bischoff.

On June 30 in Buffalo, Christian and I battled for two full-time segments between commercial breaks, maybe one of the longest matches in *Raw* history, and we came to a point where we caught each other in a double small package with both of us being in a pinned position. Nick Patrick, no longer a biased WCW official, counted three and awarded me the championship, or so I thought. Seconds later, Bischoff came strolling out and announced it was a draw and again the belt eluded me.

Performing with Christian in the marathon-type stretches was a tremendous experience. When we got in there and started working together, I discovered Christian was a master of timing, instincts, and psychology. He performed like a veteran with twice his years of experience in the ring. He taught me a few tricks, and we got along so well that sometimes it was nearly impossible to wrestle him with a serious approach. He'd be saying something funny and making outrageous faces to make me crack, and like Knobbs in the old days, sometimes he succeeded.

As amicable as Christian and I were, though, business

was business and my pursuit of the WWE Intercontinental Championship finally came to an end the following week in Montreal, Quebec, Canada: Christian country.

First, Stone Cold came out and apologized for not having been around for a while due to food poisoning and said it would be Booker T and Christian again for the IC title that night.

Christian said, "I have nothing left to prove to Booker T or his peeps," but when he tried to walk out on the match, Austin commanded him to come back and said the title would be on the line due to his constant count-out wins, and to ensure a fair fight, there was a no-DQ rule in effect.

Christian, saying the match couldn't start until he was in the ring, tried to walk away again.

Austin grabbed him and threw him inside, and the bell rang.

It was finally my time, and the crowd knew it. I swarmed all over Christian and scissor kicked him to the mat, went for the cover, and got the three count. It seemed I'd won, but it was another false finish as the ref said Christian's foot was on the rope.

I'm pretty sure Christian and I set the record for suspenseful false finishes in a single feud. Dusty Rhodes would have been proud.

We resumed the match, and Christian scored a low blow on me and almost had the pin and the victory, but I kicked out, recovered, and took control for a second. My final scissor kick nailed Christian's championship coffin.

"One! Two! Three!"

I'd finally done it.

I almost expected another last-minute swerve to take away the title, but it never happened. I was the new Intercontinental Champion.

Late into my first *Raw* IC title defense in Indianapolis on July 14, the creative guys didn't disappoint. They had Christian pin me for the title, but in another controversial false finish, a second ref ran down and contested the call. My old supermarket combatant Stone Cold came to the ring with a third official and ordered us to continue. In no time flat, I pinned Christian to rightfully retain the belt.

While I left with the prize held high, Christian threw a classic tantrum in the ring. When he made the mistake of putting his hands on the ref, Austin promptly delivered a picture-perfect Stone Cold Stunner to close out the segment.

Over the next couple of weeks, I squashed Christian's buddy and my old partner Test in Los Angeles with Steiner. It looked as if I was free of attempts at my title for a while. However, fate has a clever way of throwing a wrench into a smoothly operating machine.

CHAMPIONSHIPS	
WCW World Tag Team Championship	11
WCW World Television Championship	6
WCW United States Championship	1
WCW World Heavyweight Championship	5
WWF World Tag Team Championship	1
WWF Hardcore Championship	2
WWE World Tag Team Championship	1
WWE Intercontinental Championship	1
Total	28

The WWE went down under for a short tour. The first night in Sydney, August 1, I teamed up with Goldie for old times' sake against Jericho and Christian. It was a standard match. I combined a scissor kick and Book End on Christian for the victory, followed up with a dazzling Spinarooni, my first in Australia.

After the show, I grabbed a bite and a drink with the boys and went to bed feeling charged for the following day.

When I woke up, though, something was wrong. Really wrong.

My back was radiating with a pain I'd never experienced before. When I tried to start walking, it was as if my entire body seized and I had to lie on the floor. I finally mustered up the strength to make it to the shower, thinking the hot water would loosen me up.

It did—enough for me to limp through the next couple of shows.

I had to tell everyone what was happening with my back, and I'd wrestle as conservatively as possible. I was in pain and scared about what might have been the cause.

When the tour was over, I struggled to get on board the plane for a dreaded long flight to Los Angeles, where we had to make a connecting flight to Nova Scotia for *Raw* on August 4. As we flew, I couldn't sit or stand comfortably and opted to either lie on the floor or across three seats.

When we landed at LAX for the connection, I knew I couldn't make it through the last leg of the flight, so I called the WWE office to let them know.

The talent relations agent was dismissive. "Well, just continue on to Canada because we can still use you for pre-taped promos."

"I don't think you understand. I can't go. I'm lying here in customs at LAX and can't go any farther. I'll just book my own flight home."

The agent repeated what he wanted me to do. He obviously wasn't getting it, so I hung up. Honestly, I was ready to quit then and there.

I turned to Chris Brennan, one of the WWE trainers. "Here," I said. "Take the belt and give it to whoever you want to. I'm going home."

"Okay, okay, just calm down, Booker. Think about it for a minute. Is this really what you want to do?"

"I'm out of here, man. Whatever's wrong with my back is serious, and I've got to get it checked out."

I booked the first flight to Houston. Sharmell met me at the airport, and I went straight home to bed.

The company called me that first week and asked if there was any way I could manage to make a Sunday house show in Des Moines on August 10 and officially drop the title to Christian. I said I'd be there.

On August 10, in the midst of mind-numbing pain, I attempted to hide my hobbled state and made my way to the ring for a quick championship loss. In the shortest and least action-packed match of my career, I wasted no time in neutralizing Christian with some kicks and punches and then dramatically missed the scissor kick, landing with the pain of a thousand daggers in my spine.

Christian took his cue, picked me up for the Unprettier, and covered me to regain his IC belt.

As Sarge and some other guys from the back came and helped me out of the ring, I couldn't hide the pain from the people who saw me up close. Little did they know that what they witnessed couldn't have been more authentic than if they were wheeling me out on a stretcher, which would've been better now that I think about it.

The next night on *Raw* in Moline, Illinois, my entrance music hit. To everyone's confusion, out walked Christian with the IC title. He announced to the world he'd beaten me the previous night and was seeking a new challenger, which turned out to be little Spike Dudley. While I watched, laid up in my bed, Christian destroyed Spike in a matter of minutes.

When I saw the doctors, they told me I had a pinched sciatic nerve, which caused the unbearable pain from the middle of my back all the way down to my toes. It was decided I would have a cortisone injection. The doctor asked me if I wanted to see the five-inch-long needle he was going to jab into my vulnerable spine. No way. They anesthetized me, and

BOOKER T. HUFFMAN

I was completely out for the procedure.

Afterward, it was all a waiting game at home to see how well the steroids did their job. In the meantime, I relied on Sharmell for everything. I couldn't make it to the bathroom on my own even with crutches. If I tried to brave the trek to the kitchen, the progress was about a single step every twenty to thirty seconds while I held onto the wall. It was brutal.

As it turned out, the injection didn't work.

I thought my career was over.

The doctor said he wanted to try it again with a different anti-inflammatory agent, which at first sounded like an unnecessary risk just to wind up with the same result. But I thought about the quality of my life and the possibility of returning to the ring.

Finally I said, "All right, let's go."

So they put me under one more time, and once again I returned to my bedroom to recover.

Some of the boys, like Hayes, Goldie, R.V.D., and Nick, checked in to see how things were going, sending positive thoughts and well wishes. They worked, too, because day after day I started feeling better.

Within a couple of weeks, I morphed into a sturdy thirty-eight-year-old, ring-ready Booker Man. It was late September when I started working out, amazed at how quickly everything came back to form. The more I trained, the more I thought about returning to the ring.

After believing my career was over, now I was setting my sights on a comeback in another few weeks.

I made my official return on October 13 at *Raw* in Pittsburgh for a Tables Match, of all things, with Shane McMahon and The Dudley Boyz against Christian, Jericho, and La Résistance, a new heel team comprised of René Duprée and Rob Conway who portrayed despicable Frenchmen.

At first, I thought the creative guys were ribbing me. A Tables Match after what I'd just gone through? But they weren't. So with the intention of having absolutely zero contact with the tables whatsoever, in pure irony, I wound up being the one who claimed the match for our team by spine-busting Conway through the table.

Six days later, I was surprised to learn Road Warrior Hawk, Mike Hegstrand, had passed away at the age of forty-six in his sleep at his home in Indian Rocks, Florida.

When I heard of his death, I thought how amazing his career had been with Animal in The Legion of Doom: The Road Warriors. They'd revolutionized tag team wrestling in the eighties, just as I believe Lash and I did in the nineties with Harlem Heat.

I was saddened to hear we'd lost another one of the good guys.

On October 20 at the beginning of *Raw* in Wilkes-Barre,

Pennsylvania, the WWE paid tribute in a moment of silence.

About eight years later, when Hawk and Animal were inducted into the WWE Hall of Fame, I knew they deserved it for their undeniable contributions as one of the greatest professional wrestling duos of all time.

Later that night, I not only defeated Orton by count-out but made the announcement I'd be joining Stone Cold's team of HBK, R.V.D., and The Dudleys at Survivor Series 2003, where his job as Co-GM of *Raw* was on the line against Bischoff's team of Christian, Jericho, Orton, Steiner, and The World's Strongest Man, Mark Henry.

So on November 16 at the American Airlines Center in Dallas, I struck first in the match and eliminated none other than Scotty Steiner. Before there was any time to celebrate my victorious moment for the team, Henry took me out with the World's Strongest Slam, setting up a brief feud. HBK appeared to be our sole survivor at the end but was defeated despite his tremendous effort, thus ending Stone Cold's tenure as Co-GM of *Raw*.

I'd get my revenge on Henry. The six-feet-three, 385-pound two-time Olympic weight lifter and gold medalist at the 1995 Pan American Games had signed with the WWE in 1996. He was still relatively green in the ring by the time I started performing with him, but he told me he was a fan of mine and had admired my work in WCW for years. We formed a quick bond.

That particular night on *Raw* in Beaumont following the PPV, I hit Henry with a missile dropkick but was eventually caught in his World's Strongest Slam finisher, which pancaked me. I kicked out of it at the last second and later pinned him, using my legs on the ropes for leverage and every advantage at my disposal against the younger behemoth.

He got his chance to return the favor a week later in Utah, where thanks to Bischoff's inventive *Raw* Roulette Wheel, I squared off with Henry in a Salt Lake City Street Fight.

That night, I tried to surprise the big man early by hiding on the stage and then pouncing as he made his way up, but once we got back in the ring, he took over. He threw me into a trash can set up in the corner and then smashed me repeatedly over the head with it for the winning cover.

With our single wins against each other, it was decided Henry and I would put an end to the feud on December 14 at Armageddon. It was time for me to step up and display the ring-leading command of a five-time WCW Champion.

It seemed the WWE disliked cold weather as much as I did and booked many of our winter events in warm cities. We flew to Orlando for the PPV, which suited me fine.

I started the match by hammering Henry into the corner with punches, but he merely pushed me off like a cruiserweight and clotheslined me off my feet. We took the action outside, where I led him around, acting hurt. Then, after turning one of the corners, I surprised him with a back thrust kick.

But my advantage wouldn't last. Mark quickly took control, throwing me into the ring steps. Eventually the two of us made it back in, where I delivered a missile dropkick. Henry recovered and grabbed me like a rag doll in a huge bear hug. In the closing moments of the match, he threw me into the corner and avalanched me before picking me up for a botched powerbomb, in which I kind of slipped through his arms.

I was able to get up, kick him in the stomach, scissor kick him for the second time, and put a closure to the rubber match of our series.

With the year slowly winding down, it looked as if I might've been heading in a new direction by the very last *Raw* of the year in San Antonio on December 29, my son's twentieth birthday.

Randy Orton, the reigning IC champ, was in the ring running his mouth about Mick Foley, saying he was a coward for not attending. I made it clear my New Year's resolution was to whup his ass and take the title. As soon as I threw the gauntlet down, Mark Henry attacked me from behind and left me on the stage.

Randy walked past and accepted the challenge. The funniest part of working with Randy had nothing to do with the match itself. It was in the hours leading up to the broadcast.

Before that show, at about 5:00 p.m., Randy came up to me. "Hey, Book, so what are we going to do in there?"

I kept walking as he followed. "I don't know yet. Come find me in an hour."

An hour later, Randy was front and center again. "So what are we going to do in there?"

I looked at him, barely. "Man, let me get a Red Bull in me. Come back in thirty minutes, and we'll figure something out."

Half an hour later, Randy was following me again. "Okay, so what are we going to do in there?"

"You know what, Randy? I need another Red Bull, and then we'll talk, okay?" I thought it was amusing and took it in stride.

Finally, right before going out the curtain, as his entrance music was playing, Randy was in a panic. "I have no idea what we're going to do."

I smiled at him. "Don't worry, man. Me neither. We're going to call it in the ring."

We went out there, and I started off aggressively, leading him around the ring. Without a hitch, we seamlessly switched it up as the crowd soaked in the physical story developing in the ring. Just as things got going, Kane's entrance pyro went off and distracted me toward the ramp, giving Orton the chance to roll me up out of nowhere for the pin.

The next thing I knew, The Big Red Machine was all over me with a beat-down from hell, concluding my last appearance for 2003.

When I went up the ramp and through to the back,

Randy was waiting for me. "Holy shit, man, that was awesome! Is it always supposed to be that easy?"

I smiled. "Yes, it is. Happy New Year!"

Brandon had been on my mind for the last couple of months. Sharmell had been encouraging me to give him a second chance and have him come back home. I could do that with one stipulation: if he didn't mess it up. Sharmell even wanted to help Brandon get his GED.

Brandon moved back in that winter into the best conditions a young man could ever dream of. I felt if he was serious and could be trusted, the world still offered him tremendous promise, but he'd have to work for it.

Sharmell and I were committed to providing all the support he'd need. The rest of the journey was up to him.

When he came back into the house, our relationship was relatively normal, almost as if he'd never left, and we were all in good spirits about the whole deal. Sharmell really liked him, and the three of us would go out to eat or hang out when I was home. While I was on the road, Sharmell helped him transfer what credits he did manage to gain and got things rolling with his GED program.

As far as I was concerned, it was now or never with my son. Brandon had a lot of catching up to do, but at least he was on his feet and starting to run in the right direction.

21

TURNED HEEL

For me personally, 2004 started off on the wrong note. Creative put together a CD of original music for us WWE Superstars to utilize as our entrance themes, and mine was completely off. It was this generic elevator music version of a rap song that should've been in a late-eighties movie set in the hood. When it came on after my dramatic "Can you dig it, sucka!" opener, the slow tempo flattened the intensity of my entrance, especially the pyro.

The whole thing threw me off, so I let Vince know. "I can't do it. It's just not me. I need the original song to start out the only way Booker T starts out: hard and driving. That rap is stereotypical and clashes with everything I am."

He said I'd have to live with it for a couple of months until after the CD was properly promoted, and then I could switch back. It was better than nothing, so I went back to work.

On the first *Raw* of the year on January 5 in Memphis, I got my hands on Kane for interrupting the match with Randy and putting the boots on me. He was in the ring cutting a promo about how I'd ruined his shot at WrestleMania the previous year after eliminating him from Royal Rumble 2003. I ran down and sent him flying over the top rope with a standing side thrust kick. I picked up the microphone and told the big man I'd eliminate him this year as well.

The following week in Uniondale, New York, at the Nassau Coliseum, we faced off again only for Kane to DQ himself by repeatedly throwing me into the steps before Tombstoning me in the ring.

On January 19 in Green Bay for *Raw*, I teamed up with R.V.D. against Matt Hardy and Christian. Our lightning-in-a-bottle chemistry proved to be a perfect combination as Rob pinned Christian after his Five-Star Frog Splash, establishing our entry into the Rumble on January 25 in Philly.

When it was time for the big PPV, I was buzzed in as number eleven and ran down the aisle as intensely as ever. I hammered Steiner, who was the closest, before running toward Randy with a scissor kick.

Next thing I knew, Kane was buzzed in and got his hands on me for a big chokeslam. Just as I was recovering, The Undertaker's gong went off, signifying he was on his way to the ring, which stopped Kane dead in his tracks. I took full advantage and dumped over The Big Red Machine first. When he landed, he glared up to see it wasn't The Undertaker who was coming out; it was little Spike Dudley, who received a chokeslam on the ramp for his gag entrance.

A few minutes later, Randy tossed me.

I couldn't have been happier walking out of the Rumble into the back after a job well done.

I had a rare day off afterward during *Raw* in Hershey, Pennsylvania.

I returned the next week to assist Matt Hardy, who was in a long losing streak, in Penn State.

On February 9 in Portland, I was included in a Triple Threat Match for the IC title against R.V.D. and Randy. We all three hit it hard, and the next thing I knew, Rob was coming off the top on me with the Five-Star Frog Splash. The impact hurt R.V.D. as much as it did me, and he rolled out of the ring, allowing Randy the opportunistic cover on me to keep his belt.

In Bakersfield on February 16, R.V.D. and I took on Flair and Batista for their WWE Tag Team Championships. I had Flair in a position to combine a scissor kick and a Book End, but Randy appeared at ringside and pulled me out, smashing my leg with a chair. Mick Foley came to the rescue and brawled with Randy and Batista into the crowd. Back in the ring, Flair took advantage of my beaten leg and hit me with the figure four in the center. R.V.D., always being the bombardier with a predator's instincts, jumped to the top and splashed Flair. I rolled up and over for the pin, and R.V.D. and I were the new tag champs.

I really enjoyed working with Rob, and over the last couple of years riding to cities together, we'd become friends. Teaming up with him was interesting because the dynamics were so much different than with anyone else, including Lash. Lash was the power smasher while I carved everybody up with my speed and long-legged kicks. Rob was the aggressive high flyer while, at that point in my career, I was mostly on the ground with agile strikes and kicks. The fans loved our complementing chemistry, and I believe our run heightened both of our positions in the WWE.

CHAMPIONSHIPS	
WCW World Tag Team Championship	11
WCW World Television Championship	6
WCW United States Championship	1
WCW World Heavyweight Championship	5
WWF World Tag Team Championship	1
WWF Hardcore Championship	2
WWE World Tag Team Championship	2
WWE Intercontinental Championship	1
Total	29

On February 23 in Omaha, we were scheduled to face Rob Conway and René Duprée of La Résistance.

Those days, it seemed Duprée was having a seriously difficult time assimilating in the locker room. The kid endured several weeks of ribbing. Being a rookie in his first full year with the WWE, René wasn't making a lot of money at the time. He obviously took notice of professionally dressed performers, like me, coming in and out of the building and decided he had to get on board. So he bought himself a really expensive pair of leather shoes and a couple of designer suits. In his mind, that must've heightened his status to a level that might get him noticed.

It did. One night after a match, René came back to the dressing room and couldn't find his shoes. He looked everywhere and finally deflated with a sigh after finding them in the shower completely soaked. He sloshed out of the building.

The very next night, again Duprée came back from the ring and this time his shoes and suit were in the shower. He was hot about it.

I was just shaking my head and looking at the ground. I *love* shoes and suits and have quite the collection of both, and if someone had done that to my clothes, there would've been a problem in that locker room.

Whoever was gunning for René was relentless, but after a few similar instances, it eventually came to a grand finale.

After jumping rope in the corridor, I walked into the locker room and smelled the unmistakable, overpowering odor of industrial glue.

René came in, staring at the wall.

I walked over to where he was and looked up to see his expensive designer suit perfectly glued to the wall with its arms and legs spread as if for jumping jacks. Man, that one was brutal, and I definitely felt some sympathy for the rookie.

You could see the toll all the ribbing took on Duprée, who was completely beaten down. In two weeks' time, he must've aged twenty years. Although he was finally let off the hook, I don't think René ever found out what he'd done to deserve any of it in the first place.

I turned thirty-nine on March 1, and I had plenty of fire burning stronger than ever. There was still more to prove: many Spinaroonis and thousands of people who needed to be reminded of my five-time WCW Champion status.

R.V.D. and I started our official Road to WrestleMania that month, defending our WWE tag belts in my old town of Atlanta against Matt Hardy and Test. Test accidentally smashed Matt in the face with a big boot, which allowed Rob to hit the top-rope Five-Star Frog Splash while I dove in for the pin and the victory.

On March 14, R.V.D. and I descended upon New York City together to participate in WrestleMania XX in the arena that started it all in 1985, Madison Square Garden.

Manhattan's always got a crazy, overwhelming vibe, but when WrestleMania is in town, the frenzy takes on Olympic proportions. Fans from all over the world fly in and book all the hotel rooms in the area for a full week of shopping, eating, and sightseeing. WrestleMania brought an enormous economic windfall with it.

One of the nights, Rob and I were leaving the hotel via the escalators and could see a ton of fans hanging around in the lobby. Rob had stopped shaving and wasn't brushing his hair. He wore sunglasses and had tucked his ponytail into his skullcap.

He tapped me on the shoulder. "Hey, do you think they'll

recognize me?" He was serious.

"Man, who isn't gonna know you're Rob Van Dam?"

We both laughed, and sure enough, throngs of fans swarmed in for autographs and pictures.

That night R.V.D. and I defended our WWE Tag Team Championship in front of a sold-out Madison Square Garden. Eighteen thousand fans were primed and ready to see history made. We competed with La Résistance, The Dudleys, and Garrison Cade and Mark Jindrak in a Fatal 4-Way Match. We were ready to release our lightning yet again and walk to the back with the belts.

When we got going, I found myself taking big shots from almost every guy and was sure to return the favor. I tagged Rob to catch a breather. The match broke down into chaos at the end with almost everybody in the ring, which worked to our advantage. I caught a lost Rob Conway with the scissor kick, which was nicely followed by a Five-Star Frog Splash for the victory.

The next night on *Raw*, we gave The Dudleys a rematch at the Continental Airlines Arena. After an all-out war, I scored the win with a Book End on D-Von.

In Detroit on March 22, they announced another *Raw/SD* lottery draft. Since R.V.D. and I were drafted over to *SD*, we were booked to lose and ceremoniously drop the tag titles to the team of Bischoff's choosing, which turned out to be Flair and Batista. It wasn't the greatest of nights for me. Late in the match, Rob accidentally coldcocked me with his springboard sidekick, which led to me eating Batista's sit-out powerbomb for the crushing defeat.

Heading over to *SD* proved to be an interesting change of pace. Creative saw it as an opportunity for me to turn to the dark side and go full-out heel. Where they got it right was the method of vilifying me, and I knew exactly how to go about it.

During my first appearance on *SD* on March 25 in Grand Rapids, I came out to the ring to greet GM Kurt Angle and let him and the fans know exactly what switching brands meant to me. I told them I was brought against my will, taken away from the *Raw* fans, who truly appreciated me, and relegated to the B team of the company. I said I was better than the entire roster, especially "Latino Heat" Eddie Guerrero, the WWE Champion. I was having a great time hamming it up as an egomaniac.

Angle tried to placate me, saying I was a great WWE Superstar and that *SD* was the major leagues. He asked the people to give their ovation but received nothing but boos.

It was a success.

Because I specifically mentioned Eddie in my promo, we had a backstage confrontation that led Angle to book us in a championship match that night. Hardcore Holly, also offended by my disparagement of the *SD* brand and roster, said after Eddie was finished with me there was an entire list of guys who were next in line, including himself.

I thought it was great. I was on the show for the first time, and within an hour I'd already gained the hatred of the fans, put a target on my back, and gotten a shot at the crown. It sounded like I was going to be busy for a while. It was good to be a heel and the biggest star on a new show.

I went right out there and mixed it up with Eddie for the gold. We had a brilliant and long match that exceeded even our expectations. Going back to WCW, Eddie and I had always worked well together, everything clicking into place. We matched speed, technical moves, and a full array of reversals and high-flying maneuvers before Eddie got me down and went for his own frog splash for the finish. Just as Eddie went for the pin, Bradshaw came out of nowhere and gave him a Clothesline from Hell, which DQed my efforts for the WWE belt.

On April Fools' Day, for *SD* I complained to Angle about JBL's interference and the crowd having booed me for the first time in my WWE career. He attempted to console me by booking me into a match against Hardcore Holly.

My first impression of Holly back in my first year at Madison Square Garden was that he was too much of a tough guy, but now that I got to know the true person and performer he was, I liked him a lot. Behind the rough exterior was a great guy and talented professional in the ring. All the new guys coming in were generally afraid of Holly, but that was just a matter of perception. Holly was like a drill sergeant who always shot straight with everybody. In due time, if they survived the WWE long enough, those same guys realized he might've been the single most important veteran in the locker room to learn from.

That *SD* performance with him was easy and smooth. We nailed our moves, shared taking the lead, entertained, and put each other over. I pinned him by holding on to his tights for leverage, a classic heel maneuver in the vein of guys like Flair.

A week later in San Antonio, continuing the heel makeover, I started to treat Rob like a liability. In a tag match with him against Big Show and Charlie Hass, I avoided Rob's tags and walked out of position when he needed me most. Ultimately, I hopped down from the apron and went to the back, effectively leaving R.V.D. holding the bag as Show chokeslammed him for the win.

On April 15 in Indianapolis, Angle saw an opportunity to give R.V.D. restitution for my desertion and declared we'd face off that night. I went into the match against my buddy with a vicious expression and pummeled him into the ropes, where he got tied up. I was relentless while his guard was down, and I legitimately busted his nose open as he freed himself and dropped to the floor.

The referee stopped the match while I hit a Spinarooni to an overwhelming chorus of boos.

Backstage afterward, I was concerned about Rob's nose

and apologized.

"Nah, it's cool, man," he said. "It's just something that happens. I know you've eaten plenty of my feet to the face."

We both laughed. He was right.

R.V.D. was granted a rematch on the next *SD* on April 22 in Kelowna, British Columbia. It looked as if he had me in the end with a Frog Splash. Just as he was about to launch, Heyman secretly ignited a pyro explosion on the stage that allowed me to roll Rob up for the pin.

Later on in the evening, I made my way to the ring and grabbed the microphone, declaring, "I'm the biggest star on *SD*. I will become the most famous man in America!"

Then the air was filled with the unmistakable sound of The Undertaker's entrance gong, and I took off running, fear streaking my face.

I wasn't sure whether I'd have a run with The Undertaker on April 29 in Oklahoma City, but after hearing his gong that night, I definitely wanted it to happen. After a solid match with Billy Gunn, in which I clipped him with a scissor kick for the win, The Undertaker approached the ring, with Paul Bearer carrying the urn.

At WrestleMania XX, The Undertaker had abandoned his biker Big Evil image and returned to his roots as The Dead Man, so The Undertaker I was getting was pure vintage.

I got on the mic. "I just had a grueling match, and I'm gonna get the hell out of here!" As I took off running, I snatched the urn from Bearer and cracked The Undertaker upside the head with it before leaping the barrier and retreating through the crowd.

I knew exactly what I was getting into, so it was important to make the concept right. Not everybody gets a feud with one of the most legendary figures in professional wrestling history, and it can definitely take you to another level in the company. Most of all, I was having some fun as a heel being scared of The Undertaker's deathly powers, which was not a hard thing to do by any means.

For the May 6 *SD*, we went completely nineties with The Undertaker by filming some segments where I first went to a creepy voodoo shop and asked the psychic there how I could defeat my undead foe. She told me to go to the cemetery and find the dirt of an unmarked grave, which would fend off The Undertaker's mystic forces.

In the next scene, I was at an actual cemetery in the dead of night searching for the grave with a little flashlight. Every time I heard something, my eyes bugged out. "What was that?"

I finally found the grave and got down to collect a few handfuls into a little bag, and then another eerie sound in the dark spooked me. I took off running with a yellow streak down my back.

As I left the shot, a lightning flash went off and The Undertaker's gloved hand punched up through the soil.

It came off great, and I was having exactly the kind of fun I'd been anticipating.

The final week before Judgment Day 2004, believing the dirt from the graveyard would allow me to cast a spell over The Undertaker and make me stronger as well, I took on The Full Blooded Italians (F.B.I.), Nunzio and Johnny Stamboli, in a 2-on-1 Handicap Match.

Since they had been injured the previous week by The Undertaker, I beat them both easily at the same time, then declared, "I'm just as strong as The Undertaker!"

Just then the image of The Undertaker appeared on all the big screens, while the ring filled with mist. From the top of the stage, Paul Bearer came out and began taunting me with the mysterious urn he always carried. Before I knew it, The Undertaker rose out of the floor of the ring, and I hightailed it out of there just as fast as I had the previous times.

When the big night arrived for Judgment Day 2004 in Los Angeles, nineteen thousand strong watched my entrance. I acted like I was trying to be confident, as if the magic dirt might have an effect on The Dead Man, but I kept looking around with trepidation.

The Undertaker slowly crept toward the ring, and when we finally locked up, it was another amazing experience working with The Undertaker's style. He has a great approach to his communication and signals in the ring, and he's as smooth and nonchalant as any pro I've ever worked with.

He hit all his classic tricks, sitting up after repeated beat-downs, just like Jason in *Friday the 13th*, taking my arm as his guide while he walked along the top rope and performed his flying lariat. I blasted The Dead Man with a hard scissor kick, but he kicked out, chokeslammed me, and signaled for the Tombstone.

He lifted me up with ease, as all the flashbulbs in the crowd went off, and drove my head straight into the canvas. I was Tombstoned for an honorable loss to one of the industry's best.

Losing to The Undertaker is never a loss but a tactical and character victory everybody wears with pride. I couldn't have been prouder of our entire angle.

In the back, we thanked each other for a good time. Imagine that—eating a Tombstone for a clean pin fall being a good time. It was a *great* time.

Over the next couple of weeks on *SD*, they had me running around backstage telling anyone who'd listen that I was getting another shot against The Undertaker because my magic grave dirt had been tampered with. Guys like Sho Funaki and Scotty 2 Hotty were less than sympathetic, so they each caught a quick squash match that quelled my anger.

On May 27 in Milwaukee, I was selected as one of many wrestlers to surround the outside of the ring during John

Cena and René Duprée's Lumberjack Match for the United States title. Every time Cena got near me, I'd grab his feet and trip him up or distract him any way possible. Also during that match, Paul Heyman and The Dudley Boyz kidnapped Paul Bearer so Heyman could assume control over The Dead Man, effectively ending my potential rematch.

The following week in Toronto on June 3, I started off the show professing my innocence in the abduction of Paul Bearer, only to be interrupted by Cena. He took exception to my participation during the match with Duprée and got in my face. During the ensuing scuffle, both John and I fell into GM Kurt Angle, who was ringside in a wheelchair, healing fake injuries from an attack from Big Show. Just as we settled down, Heyman came down to discuss having kidnapped Bearer, so I casually left.

At the Nassau Coliseum on June 10, Angle was in the ring and demanded Cena and I come down and immediately apologize for unintentionally assaulting him during the last show. I thought it was pretty funny that they had me apologize five times in parody of my five-time WCW Champion catchphrase. Cena refused to apologize and was penalized by being booked into a Triple Play Challenge where he had to face R.V.D., Duprée, and me in three separate five-minute matches.

I was up first and demolished Cena for the entire time limit, but before I hit him with a finish and a cover, the bell rang.

Cena and I were on a planned collision course for a United States title run together.

Before that single feud fell into place, Angle set up a series of No. 1 Contender's Matches over the next couple of weeks, starting at The Great American Bash on June 27 in Norfolk.

R.V.D., Duprée, Cena, and I were pitted against each other in a Fatal 4-Way No. 1 Contender's Match for the top spot in line for the United States Championship. R.V.D. quickly hit a Five-Star Frog Splash on Duprée and me as we were both laid out, but Rob ironically hurt himself with the high-risk move and Cena was able to cover and eliminate him. Cena next dropped and pinned Duprée with an Attitude Adjustment, leaving me the opportunity to eliminate René. Cena and I brawled back and forth, but he got the upper hand and I found myself getting an Attitude Adjustment as well for the loss.

Because Cena won and was already the champ, it nullified having a number-one contender, so in Fayetteville on July 1, Angle announced a 3-Way Match between R.V.D., Duprée, and me.

During the match, I was hurt after taking some moves outside of the ring as Rob delivered a high-flying Five-Star on Duprée, but I reached in and pulled R.V.D. out of the ring and slid in to steal the victory and the shot at Cena's United States title.

The next few weeks brought a maelstrom of in-ring action that jeopardized my earned opportunity to defeat Cena for the belt. First, we had a singles match in Providence, which was DQed because Angle and Luther Reigns attacked Cena in the ring. And since John fell into the wheelchair-bound GM, he was stripped of the United States Championship.

The following week for the vacated title, I took on Duprée, Kenzo Suzuki, and Cena. Suzuki was DQed for choking, René was pinned by Cena, and I capitalized on John after Luther threw him into the outside post. I rolled him back, delivered a scissor kick, scored the pin, and assumed the title. There was never an official decision, and my hand was never raised, presumably because Luther interfered. I walked out with the belt and waited for the following week to be declared the rightful titleholder.

In Philly on July 22, I never thought Vince McMahon would be such a welcome sight, but he shed some much-needed light on the United States title. Vince came out and fired Angle for abuse of power and blatantly falsifying his injuries.

With Angle out, Teddy Long was in as the new GM of *SD* by July 29 in Cincinnati.

I'd been out there in the ring holding the United States belt, demanding that someone declare me the rightful champion.

Teddy said his run with the *SD* brand would be a land of opportunity. To illustrate that fact, there would be an Eight-Man Elimination Match that night to crown a new United

BOOKER T. HUFFMAN

States Champion once and for all. It looked as if I'd have to endure one more test of my ability to prove to the world I was the rightful United States Champion.

Cena, R.V.D., Charlie Haas, Billy Gunn, Luther Reigns, René Duprée, and I were subjected to the same ring in a chaotic tornado of flying bodies to determine the United States Champion. In sequential order, Hass was eliminated by Duprée, Duprée by Luther, and Suzuki was DQed for hitting Cena with the belt but recovered to pin Gunn and Reigns. Finally, yes, indeed, I caught John in the back of the head with a fatal scissor kick. I covered, hooked the leg, and became a two-time United States Champion.

Upon reinstating the United States title, WWE had manufactured a completely new belt to replace the WCW's gold-on-black leather version. The new one was sharp with the main center plate being the stars and stripes of the United States flag. It would've been *perfect* for G.I. Bro.

CHAMPIONSHIPS	
WCW World Tag Team Championship	11
WCW World Television Championship	6
WCW United States Championship	1
WCW World Heavyweight Championship	5
WWF World Tag Team Championship	1
WWF Hardcore Championship	2
WWE World Tag Team Championship	2
WWE Intercontinental Championship	1
WWE United States Championship	1
Total	30

The last few shows, the truth was that I'd started to get a little weary with the constant indecision over the direction of match booking. It would've been nice to have a long-term map for the journey.

Thankfully, that night it all came to a conclusion in my favor, but throughout my entire career, I'd never lobbied or campaigned myself to the creative team or sat down and discussed long-term angles or the desire to hold a championship. Belts never defined who I was in WCW or in the WWE.

I remember back in WCW, in the summer of 2000, Big Vito was told he was losing the Hardcore title to Lance Storm, and he was in the back crying, literally. "Man, I can't believe they're taking the belt from me. I've worked so hard!"

I thought he'd lost his mind and was having a breakdown. "Are you serious? You're really crying over a title belt in WCW? Get a grip, man."

He looked up with red eyes. "I made this belt what it is!"

I just shook my head and walked away.

Sure, it's nice to be tapped and informed you're going over for a belt, but a good performer never relies on a title. Once you're over, you're over with gold, silver, or nothing but your boots and the ability to call a match on the fly anytime, anywhere.

22

TRIBUTE TO THE TROOPS

Holding the United States title meant an exponential increase in my participation on each broadcast and PPV. Booker T business was about to skyrocket again.

I knew I'd still be involved with Cena's pursuit of regaining the title, and it was revealed on the August 5 *SD* in my hometown of Houston that I'd be facing him in a Best of Five Series starting at SummerSlam 2004 on August 15 in Toronto. Cena was their guy, something that was becoming clearer with each passing week, and he was excited for the opportunity to work with me in a new capacity.

At that time, John was in the middle of his whole white-guy-who-can-rap character, which drove some of the audience insane, but I honestly thought he pulled it off pretty well. The guy could rap whether people wanted to admit it or not, and he was getting himself over with his catchphrases and Thuga-nomics philosophy.

In actuality, Cena was the perfect performer within the *SD* roster to pull off the Best of Five with because he was willing to be different and had a great look. He was also meticulous about his work and took direction extremely well. I'd look at him and think, *Cena's gonna make it big.*

When SummerSlam 2004 arrived on August 15 and we faced off in the Air Canada Centre, the creative team kept both of us legitimately guessing about each performance. Not until just before going out each night did we know who'd be the victor, so we had to call our matches on the go.

That first contest at SummerSlam 2004 saw Cena go up one to zero over me in a nine-minute match after kicking out of the scissor kick, which not too many people were able to do, before dropping me with his Attitude Adjustment finisher. That move might not look like much to viewers, but I can assure you it's a jarring bump that almost induced whiplash. Not fun at all.

Eleven days later in Fresno, I tied up the series at one win each.

The next day in beautiful Sydney, Australia, on August 27, I took the two-to-one lead in the series.

After a two-week interlude, we resumed the action on September 16 in Spokane, where I tried to sneak John in the face with the championship belt while the ref was down, only to be caught by an Attitude Adjustment that allowed him to tie up the series at two wins each.

Before Cena and I could conclude our series with the fifth and final match, we took another two-week break from each other, which built up the hype for the conclusion at No Mercy 2004.

BOOKER T. HUFFMAN

On September 23 and 30, I was randomly booked into matches with Paul London, which were squashes in my favor.

The day before my first match with London, news hit that The Big Boss Man Ray Traylor had died at his home in Georgia of a sudden heart attack. He was only forty-one.

Ray, or Bubba as I called him, was literally plucked off the streets. After quitting his day job as a real prison corrections officer, he walked into the ring as a jobber for Jim Crockett Promotions' WCW. By 1987, Vince saw potential in his real-life story and turned him into the hugely successful Big Boss Man. The rest was history.

It was devastating to lose another colleague long before his time.

On Sunday, October 3, John and I descended upon the Continental Airlines Area in East Rutherford, New Jersey, for the grand finale to our Best of Five Series for the WWE United States Championship. Knowing Cena was going over for the belt, I poured on the intensity to make it a quality match and put Cena over. When one guy gets the win and a title, the other comes off looking strong in defeat. If anything, John was the one in for a tough night in the ring.

John and I squared off like two raging bulls, with serious intentions to steal the show. We went in and out of the ring, aggressively attacked each other, taking every liberty imaginable. I assumed the role of ring general, and Cena was a good follower, easygoing and fluid.

When it was time to bring it home, I went for a leaping Houston Sidekick. Cena ducked, leaving me to crotch myself on the top rope. He made an Attitude Adjustment attempt, which I reversed into a Book End, before going for the cover. He kicked out at two. I missed a scissor kick, allowing John to cover me for the two count. We got up and began trading blows when Cena took control, hoisting me up for a powerful AA. I crashed to the canvas as John covered me for the championship win.

At the end of the day, I was proud of what both John and I had accomplished in our Best of Five Series.

After losing the United States title, I lay low for a few weeks, not working too much on TV. My run with Cena was concluded, and it was just a matter of time before creative pointed me into a new angle.

By October 21, creative entered me into a program with WWE Champion JBL and his lackey and chief of staff, Orlando Jordan. Teddy Long set up a Six-Man Tag Team Match with R.V.D., Rey Mysterio, and me versus JBL, Suzuki, and, René Duprée. Before the match, in an attempt to gain favor with me, Bradshaw sent Jordan my way to deliver a greeting from the champion. I scorned Jordan, the "errand boy," and told him to get out of my face.

BOOKER T. HUFFMAN

Getting back to the Six-Man Tag Team Match, R.V.D. and Mysterio felt they couldn't trust me, assuming I went into business for myself by aligning with JBL. I played the part, staying distant and disinterested, but when they finally had no choice but to tag me in, much to Bradshaw's chagrin, I clocked him and Duprée. I quickly covered and pinned JBL but saved a Book End for Orlando.

Jordan was put into a singles contest with me the following week for a shot at JBL's WWE title where I made short work of him.

I traveled to Cleveland for Survivor Series 2004 to face Bradshaw before a packed house of seventy-five hundred. JBL worked a different style than what I was accustomed to: a big-man, brawling approach. I adapted, and we had a competitive match. We shared leading back and forth, but of course I had the obstacle of Orlando standing at ringside, causing a constant distraction. In fact, he found himself in the ring on the receiving end of yet another Book End, but Bradshaw took advantage of the interference. He knocked the taste out of my mouth with the belt and stole the pin fall to retain it.

I demanded an immediate rematch at *SD*, but because Eddie and The Undertaker were also in top contention, Teddy Long decreed there would be a Fatal 4-Way Match for the WWE title at the final PPV of the year, Armageddon 2004.

Leading up to the big main event in Duluth, Georgia, The Undertaker, Eddie, and I were subjected to various warm-up tag and Six-Man Tag Team Matches against JBL, Jordan, and their newest allies, Danny and Doug Basham, known simply as The Basham Brothers. The weeks passed like hours, and on December 18 it was time for JBL to step up and put the gold on the line against three determined veteran competitors.

The Undertaker viciously set the pace by jumping out and destroying the rest of us, even hitting three consecutive chokeslams on Eddie, Bradshaw, and me. But as he went to give JBL the Tombstone, out of nowhere, Jon Heidenreich, an imposing madman, showed up and hit The Undertaker with a clothesline and pulled him out of the ring for a cobra clutch.

With The Dead Man out of the way, JBL came running up on me with the Clothesline from Hell and stole the win.

The WWE Championship now out of my grasp, I shifted my attention to what would become an experience of a lifetime: I was booked for the second annual WWE Tribute to the Troops on December 23.

We were headed to Tikrit, Iraq, where we'd perform an exclusively *SD* card of matches at a secure military base for men and women of the United States military. We took off from New York in a Lockheed C-130 Hercules cargo transport plane, which was big enough to fit an aircraft carrier, the Houston Astrodome, and Madison Square Garden inside with still enough room to spare for Big Show. Exaggerations aside, the huge plane transported pretty much the entire roster, including The Undertaker, Eddie, JBL, Show, Angle, Mick Foley, Hardcore Holly, Rey, Heidenreich, and me.

It was a twenty-hour flight with one stop eight hours in. We landed for a three-hour layover in Germany, where we stretched our legs and hung out bowling and playing games. Then we loaded up again for the long haul to Tikrit, another twelve hours away. Many of us caught up on sleep, or at least attempted to.

Big Show knew from experience to bring his own big air mattress. He claimed a corner, blew up his bed, and went to sleep.

About two hours into Show's slumber, as he snored like a lumberjack sawing logs, someone tiptoed up to the mattress and stabbed it with a ballpoint pen before sneaking away. The air slowly rushed out with a *pshhhh*, and Show steadily sank to the floor as if he were in quicksand.

Ten hours later, when we were about to land, Show came to and lost his mind. "Whoa! What the hell happened to my bed? Oh, my back! I'm stiff as a board."

Nobody said a word as Show examined every inch of the deflated bed to determine the cause. Then he found it. "Which one of you popped my bed, huh? Somebody's going to pay—and pay big!"

Again, nobody spoke, but their gazes were darting around, each person looking like the cat that swallowed the canary.

Show conducted his own investigation, questioning everybody, but he never did find the culprit.

A caravan of armed military Hummers met us at the airport, and soldiers chauffeured three wrestlers to a vehicle. It was cold outside and not at all what I expected. At forty-seven degrees, Iraq wasn't quite the hot desert climate I'd assumed it to be. It was like Reno, Nevada, in the winter.

When I sat in the front passenger seat, I had a good view of a bullet hole in the windshield in perfect alignment with my head. It felt like we were on Mars as we traveled the desert terrain to the home base, where we'd rough it in barracks just like our hosts had been for weeks, months, and years. We ate what they ate, observed their drills. We were even invited on flights in Black Hawks to visit other bases and to target practice with an array of rifles and pistols. I made sure to hop into Hummers with my military chaperones and visit every side of the sprawling base to raise the soldiers' spirits, which also raised mine.

It brought to mind a phone call I'd received the previous year from a friend making a similar appearance in Iraq with the WWE.

"Hey, Booker! It's Termite. How are you, man?"

I hadn't heard from the former pro boxer and fellow Houston native, Maurice "Termite" Watkins, for a little while.

"Termite! Hey, I'm doing all right. What are you up to?"

Termite sounded really distant and broken up, but then it all made sense as he continued. "I'm over in Iraq visiting the troops and having a great time with these young men and women, and I've got somebody here who wants to say hello. Is that cool?"

I didn't hesitate. "Put them on."

It was a young soldier who was excited beyond belief to speak with me. He briefly chatted me up, asking me basic questions about my career and how things were going in the States, and I could tell it meant a lot to have a piece of home transmitted through our call together.

Before he had to go, he asked, "Do you think you'll come over here with the WWE next year for a show?"

I thought about it. "Yeah, man. If they go again, I'll be there. But do me a favor. Be safe out there, and keep your head down. I'll see you soon."

It was a great memory, and as I lay down that night in Iraq, I hoped I'd have a chance to shake that soldier's hand.

Before I fell asleep, a mortar exploded not far from the base. Even though we felt safe among our heroic brothers and sisters, feeling the concussion through the ground definitely unnerved us and made it impossible to get a good night's rest before the big day.

I felt even greater respect for the men and women trying to sleep there night in and night out.

When it was showtime, I got my two Red Bulls in me and jumped rope. In the cool temps, I was burning up with a cold sweat and ready for my show-opening bout with René Duprée. It was a truly special moment to walk out to the thunderous reaction from the rows of helmeted young soldiers and service people.

René and I put on a furious performance, which we dedicated to our deserving audience. We were well aware we were bringing them comfort from home, if only for a few golden moments of escape, through our brand of entertainment. I got the pin with a super airborne scissor kick for the victory and pulled out a dizzying Tribute to the Troops Spinarooni.

The most memorable image I have of that match came after I won and jumped onto the top turnbuckle with my hands raised, looking down at the troops as they cheered for me. In my heart, I was cheering for them. It was an emotional moment that will never leave me.

That night before we left, I decided to take the short walk to the little latrine they used for washing up at the edge of the base. Because we were literally in the middle of nowhere, there wasn't any ambient light from nearby towns. Nighttime in the desert of Iraq is pitch black. You can't see your own hands and feet. To remedy this, each person was given a little green glow stick. They put one around my neck and said, "The creek is fifteen paces that direction. You'll see it no problem."

As I carefully ventured ahead, a green light passed me. Two paces on, another green light drifted by. Another green light came near, and I could hear the bustle of the latrine ahead, but this third light stopped just past me and reversed toward me.

"Hey! I know you!" The man was almost completely blanketed by the darkness.

"You do? How's that?"

"Last year Termite Watkins put you on the phone with a soldier and you were kind enough to speak with him for a minute. Remember?"

I couldn't believe it. "Are you kidding me? Hell, yeah, I remember. What are the odds? I told you I'd come!"

He laughed. "You told me to keep my head down. I'll tell you what, that's exactly what I've been doing. When I heard the WWE was coming and saw your name on the list, I couldn't believe it."

And there we were in the middle of Iraq, two Americans doing everything in our capacity to try to serve. As we parted ways, I reached down and picked up a decent-sized rock to commemorate everything I'd experienced in my couple of days in Iraq. Later I wrote *2004* on it in marker. It's sitting on my desk now, and it always will be.

On our return flight, Big Show tried desperately to repair his bed with duct tape and any other adhesive he could get his big hands on. Finally, he fixed it.

As soon as he went to sleep, the ripper sneaked back over and popped it again.

Sweet dreams, giant friend.

When I was finally back on American soil and walking through the doorway of my home in Houston, the inevitable was awaiting me. Sharmell told me she hadn't seen or heard from Brandon for the last twenty-four hours. I was not only worried; I was disappointed that he might've messed up again.

Prior to this disappearing act, Brandon truly seemed to be doing well for himself. He was close to earning the GED Sharmell had been helping him with. To show him how proud I was, I'd taken him to the local Chevrolet dealer and bought him a Suburban. He was beyond excited, and honestly so was I, but to give him a little responsibility and help build his credit up, I left a few thousand dollars on the note for him to pay off.

Not more than a few days later, I came back home and saw a Jaguar sitting in the driveway.

"What is that outside? Where's the Suburban?"

Brandon was too cool for the room about it. "Aw, Dad, it's no big deal. I traded it in even for something a little more my style. You don't mind, do you?"

It did bother me, but I let it slide, though I wondered what might be coming around the corner with him.

That night when I got back home from Iraq, I was lying in bed worrying about Brandon's disappearance when the bell at the gate sounded. I looked outside to view the last thing anybody, especially me, wanted to see outside the house: several police cars.

I got dressed and went outside to buzz them in. As they drove up the driveway, there was Brandon in the backseat of one of the cars. He got out and said he was robbed of his wallet, taped up, and thrown into the trunk of his own car while the perpetrators committed another aggravated robbery across town.

I felt sick to my stomach. I saw no signs of his being taped up or struggling—no messed-up hair or clothes, nothing. I sensed he wasn't being honest but thanked the cops and asked them to keep me posted on the status of the car and Brandon's wallet.

The entire night, I stayed up talking with Sharmell. She didn't believe Brandon either. Without concrete proof, I decided I had to let it go and wait to see if the tall tale caved under the pressure.

And it did.

While I was back out on the road, my nephew Kevin, Billie's son, called. I loved and trusted Kevin and had asked him to stay at my place when I was out of town. It gave me peace of mind to have a responsible man there in my absence.

"What's up, Kevin?"

"Book, if Brandon's wallet was stolen, how is it sitting in

his room right now?"

It felt like a giant dagger stabbing me in the back. My son had made a fool of me for the last time.

When I got home to confront Brandon, Sharmell told me the cops had already put two and two together and picked him up. He was sitting downtown at the county jail for a few days.

I received a call from the father of one of Brandon's friends. As it turned out, it was Brandon and this man's son who committed the crime of aggravated robbery at some local business and then cooked up that whole story. "So what do you want to do?" he said. "Do you want to get separate attorneys for them, or do you have someone in mind you'd prefer using for both?"

"Listen, you can do whatever you want to do, but I'm not doing a thing. He chose to break the law, and now he's going to receive the full extent of the law."

The guy was silent, more than likely shocked, but he didn't have a clue about my past, let alone what had transpired between Brandon and me over the years.

The man wound up paying for both boys' legal assistance.

Brandon came home a couple of days later.

"Get your things, and get out now," I said. "I don't care where you go, and I don't want to know once you're there. Just get out."

As I watched him pack, he didn't even look at me. He seemed interested only in making sure he secured his PlayStation.

BOOKER T. HUFFMAN

A few minutes later, he was ready. The door hit him on the way out for the very last time. Brandon had followed in my footsteps, all right, down to robbing a store. I couldn't believe it. The circle had been completed. I'm sorry to say, Brandon and I barely speak to each other these days, and I'm not sure if some grand miracle will ever occur to change his lifestyle, as it did for me.

And that was the end of 2004 for the Huffman household. Happy New Year to us, right?

23

Trying to put the dismal end of 2004 in the rearview mirror, I hit the road once again.

Teaming up with Eddie, I chased the belts around the waists of The Bashams. But we weren't alone. R.V.D., Rey, Mark Jindrak, Luther Reigns, and Orlando Jordan were also in contention. To accommodate the masses, Teddy booked most of January with standard Four-Way and Six-Man Tag Matches for the titles leading up to the Royal Rumble 2005. Eddie and I failed to capitalize each week.

Royal Rumble 2005 came on January 30 in Fresno, where I entered the ruckus at number ten and immediately went after Middle Eastern sympathizer and anti-American heel Muhammad Hassan. Nobody wanted him in there, so in a group effort, he was easily tossed out to the delight of the roaring crowd in the Save Mart Center. I turned my attention to Luther Reigns and Orlando Jordan, dispatching them both from the match as well, only to be double-teamed by Rey and my own partner, Eddie.

After the Royal Rumble, I took a real leap of faith. Over the last couple of years, the more I was away from Sharmell the more it had become clear we would be together forever. On a cold but calm day in February, Sharmell and I got married in her hometown of Gary, Indiana, in an elaborate ceremony filled with our families and personal friends. My brothers, sisters, nephews, and nieces were all in attendance as I exchanged vows with the love of my life, Sharmell Sullivan-Huffman.

The ceremony was fairly big news in Sharmell's hometown, and the local press covered it like a royal affair.

Because I had to get back on the road almost immediately, we had to postpone our getaway until later that year, when we'd fly to St. Thomas in the United States Virgin Islands and walk the crystal shores as husband and wife.

In the meantime, I went right back to work. Teddy announced he'd established yet another No. 1 Contender's Tournament, in which the winner would face WrestleMania XXI's WWE Champion.

Backstage I told Eddie in a taped segment it was every man for himself at the Rumble. That night, we went out heel versus heel in a contest that turned into a mockery when Eddie followed his Lie, Cheat, and Steal philosophy by faking a knee injury. But when my back was turned and I looked at the big screen, it was clear he was playing shenanigans on me. I dodged his antics and scored a victory with a quick pin.

In the second round, Cena handily destroyed Orlando Jordan and moved full speed ahead to Cleveland and directly into a semifinal match with me on February 17.

Before the night's show got under way, however, things backstage didn't kick off the way they normally did. I went through my pre-show rituals, jumping rope, warming up my arms and chest with rubber exercise tubes, and going for my Red Bulls. But my cooler was empty!

A slow rage steadily climbed. "Who stole my Red Bull? I want to know. Now!" I looked at everybody and everything in the locker room to find evidence.

Finally, one of The Shane Twins, a new, muscle-bound tag team on the roster recently repackaged as Gymini, sheepishly approached me. "Um, Booker, I'm Mike Shane. I'm very sorry, but my brother Todd and I drank your Red Bulls. We thought it was a community cooler for the guys in the locker room. We're terribly sorry and meant no disrespect."

I was holding back my anger as much as possible but looked at Mike's brother, who was visibly shaken. "That cooler is where I store *my* Red Bulls. Everybody in the locker room knows that. Now I don't have my cans to get ready for the match. I'm going to cut you some slack since you're new. But now you know, so stay out of that cooler!"

They both apologized profusely.

The very next show on the road, the twins handed me a pack of Red Bulls and apologized again, and I let them off the hook.

Many wrestlers have pre-show rituals they do in order to help them focus on the match ahead. Although it was just two Red Bulls, for me they represented two important steps in preparing to head out to the ring.

Unfortunately, that wasn't the last time I was a victim of a Red Bull robbery.

A couple of weeks later during a house show, I went for the cooler. Again both Red Bulls were gone. "What? This isn't going to work, guys. Who was in the cooler?"

I looked at the Shanes, who put their hands up and shook their heads.

This time nobody came forward, so I took the cooler out into the hallway and proceeded to dump the ice and water everywhere in a big slick mess. "This is going to happen every time I come in here and find someone stole my Red Bulls and won't come forward. Every time. Do you hear me?"

As I sat there steaming, Kurt came walking past and slowed down enough to say, "Hey, man, listen. Do you really think this is the way a professional like you, representing the WWE, should act out?"

I turned to Kurt very slowly. "Kurt, listen to me. Now's not the time."

He looked at me and nodded and continued on his way.

Regardless of who took them, I think my point was made loud and clear, as I never found the cooler empty of Red Bulls again.

As I put the incident behind me, my journey took me to No Way Out 2005 in Pittsburgh at the Mellon Arena, where a big and unpredictable challenge awaited me. Jon Heidenreich was six feet five and three hundred pounds of former Washington Redskins power. During our bout, he lost control of himself and attacked me with a chair, ramming it over and over into my throat for the DQ loss. I nursed the injury like an Oscar winner while being helped to the back.

Because of his vicious attack, the two of us entered a short feud over the next few weeks, but his behavior offstage was what caught me off guard. Not only did Jon enjoy sitting in the corner of the locker room playing with his own action figure, having full conversations with it in front of all of us, but he would retreat to the nearest shower or closet and refuse to get out. It would be show time, and he wouldn't leave his dark sanctuary while officials would be banging on the door. For whatever reason, I was one of the very few people who could coax him out of his self-imposed exile.

Personally, I liked Jon and never had a problem with him. He listened to direction, and we worked well in the ring together. Our matches weren't exactly classic masterpieces, but we both knew how to work with each other's strengths to tell

BOOKER T. HUFFMAN

a good story.

On March 3 when we faced off in Albany, Jon went straight for a steel chair, but when he got close, I Houston Sidekicked it into his face. When I reached for the chair, the ref grabbed and dropped it, freeing me up for a quick opportunity to catch Heidenreich with a big DDT on the chair, giving me the DQ loss. I wasn't pleased with Heidenrich getting the victory over me, but I wasn't about to cry over spilled milk. I had an audience to entertain, and I knew my Spinarooni would dazzle the New York State Capitol.

I was able to finally lay Heidenreich to rest once and for all a week later in Roanoke, Virginia, in a No DQ Match, where I smashed Jon with a ferocious chair shot, pinning him for the victory.

Although I was enjoying my current direction working with Jon and in the main title pictures, something wasn't right. I was burning out and felt that my fuel tanks were running on fumes. I also missed Sharmell more than ever.

I decided to go straight to the top to tell them it might be time for me to hang up my boots. After calling a brief meeting with Vince and the new WWE Talent Relations President John Laurinaitis, I put my cards on the table.

"My heart's not in this anymore. Out of respect for the business, you, and myself, I should walk away."

Vince and Johnny asked what had prompted my sudden

decision, and I told them it was being away from Sharmell. If I weren't ready to walk out the door, I wouldn't have risked being so blunt. Throughout my career, I'd seen many guys issued a pink slip for letting their personal lives interfere with their careers.

Much to my surprise, Vince made a suggestion. "Well, why don't we just hire Sharmell and bring her on the road with you? How would you like that?"

I sat up and flashed a smile of relief. "That might just work, Vince."

With an even bigger grin, he stood, buttoned his coat, and shook my hand. "Then it's settled. If Sharmell's a big part of your life, than she's a big part of ours as well."

In that moment, I respected Vince more than I ever thought humanly possible.

Sharmell was ecstatic to hear Vince's idea. Now we'd be together not only in Houston but also on the road.

On March 17 in Savannah, Sharmell was sitting in the front row cheering me on. I faced Luther Reigns, who I pinned after a scissor kick. Afterward, I jumped down and celebrated with my wife and all the fans at ringside.

Sharmell would begin a steady transition into a stage managerial role, becoming more and more physically involved as the weeks turned into months. We were the happiest we'd ever been. Working together brought our understanding and appreciation of each other to a level I never knew possible.

Leading up to WrestleMania XXI, I won matches over Reigns and Duprée. While creative didn't have much for my story line, the WWE producers had something even better in mind.

Because the theme was WrestleMania Goes Hollywood, they decided to shoot elaborate commercial parodies of famous movie scenes with practically the entire roster, featuring such films as *Gladiator, Forrest Gump, Basic Instinct, Dirty Harry, Braveheart, Taxi Driver, A Few Good Men*, and *When Harry Met Sally*.

I was paired with my Rumble rival Eddie Guerrero to reenact the moment from Quentin Tarantino's Academy Award–winning film *Pulp Fiction*, when Jules, played by Samuel L. Jackson, and Vincent, played by John Travolta, crash the apartment of the four young guys who stole Marsellus's briefcase. I'd never even seen the movie, so I had some homework to do.

Watching and rewatching the entire film and my scene, I was inspired by Jackson's performance but wondered if I'd be able to pull off anything slightly as entertaining. When we were finally on location in Los Angeles, our set was an almost identical version of the apartment in the movie.

Eddie and I met for costuming and makeup, and we were laughing at how funny the whole thing was—two WWE Superstars being made up like Jackson and Travolta for a commercial shoot. Eddie was always good company, and just a smirk or a raise of his eyebrows could crack me up. We were like little kids together.

Even though he was having a lot of fun, I'd noticed a shift throughout the last few months. He seemed tired all the time. No matter where I saw him, whether in the arena or back at the hotel, he was just drained. I attributed it to the wear and tear of the business finally catching up with him. He'd always seek out a secluded spot in the back where he could be alone in silence, usually with his Bible. By that time in his life, he was very religious. I wondered if he was trying to clean his closet of whatever skeletons may have been hiding in there. But he was always all smiles and a true friend to anyone who approached.

And rest assured, when his music hit and it was time for him to jump into yet another chopped Latino Heat–style low rider for his entrance, Eddie sprang to life for the fans. He was like a completely different person.

During our commercial shoot, Eddie set my mind at ease. As I made every attempt to deliver the long series of memorized dialogue, I was nervous. While delivering some of the lines, I'd look up at Eddie. The second we made eye contact, we'd have to cut action because we were cracking up, and it was infectious among the entire crew and other actors.

We finally wrapped shooting that day, and the team produced a truly magic moment between Eddie and me that will always be a part of WrestleMania history.

On April 4 in Los Angeles, almost twenty-one thousand people filled the Staples Center to be part of WrestleMania XXI. It seemed like every time I turned around, there was a different celebrity saying hello, including my *Ready to Rumble* buddy and fellow former WCW Champion David Arquette. Other visitors included Sylvester Stallone, Adam Sandler, Rob Schneider, The Black Eyed Peas, Ice Cube, Billy Corgan of The Smashing Pumpkins, and even Macaulay Culkin. It was a weird role reversal meeting film and music stars out of their natural element, much as I was on the set of *Rumble.*

There was no way around it; WrestleMania was the hottest ticket in Los Angeles. Having felt like a bastard stepchild of the entertainment industry for the majority of my career, that weekend I saw the international impact WWE performers really had on pop culture.

Since creative hadn't written anything for me going into the year's biggest event, I was left off the PPV card for the first and only time in my active WWE career. I looked at it as a low-pressure night.

It might've been easy for someone else in my position to approach the writing staff and complain, demanding a place on the card, but that was never in my wrestling DNA. Without saying a word about anything, I was approached by the producers themselves.

"Booker, we've got something interesting for you to start

off the show. It won't be part of the broadcast, but we're going to have you be in the first WrestleMania Thirty-Man Inter-promotional Battle Royal consisting of *Raw* and *SD* talent."

It suited me just fine. "Cool. Let's do it!"

Before I knew it, I was surrounded by twenty-nine other guys, such as The Hurricane, Gene Snitsky, Hardcore Holly, Billy Kidman, Scotty 2 Hotty, The Bashams, Heidenreich, William Regal, Paul London, and Val Venis. When it came down to it, I eliminated The Masterpiece, Chris Masters, and collected another WrestleMania win.

Since John Cena took the WWE Championship from JBL at WrestleMania XXI, he along with Eddie, Big Show, Rey, Angle, and I were the top contenders. They had Teddy announce on April 7 yet another No. 1 Contender's Tournament starting that night in San Diego as JBL defeated Rey in the first match. Eventually Angle defeated Eddie.

That left me to take on Show at Madison Square Garden on April 21. Only a few minutes in, JBL and Angle ran in and attacked us. By having the match thrown out, they thought we would be eliminated and the tournament finale would be the two of them facing off. They were wrong.

Teddy quickly booked a Fatal 4-Way No. 1 Contender's Match for the following week on April 28 overseas in Birmingham, England. That night JBL, Angle, and I decided to triple-team Show and remove the threat. Kurt managed to impressively get him up on his shoulders for an Olympic Slam right through the commentary table, causing our giant problem to be counted out.

I was next to be eliminated after JBL slid a chair in the ring while the ref was distracted, allowing Angle to whack me with it for the pin. In the chaos of the match, the ref was knocked out, which The Bashams took as an opportunity to come down and attack Kurt. While he was distracted with them, I took advantage by reentering the ring and returning the favor to the Olympian with a devastating chair shot of my own. JBL saw his moment and covered Angle to become the top contender to face Cena for the belt.

In Trenton, New Jersey, on May 5, Kurt sneaked up behind Sharmell backstage as she watched me destroy Orlando Jordan. Kurt told her he was challenging me for a match at Judgment Day 2005 later in the month.

A few segments later, Kurt was in the ring and demanded my reply, but I was drawn out to confront him only after he called my wife a gutter slut. No one calls my wife a gutter slut. I sprinted to the ring full of rage and furiously leveled Angle and held him as Sharmell ferociously slapped him several times to teach him some manners.

Kurt managed to wrestle free of her and uppercut me with a low blow to the crotch before giving me a devastating Olympic Slam.

Sharmell tried to run but fell and hurt her ankle. Before Angle could go after her, several WWE officials stormed the ring and saved her.

Angle had crossed the line and was going to pay.

Sharmell loved getting involved in TV segments with overinflated acting as much as I did. She was a natural at it, and we were having the time of our lives performing for the world together.

On May 12 in Reading, Pennsylvania, we decided not to wait until Judgment Day and main evented *SD* in a brutal match between the obsessed Olympian, Kurt Angle, and the furious husband, me. I had the upper hand initially, but Kurt eventually swarmed with a huge offensive and had me down long enough to jump out of the ring and run backstage. Like a mad stalker, he barged into my dressing room and scared the hell out of Sharmell, who started screaming like a woman possessed. By the time I came to and made it back there, Kurt jumped out from behind and knocked me out against the wall. In true over-the-top B-movie dramatics, Sharmell crawled toward my broken, unconscious body, shrieking as the camera faded to black. This twisted triangle had to be resolved once and for all at Judgment Day on May 22.

Before the match at the Target Center in Minneapolis, we agreed to put it all out there to ensure it would be an instant classic among the three of us. With that in mind, I was whacking Kurt around the ring with every punch and kick I knew and some I just made up, sending him pinwheeling around the ring with a battered and bloody face. Kurt eventually came back with a full gauntlet of stiff offense and went for an Olympic Slam, which I reversed into a roll-up pin for a three count by Charles Robinson. I had won the match and shown Kurt that you don't mess with my family.

Only I wasn't supposed to win just yet.

Robinson had gotten totally lost and botched the finish.

Kurt tried as hard as he could to kick out at the last second after he realized Charles was really going for the third smack on the canvas. When we both knew what had happened, Kurt yelled at Robinson, "What the fuck? What did you just do?"

Then he looked at me, and I had no choice but to keep performing and celebrate the win. But inside I was thinking the same thing he was.

We had to follow through with the events that were planned to happen about eight minutes later, after I would've pinned him with the scissor kick: Angle ran over me like a freight train, giving me the Angle Slam and knocking me almost unconscious. He then tossed my lifeless body out of the ring as he went after Sharmell.

Angle grabbed her by the hair and rolled into the center of the ring, where she sat in fear, yelling for me to help. In cold and calculated fashion, he then went under the ring and produced a pair of handcuffs, which he slapped on the top rope, and then attempted to secure the other end to Sharmell's arm. Thankfully, I recovered in time and started pounding on Angle. I then dragged him over to the open handcuff and locked him onto the top rope. As Angle cowered in the corner, I gave him a justified beat-down before turning him over to Sharmell, who slapped him mercilessly over and over again. Then, for good measure, Sharmell stepped back and charged, kicking Angle square in the groin. He crumpled to the ground, a mess of blood and tears.

We celebrated and went backstage and waited to see what would happen.

As soon as they came through the curtain, Kurt was screaming at Robinson. "Did you forget your brain backstage? We rehearsed that over and over, and *you* messed it up?"

Charles repeatedly apologized, saying he got confused in the middle and thought it was the finish.

Angle was still huffing, not sure what he was going to do, but eventually he cooled down enough to walk away.

He and I talked about it a little later and agreed it was a disappointing end to a great angle that could've been our one and only chance to face each other on a WWE PPV. Now there was unfinished business to attend to with some sort of professional closure.

On June 9 in Kansas City, we transitioned into a match together to end the feud. We wrestled a battle very similar to the one planned for Judgment Day. When it was time to bring it all home, Kurt brought a chair into the ring and took a big swing as I ducked out of the way, effectively allowing it to bounce off the top rope and smash him in the face. I took full advantage and gave him the proper scissor kick finish we'd both been waiting for, and backstage we walked away happy.

On June 30 in Anaheim, Teddy once again activated me in the title landscape. During the WWE draft of 2005, the WWE Champion John Cena was drafted from *SD* to *Raw*. *Raw* already had Batista as the World Heavyweight Champion, so the *SD* brand was left without a major title. To rectify this, Teddy announced a six-man match for a newly created *SmackDown* Championship. The draft lasted for a month, with newly signed draftees showing up every week on both *Raw* and *SD*. It kept the fans engaged. They didn't know who would be traded to what brand each week. Fortunately, I was booked into the Six-Way *SD* Championship Match for the belt with The Undertaker, JBL, Chris Benoit, Muhammad Hassan, and Christian, who'd just been drafted from *Raw* in exchange for Big Show.

Unfortunately, I didn't last long after The Dead Man DQed himself by going after Hassan with a chair. Hassan eliminated himself by running out like a coward. Benoit was next to go, getting pinned by Bradshaw. When I wasn't paying attention, Christian tagged himself in, courtesy of JBL's turned back, and sneakily rolled me up. JBL then took advantage of the situation and took him out with a Clothesline from Hell for the win. The action was fast and furious and made JBL look strong for the title picture.

After the match, JBL was on his knees in the middle of the ring, ready to receive the new *SD* Championship, which Teddy brought to the ring in a black velvet bag. Eager for its unveiling, JBL smiled at Teddy and held out his hands in anticipation of his well-earned prize. With velvet bag in hand and moments away from showing the new title, Teddy looked at JBL and said, "I've got some good news . . . and I've got some bad news for ya, playa!"

The bad news was that even though JBL had won the match, he was not the new *SD* Champion. Because recently Teddy had found out that there was no need for the *SD* Championship. The good news was that JBL earned the right to be the new number-one contender to the last draft pick of *SD*—none other than the World Heavyweight Champion, Batista! *SD* had a major title, after all.

A week later in Sacramento for my No. 1 Contender's Match for the United States Championship on *SD* with Benoit, I lost cleanly after tapping to the Crippler Crossface.

On July 14 in Worcester, I found myself going into a match with my old IC title nemesis Christian, but it quickly devolved when we almost got into a backstage fight.

Christian had been on the bubble as of late with little to no creative direction and was feeling the pressure. It's the kind of situation that can easily make or break a guy if he sits back and allows himself to be vacuumed into the black hole of anonymity. When a performer in Christian's position sees that happening, it's important to become as proactive as possible and fire up hotter than ever in the ring. It's all up to what a guy has inside.

Creative was well aware of all this and wanted to see Christian climb out of the mire. He'd been with the company since 1998 and worked in some revolutionary Tables, Ladders, and Chairs (TLC) Matches with The Hardys and The Dudleys.

While we were standing at The Gorilla Position, one of the producers took the opportunity to inspire him: "Christian! We want you to get down there tonight and fight for your life! Show the WWE Universe what you're made of! We want to see you light up like the performer we all know you are! Kick some ass!"

Keep in mind he was saying this right in front of me, and I'm thinking, *Okay, but let's not get too carried away now.* I'd be the one on the receiving end of this newfound motivation.

As I made my way to the ring, Christian attacked me by surprise, as planned, leaving me pretty well beaten up before the bell even rang. However, when we were in there and he was hammering away at me, Christian punched me right in the eye. Bam!

"Aw, man!" I muttered while trying to blink and rub my eye to regain focus.

Then he kept on me—bam, bam, bam—but I couldn't focus on what was happening. My eye took me right out of the match. It was pretty much a squash for Christian as he laid me out with the Unprettier for the impressive win.

When I got to the back, the producers praised Christian on a job well done.

I gave him some space, but afterward I said, "What were you doing? You could've seriously messed me up. It wasn't safe!"

Christian walked me back into the hall. "Man, what they told me really affected me before the match, and it felt like my neck was on the line or something. I panicked, and I'm sorry."

I understood where he was coming from, but I said, "Instead of blindly tagging away, you need to channel that aggression into a fine-tuned performance. You'll get the same results without the backstage beef." I didn't hold it against him, and we remained as cool as ever.

24

LOSING EDDIE

It was during this time in the summer of 2005 that I decided to activate a longtime dream of opening my own wrestling school in Houston. Lash had the same goal, and we decided to go into business together, reviving the legacy of Stevie Ray and Booker T as Harlem Heat. I envisioned us being very hands-on, doing signings and appearances together to draw in business.

I knew we couldn't serve wrestlers who'd been running the roads for years and grown cynical that they hadn't made it big. I felt that type of mentality would be destructive to our goals. Instead, I wanted to draw young talent and build them from the ground up.

I wasn't sure Lash and I were on the same page fundamentally, though, and it started to prove true when he brought an attorney friend around. This guy immediately conjured up scenarios of wrestling shows and how much money we could generate. We didn't even have a building or a name yet.

I got frustrated with the guy right away. "Man, you just

don't get it. This school isn't about going to some field and pitching a tent with a ring underneath it."

Lash shook his head. My brother and I just didn't see things eye-to-eye.

However, we continued to move forward, and Lash and I decided to open a joint bank account under the business name of Stevie Ray and Booker T's Pro Wrestling Academy, which we called the PWA.

We planned to invest five thousand dollars each and use the capital to find and lease a building and purchase everything else we needed, from the ring to lights and basic furnishings.

We finally found the appropriate building, an old warehouse at 2301 Commerce in Houston, and quickly signed the lease papers. We even had a painter create a giant, colorful mural in a graffiti design with our names tagged right at the top. We loved it. It felt like our bond from the old days was being revitalized. An added bonus for me was having Sharmell as my right hand with any PWA business. I was excited to have my family together and looked forward to working with them.

I went back on the road only a few weeks before our grand opening. Lash was in charge of cleaning everything up and securing all the accessories to bring the PWA dojo to life.

However, when I came home, I found the school in a mess, and the finances hadn't been maintained as we'd discussed. I stepped in to handle the money and the rent so we wouldn't lose the building or our shared dream. It was disheartening to see Lash's involvement fade away, but my determination to see the PWA come to life consumed me.

Every day Sharmell and I had off, we stayed morning to night in the sweltering heat, cleaning the fifteen-thousand-foot warehouse for the big day. We were behind schedule, and the pressure was intense. When the grand opening finally did arrive, we pulled it off—but not without strife.

Sharmell and I were there all day greeting guests and potential students while signing autographs and posing for pictures.

Lash was supposed to be there to deliver Harlem Heat to the people as advertised. When he did show up a couple of hours late, he nonchalantly walked in like nothing was wrong. In tow were a bunch of guys I knew from back in the WWA and all over Texas.

Feeling a little burned, I asked him if we could talk in the back, and we went for a walk. "What's going on, man? You show up late and with a bunch of cronies who never drew a dime? You knew from the start what I wanted to do, and this is the complete opposite."

It was the first and only time I ever went off on my brother.

Lash stared at me. "Whoa there, Junior. *You're* blowing up on *me*?"

I cut him off. "We're not kids anymore! How could you be surprised by my reaction? What's the deal? Do you want me to buy you out or the other way around?"

He didn't say a word but simply walked away, gathered his boys, and left.

I thought of when our mother died when I was thirteen. Lash, then eighteen, packed up and sought refuge with his buddy down the street. I felt abandoned. It hurt back then, and now it did again. Both times, I wondered what we could've done differently to stay together.

I assumed full control of the PWA and reluctantly had his name removed from the mural, which now simply read, Booker T's Pro Wrestling Academy. It wasn't at all how I imagined things would transpire. Two brothers broke up that day. And it would be eight long years before we would speak again.

I picked back up with the WWE at the end of August and entered a program with Christian and Orlando Jordan along with Chris Benoit, who was carrying the United States title since whupping Jordan at SummerSlam. The four of us, and eventually also JBL, became embroiled in a heated fight for the belt through September and into October.

Week after week on TV, we were in constant variations of triple threat and Fatal 4-Way No. 1 Contender's Matches to determine who would go for the gold at No Mercy 2005 on October 9.

The championship match at the PPV wound up being yet another Fatal 4-Way in my own backyard at the Toyota Center in Houston. Although I had many near falls for the title, a two count was as close as I got that night. The hometown guy losing tradition was still in full effect.

That night Benoit's trademark buzz saw of aggression proved too much as he caught Christian in the sharpshooter in the center of the ring. There wasn't much Christian could do as he tapped out, allowing Benoit to pick up the victory.

On the next edition of *SD* in San Antonio, I seized my opportunity to face Chris one-on-one for the title by beating JBL, Rey, and Christian in our one hundred fifty-seventh four-way dance. With the help of Sharmell tripping up Mysterio, I nailed the scissor kick on the back of Christian's neck and was immediately thrust into a position to gain some gold after a lengthy dry spell.

In Reno on October 21, Chris and I faced off yet again. We knew each other's set like clockwork, and after our masterful exchange of follow the leader, Sharmell hit him with a low blow behind my back. When I saw him doubled over, I knew it was my night. I scissor kicked him and claimed the United States title for the third time.

Following up on my big win, Benoit relentlessly pursued me for the next four weeks in rematch after rematch as I edged him out consistently to maintain the belt.

CHAMPIONSHIPS

Championship	
WCW World Tag Team Championship	11
WCW World Television Championship	6
WCW United States Championship	1
WCW World Heavyweight Championship	5
WWF World Tag Team Championship	1
WWF Hardcore Championship	2
WWE World Tag Team Championship	2
WWE Intercontinental Championship	1
WWE United States Championship	2
Total	31

LOSING EDDIE

On Monday, November 14, I arrived in Minneapolis the day before our *SD* tapings. As I walked into the Target Center that night and looked around, the mood was solemn.

"Hey, what's going on?"

Someone spoke up. "You didn't hear yet? Eddie died on Sunday."

My breath was knocked out of me.

I slowly got more information. Eddie's nephew and tag team champion partner, Chavo Guerrero, arrived in Minneapolis that Sunday morning and checked in to the Marriott City Center Hotel, the same one Eddie had been at since the previous night. While he was signing in, the front desk informed him his uncle hadn't responded to his requested wake-up call, so he asked for a key card to the room. Chavo made his way to the door and let himself in after knocking several times to no reply. Once inside, he found Eddie lying on the bathroom floor unconscious. He desperately tried CPR to no avail and immediately called 911. When the police and paramedics arrived, they found Eddie had, in fact, passed away. There was nothing Chavo could've done. The autopsy would later reveal the cause had been acute heart failure. He was only thirty-eight years old.

The thought of Eddie being gone was unimaginable. I found a private space and wept for the loss of my colleague of so many years, Eddie Guerrero, a passionate performer, a man of faith, and an amazing friend.

It particularly tore me up to think of Chavo having found Eddie and how that image would haunt him for the rest of his life. I know I personally wouldn't have been able to handle it with as much poise and presence of mind as Chavo showed in the hours and days immediately following.

For *Raw* and the *SD* taping the next day, both shows were Eddie tributes, which featured interpromotional matches between brands and many pre-taped personal moments with WWE Superstars who wanted to memorialize him on air.

The tone was quiet and reflective everywhere I went in the locker room. I barely spoke as images of Eddie's smiling face flashed in my memory. When it was my time to speak to the camera, I had Sharmell at my side. I made it clear to the Guerrero family that if they ever needed anything, the Huffmans would always be there, just as Eddie had been for anyone who needed someone to talk to. I said I believed in God and knew we'd see Eddie again someday. When the tribute shows were complete, we knew the show had to go on and Eddie wouldn't have wanted it any other way.

We all boarded our international flight to Europe, leaving our friend behind for the first time. Even though the cloud of Eddie's death stayed with us on the trip, we went out and performed in his honor in every move and sequence we collectively made.

A few weeks after, many wrestlers honored the memory

of Eddie by wearing black bands with the initials *EG* around their arms. Years later, Eddie's memory and contribution to this business are still alive and well, as fans worldwide will erupt into chants of "Eddie Eddie! Eddie!" whenever reminded of him.

In Sheffield, England, I again defended the United States Championship against a still very distraught Chris Benoit. He and Eddie had been like brothers since way back in the WCW days, when I'd first met them. The death of Eddie left a huge void in Chris's life, and it was clear just how much he missed his friend.

We went out and hit it hard, with the finish coming as a controversial double pin. Chris and I managed to twist each other up into a pretzel-like dual cradle, with our shoulders flat on the mat. A ref raised Chris's arm and another ref raised mine, which incited an argument. Teddy Long marched out to listen to us and watch the replay, then made his executive decision: the only way to settle the title dispute was another Best of Seven Series, just as we'd had in WCW for the Television Championship.

Prichard and the other agents had talked to us in the back the previous week. "Would you be willing to do the Best of Seven again?"

Chris and I looked at each other in disbelief.

"You're kidding us, right?" I was half smiling.

They were 100 percent serious.

Could we pull it off again?

I doubted Chris and I could live up to the physical standard we'd set so long before in WCW. There was no way I could beat myself up as I had before, but I wasn't in this business to produce something second-rate.

To my horror, that's exactly what happened.

Everything started out well enough as Chris and I worked magic for match number one at Survivor Series 2005 on November 27 in Detroit. As in the past, the creative guys kept Chris and me in the dark about who would come out on top each night until just before the show started.

In the beginning of that first match, I found myself using my old buddy Bret Hart's excellent heel tactic of bailing out of the ring when Benoit started turning up the heat a little too much. As usual, we eventually settled into a rhythm and were both giving a great performance. When it came to the end of the match, Sharmell distracted Chris while he was on the top rope for his diving headbutt. This allowed me time to get up and start attacking him while he was precariously perched up high. As I mounted the ropes to grab him for a superplex, Benoit hit me repeatedly with fists and headbutts, showing everyone why he was called the Rabid Wolverine. I fell hard to the mat as Chris dove off the top rope for his flying headbutt. At the last second before he connected, I rolled out of the way, and he came crashing to the mat. Taking advantage of the moment, I cradled him, putting my feet on the ropes for leverage, with Sharmell helping to keep them in place. Three seconds later, I'd won the first match in the series.

Two days later in Cincinnati, I took another match.

We broke into the third clash on December 9 in Columbia, South Carolina, where I took my third win after crashing Benoit with a steel chair, which Sharmell provided, followed by a scissor kick.

I was now up three matches to zero and feeling pretty good about what we'd been able to deliver so far.

At Armageddon 2005 on December 18 in Providence, Chris defied the overwhelming odds. Sharmell had brought a broom to ringside to signify my clean sweep and was determined to use it. When the ref was accidentally knocked out, Benoit put me into a grueling sharpshooter, and I immediately began to tap out. But since the ref was out cold, he didn't see it.

Sharmell saw it as the perfect time to wield her broom and made her way into the ring to give Benoit a surprise whack to the back of the head. But the impact didn't faze Chris, who broke the hold and stood up, glaring at her. As he cornered her in the ring, I moved in for a Book End, only to have it reversed into a powerful DDT. Stunned, Chris turned me over and slapped on the Crippler Crossface one more time for the submission victory. He now had one win to my three.

Everything was going well, and I enjoyed the new dynamic Sharmell was able to bring to our series.

We took a break for Christmas, but meanwhile I did a house show on December 26 in White Plains, New York, facing Matt Hardy. Since I was embroiled in an epic saga with Chris and our integrity was hanging in the balance, the logic of pairing me with Matt for a match on the road escaped me. Working with Matt wasn't the issue—he and I always delivered. But I didn't understand disassociating what was happening on the road from what was happening on our TV programming.

As we were out there exchanging basic moves, Hardy shot me over for a hip toss and caught me off guard. I was expecting a hard toss once I jumped with him, but there wasn't any real power behind it. All my momentum turned into a short-distance flip across the ring, causing me to land on my shoulders in an awkward position, my legs jarring apart. Bang, pop!

Instantly I tried to get up but had to lie right back down while the pain of a shotgun blast to the groin lit me on fire. *I'm hurt*, I thought. *There goes the Best of Seven.*

I yelled up to Matt, "Cover me, man. I'm done."

Matt looked at me and shook his head. "I can't, man. You're the champ."

Nick was refereeing that night and leaned over. "Come on, man. Can you make it through at least one more spot and get the pin?"

I stayed on the mat for what seemed like an eternity, staring at the lights, and I started laughing out loud. Matt and Nick probably thought I was insane with shock, but I was thinking, *Unbelievable. All this time I'm deathly afraid Chris and I won't be able to live up to the ghosts of the Best of Seven Series past, and what does me in? A groin pull in White Plains.*

I regained my composure and rolled out of the ring to take a ten-count loss to Matt.

After staggering on my own to the back, I collapsed onto the floor in excruciating pain, still laughing at the absurdity of it all. After the trainers got a good look at me, they determined I'd be out of action healing for six to eight weeks, effectively ending Chris's and my run at recapturing our WCW glory days.

At the *SD* tapings in Uncasville on December 27, I hobbled out on crutches and announced to Teddy and Chris that the doctor wouldn't let me compete for almost two months. When Long was about to award that night's match number five to Benoit by forfeit, Chris refused and demanded to win it in the ring, and that's when we activated the management's solution of using Randy Orton as my substitute.

Randy stepped up and proceeded to give the performances of his life, but as the story line went, he dropped two straight wins, allowing the three-to-three score card.

It all came down to a tiebreaker in Philly on January 13,

2006, for the seventh match for the belt. Sharmell and I made our way to ringside to watch the grand finale, but Benoit protested and made the ref ban us to the back.

After a long, grueling performance and a failed attempt by Orlando Jordan to help Randy win, I took matters into my own hands. As Chris locked the Crossface on Orton for certain death and a title win, I smashed Benoit across the head with the belt, allowing Randy to cover for the win and my fourth United States title.

Randy had delivered. As a result, he'd risen to a higher level in the company and the minds of everyone backstage and in the arena. Afterward, I congratulated him on a job well done.

For the next few days, I concentrated on healing to get back to the ring right away. I was the new champ, eager to defend my title. On January 19, I returned for a house show and teamed with JBL versus Benoit and Rey in Mexico City. At one point in the performance, Mysterio gave me a moonsault. When I caught him, the stabbing pain in my groin was immediately reactivated.

I'd come back too early once more. I was out again for the

CHAMPIONSHIPS	
WCW World Tag Team Championship	11
WCW World Television Championship	6
WCW United States Championship	1
WCW World Heavyweight Championship	5
WWF World Tag Team Championship	1
WWF Hardcore Championship	2
WWE World Tag Team Championship	2
WWE Intercontinental Championship	1
WWE United States Championship	3
Total	32

next ten days, cursing the world. But there was no way I was missing the Royal Rumble 2006 in Miami. The trainers gave me tight compression shorts to support me through a brief appearance at the Rumble.

I wore the compression shorts under a pair of long white tights like the ones I wore in WCW and entered the Royal Rumble at number thirteen. Once I got in there, it was clear my injury was still a huge factor as Benoit almost immediately tossed me over for the elimination.

I sat out for the first few weeks in February and watched as the newly signed Fit Finlay successfully subbed for me in a title match against Chris. After our WCW wars in 1998 over the TV title, here the three of us were again. It was a DQ loss because Sharmell swung one of my crutches at Benoit.

Teddy then told me I had nine days to get healthy enough to defend the belt at No Way Out 2006 against Chris, who'd become the number-one contender, or it would be vacated once again. And there was no way I was going to let that happen.

At No Way Out 2006 in Baltimore on February 19, Benoit and I locked up for the definitive chapter in our United States title history. As the match was set to begin, I announced that due to my injury I wouldn't be competing and the championship would be forfeited to Chris.

Benoit wouldn't have it, and he grabbed a mic: "Coward! Coward! Coward!"

The crowd picked up the chant and continued to taunt me.

But in classic heel fashion, as soon as he turned his back, I ran up, attacking him, and the bell rang.

He quickly took control, working me outside the ring and then again inside. He eventually tried to tie me up in a sharp-shooter as Sharmell got onto the apron to distract him. As I struggled to get out, I used my legs to launch Benoit toward the ropes, which knocked Sharmell to the ground. When he ran back toward me, I tried to nail him with my scissor kick, but Benoit ducked, taking me down for another sharpshooter. I was in agony as I hung on, trying to endure the painful hold. Wasting no time, Chris released the hold and pounced on me for a Crippler Crossface, leaving me no choice but to tap and drop the belt.

Working with Chris almost exclusively over the previous months, both together in a tag team and against each other in a lengthy feud, was about as good as it got in the business. We did it all, as we had so many times in WCW nearly a decade earlier. Although our bodies weren't as spry as they once were, our mental focus and execution were razor sharp, and now we had the advantage of maturity in our craft.

Guys like Eddie, Chris, and I were part of the heart and soul of WCW, and we brought that same lifeblood with us to the WWE. We'd lost Eddie, but we knew he was with us in every new step we took as we honored his legacy and the company.

In the weeks leading up to WrestleMania XXII in Chicago on April 2, Sharmell and I had some pretty memorable and entertaining moments on TV with the newest supernatural WWE Superstar, The Boogeyman.

Sharmell and I had slowly developed a side program with him during the Best of Seven Series, where he'd harass us with his bag of tricks, usually his favorite snacking delicacy: giant earthworms.

I liked Boogey a lot and took him under my wing when he joined the WWE, which could've come a year or more earlier than it did. Boogeyman was a contestant on the reality show *WWE Tough Enough* as Marty Wright and had fabricated a little tale about being only thirty years old. I'd watched it at home and almost spit my Texas chili out. "Thirty! There's no way he's thirty! That guy's older than I am."

He was forty at the time. He was ceremoniously booted from the program, but after some time, they realized his talents could be utilized and gave him a contract along with The Boogeyman character.

I liked his character, look, and attitude. Marty deserves full credit for everything he came up with for Boogeyman to get over with the crowd. I simply got in the ring with him and told him to let his great creation work more to his advantage and not use so many moves. He'd have a successful match every night by concentrating on developing intense ring presence.

He did great with what he brought to the table, such as his smoking staff and creepy entrance strut. As Eddie Gilbert had recommended to me and Lash in the WWA, I encouraged Marty to wear a suit to build his confidence, which he did.

Our WrestleMania XXII program slowly but surely began as Boogey relentlessly stalked Sharmell and me. No matter where we were backstage or in the ring, he'd suddenly appear, either hanging upside down or causing me to run for my life out of pure superstitious fear, leaving Sharmell in the dust. He once filled the entire trunk of our car with worms, and he always found a way to get those suckers near or on Sharmell, even kidnapping and burying her in them backstage.

For one segment, to shield herself, Sharmell put on a bee-keeper's suit complete with screened mask. We laughed hysterically backstage as she put it on. No matter what scenario we were placed in with The Boogeyman, we had a lot of fun with him.

As his staged harassment increased, I took up a campaign of writing protest letters to the president of the NAACP, acquiring restraining orders, even complaining to the WWE brass, none of which was effective.

Teddy Long booked us for the inevitable clash at Wrestle-Mania XXII, but the match was in real jeopardy by the time we walked into the Allstate Arena in Rosemont, Illinois.

Marty pulled me aside with a serious look on his face. "Listen, man, I tore my right biceps at the house show the other night. I don't want to tell anyone. I'm worried they might release me. I can't work."

Being in a match at WrestleMania is every wrestler's dream, and I could understand why Marty was concerned about blowing such a huge opportunity by not being able to work. I told him to calm down and get ready for the show. "When we get in there, I'll do everything for you. Protect your arm, work safe, and no one will know."

Before the match, the cameras cut to the back, where Sharmell and I were about to make our entrance. We looked around nervously as Sharmell said, "Baby, I'm scared. Please don't make me do this!"

I tried to reassure her. "Don't worry about this, a'ight?"

But she was unraveling fast. "Why are all the freaks around here always drawn to you?"

"Come on now, baby, I ain't no freak magnet! Come on, let's get this done." As I did my best to make her feel secure, we made our way down the hall, only to run into one freak after another.

The first was the pirate Paul Burchill, who was standing on some trunks having an imaginary sword fight. When he saw us, he paused long enough to say, "Arr, me matey," before continuing to battle his unseen foe.

We made our way past him as I told Sharmell, "Don't worry about this. I'm your man!"

But we didn't make it far before we met "The Million

Dollar Man" Ted DiBiase and Eugene, who was dribbling a basketball while DiBiase counted: "Ninety-six, ninety-seven, ninety-eight . . ." and before Eugene could get to ninety-nine, DiBiase kicked the ball out from under him. It was a classic re-creation of Ted's heel run in the eighties, when he would offer money to people for performing menial tasks. DiBiase taunted Eugene, saying he was close but he didn't get the money. Upon spying Sharmell and me, he looked at me and said, "Hey, Booker, want to make a thousand bucks?"

"I don't want no thousand bucks, man." I looked at him with disgust.

"Everybody's got a price for The Million Dollar Man." He laughed at his own cockiness.

We pressed on, hoping to put the freaks behind us, when we heard the sounds of ecstasy coming a little further up. We were disturbed to find The Fabulous Moolah standing over Mae Young, who was having her foot licked by Snitsky. We nearly vomited when Snitsky asked if we wanted to join in.

"Somethin' just ain't right," Sharmell said.

I said, "I feel like I'm in *The Twilight Zone* or somethin'. What the hell is going on around here?"

Looking for answers, I spotted a woman up ahead. "Excuse me, ma'am. Excuse me . . ."

To my horror, it wasn't a woman standing there but Goldust. He was dressed in full paint and a body suit along with a blue dress and a black curly wig.

"Da hell you doing here?" I asked.

Goldie proceeded to tell me that he'd gathered all the freaks there to help me unleash my inner freak. He said that just like The Boogeyman took his worms and put them in his mouth, I needed to take the worms and "put them in my . . ." and Goldie leaned in to whisper the rest in my ear, leaving it up to the viewers' imaginations as to what he'd said. "It's the only way you're going to beat him," he said matter-of-factly.

"Tell me you didn't just say that," I yelled. "You didn't just say that! Baby, let's get the hell out of here!"

We quickly made our way out of the hall of freaks and to the arena.

Sharmell and I walked carefully to the ring with terrified looks on our faces. Instead of my usual pre-match showboating on the ropes, I looked worried and scared, even breaking down into tears and hiding behind Sharmell as The Boogeyman entered the ring.

Once the bell rang, we pulled out a decent match with no one suspecting Marty's injury. I put twice the effort into the performance, making him look monstrous and indestructible. When he got me up for his Falling Chokebomb, I made myself as light as air for the execution and his first and only WrestleMania victory.

It was my pleasure to help put Marty on the map that night by giving him the rub, as so many had for me in the past.

BOOKER T. HUFFMAN

With WrestleMania XXII and my feud with Boogeyman in the record books, creative decided to move me on and resurrect an event customized just for me, King of the Ring. It had been my very first appearance for the company back in 2001, and it had been decommissioned altogether after 2002.

In Green Bay at *SD* on April 14, the event was announced, and my throne, cape, and crown were showcased in the ring. I immediately went with Sharmell and deemed *SD* a Boogeyman-free zone and boldly predicted I'd win the KOTR and eclipse former victors like Bret Hart and Steve Austin. Feeling confident and cocky, I put on the cape and crown for the first time.

Sharmell paraded me around, introducing me before my loyal subjects. "King Booker!'"

At my first KOTR Tournament Match in St. Louis at *SD*, which aired April 21, I defeated Matt Hardy with the help of Sharmell and advanced to the next round. I was on my way to legitimatizing my crown.

Before moving on, though, the KOTR tournament would be interrupted briefly while we headed to a European house show tour with stops in England, Italy, and Germany.

In Germany during the WWE's three-day *SD* roster visit, one of the most popular events of my career would intersect with my real life.

25

THE RISE OF KING BOOKER

Dave Batista, "The Animal" of the WWE, had been irritating many of the men and women in the locker room with his attitude toward the rest of the roster and his relationship with one of the WWE Divas, Melina. He even said in an interview with *The Sun* that the *SD* guys had no passion, pride, or dedication. That kind of statement regarding your own company is bad for business, and it reminded me of what Russo was doing when WCW tanked.

When I first met Batista in late 2001, he'd been coming up through the development system at OVW with Brock, Orton, Cena, and even Sharmell before her knee injury. As he was finally integrated into the company, working dark matches before *Raw* and *SD*, I found him to be very down-to-earth, respectful, and likable. He did all the right things, took his cues, and listened and learned.

His newly developed friendship with Hunter led him to the Evolution stable along with Flair and Randy. We had quite a few matches in his earliest days on *Raw* and on the road. We got along great, and I shared as much advice and insight as I could in our short times together. With his intensity and bodybuilder size, he'd become a major WWE Superstar.

But by the spring of 2006, I barely recognized him. A bigger issue had been developing over the last few months that would lead to a real clash between the two of us.

Batista had been messing around with Melina, John Morrison's girlfriend, in front of everybody, including Morrison. They'd be out at the bars and clubs all over each other and sharing hotel rooms on the road, while John was too passive to do anything about it. It bothered everyone.

The boys were giving John a hard time for not doing anything, and there was no question he was really upset but unsure what to do.

As a result of all this, both Batista and Melina developed serious heat with all of us. We decided in Germany to handle things in our own system, Wrestlers' Court, where we dealt with crimes against the code of the locker room.

Since Dave wasn't on that tour, that left Melina, who had no idea she was about to be taken into custody and placed in front of the Honorable Judge Undertaker before a jury of her peers. She was grilled by prosecuting attorney Bradshaw and me. It was time for an admission of guilt.

We officially charged Melina with Divaism, the flagrant act of running around on one's husband or boyfriend, shaming the Divas' division and locker room.

It was really only an elaborate joke and a way to tell Melina what needed to be said, put it in the past, and move forward.

When we got back to the States, however, Dave wasn't happy at all. There was tension in the locker room while we stayed on our separate sides at the first *SD* taping since our return home in Cincinnati on May 2.

The following Saturday, May 6, most of the WWE rosters from both brands traveled to Encino, California, for the big commercial shoot for SummerSlam 2006.

We were staying at a mansion the company had rented out. It was beautiful with sprawling grounds, amazing scenery, and a giant swimming pool. Rey Mysterio, JBL, Randy Orton, Finlay, Ricky Steamboat, Matt Hardy, Tatanka, Melina, and others—virtually every WWE Superstar and Diva—were all having a great time, enjoying a perfect California day. JBL was acting crazy in the pool, and he tossed a producer in. Every time the producer tried to get out, Bradshaw grabbed him and threw him back in. The producer and all of us were cracking up.

In the midst of all the insanity, Dave, who'd arrived late, came out to the pool area and stood there scanning the scene, not saying a word to anybody. Rey and some others went up to break the ice with a hello, but Batista simply stood brooding.

Tatanka, a guy I really respected, was in the pool next to me. He leaned toward me and said quietly, "Look at him standing there, big-timing as usual. He doesn't even have the respect to come over and say hi to the boys."

Later on, we had some lunch around the patio tables, and I excused myself to the bathroom. While walking toward the house, I noticed Dave heading my direction. Before we passed each other, he veered to the far left to go around me.

I stopped and yelled out, "Hey, Dave!"

He turned around.

As politely as possible I said, "Here's the thing. You don't like me, and I don't like you, but the fact is we have to work together. But I'll make it clear: if you cross me, I'm going to kick your ass and there ain't nothing you can do about it. The best thing possible would be to keep your distance."

All the boys outside stopped eating to watch. You could hear a pin drop.

I saw him heating up as I walked away.

When I came back and sat to continue the good time we were all having, he stomped toward the table. "What's your problem with me, man? Do you find me to be a challenge because I'm the top draw on the card and have done more in the last couple of years than you have in your entire career? Are you jealous?"

"Are you kidding me? You're going to stand there and disrespect all the boys by saying that?"

Then in an act of machismo, he asked me to walk with him outside the gate and settle it.

I said, "Man, get out of here. If you're going to do

something, do it right now. This isn't the school playground."

He glared at me. I'd called his bluff, and he didn't do anything. To me it was obvious he was only charging off at the mouth because all the agents like Finlay and Steamboat were gathered around.

I went back to my plate, and he walked away.

Shortly after, one of the producers came to me and said, "Booker, we need you to get ready for a shoot. Can you get dressed?"

"Absolutely." I made my way to my tiny bedroom and started undressing. I was down to my underwear and nothing else, not even socks, when Batista walked in wearing his wrestling gear.

"Talk that shit you were just talking out there, Booker. Go ahead."

I laughed. "Whoa, man, you're going to come in here and catch me in my drawers? Come on. If you want to do this, get out of here and let me put some pants on. I'll be right out. This is ridiculous."

He stared a hole through me. "There's not much room in here anyway. I'll be waiting just outside for you."

"Okay, I'll be out in a minute," I said, rolling my eyes.

I casually put on a pair of pants and a white shirt, no shoes or socks, and took my Paul Boesch, diamond-encrusted ring off my left hand and placed it on my right. As I opened the door, I was fairly annoyed he was wasting my time and delaying the shoot. I took two steps out, and there he was. "Well,

I'm out here. Now what are you going to do?"

"Talk that same shit you were outside," he said again.

"Man, if you're going to make a move, go ahead and do it. Otherwise, I'm going to film my spot. I've got business to attend to. That's why we're here."

Rey came in and said, "Come on, Book! Don't do this!"

"Rey, please step back. If he's going to do something, let him do it."

Dave took a big, slow swing at me.

I stepped to the side, and he fell forward, striking nothing but air.

I thought he was joking. It was a total goof punch with nothing behind it. "Man, you don't want this. Let's go about our business."

I started to walk away when he threw another shot, just as poorly timed, and again I slipped out of the way as his arm passed me.

As much as I regretted it, in an effort to put this thing to a quick end before it got out of control, I took two steps back, quickly stuttered up, and punched him right in the chin.

All of a sudden, I felt arms around me and heard yelling. "Book, stop it! He's had enough!" It was Finlay.

I looked back and saw Melina's boyfriend, John Morrison, also there helping pull me off, which was crazy. Part of me wanted to kick his ass for not handling his own problems.

Sharmell was finally in there too, furiously looking for

Melina because she wanted a piece of the action too, but that girl was long gone.

I told Finlay, "Okay. I'll lay off."

But before Finlay let go of my arms, Batista reached up and—boom—punched my left eye.

I started chuckling that he'd sneaked one in on me like that, which was the only shot he managed during our little escapade.

I told Fit this had to be finished, and he stepped back as I took Dave right back down.

Even Sharmell laid in a couple of kicks on him.

Finally, Finlay again stepped in.

"Okay, Book, that *is* enough. He can't take any more."

I looked down at Dave, and Fit was right. He was pretty well beaten up, and it was obvious this thing was over. His face was a mess, and it was clear he wasn't interested in continuing any more than I was.

Before I left, I turned to Dave and said as if we were out in the school yard, "If this beef of yours continues, every time I see you and the boys ain't around, I'm gonna beat you up again."

As he started to get up, he muttered, "Well, that's really mature."

To which I responded, "Yeah, well, it was really mature for you to call me out to a fight too."

I walked away, cleaned up, and went on to the shoot. Once I'd had a chance to think about it, I started having concerns about what had just happened, knowing full well I could've walked away and been the bigger man instead of resorting to physical reprisal with one of the top guys. What would Vince or anybody else in the WWE think? The last thing I wanted was to reflect poorly on the company and the business.

The next day, Johnny Ace invited Dave and me to breakfast at our hotel to talk about the situation. We knew we had to work together or lose our jobs. Dave even said he regretted the fight. For the sake of the business, we put it behind us.

Before the *SD* taping in San Diego on May 9, Vince called me into his office and wanted to hear the details for himself.

I told him if it ever happened again, I wouldn't *try* to walk away from a fight. I *would* walk away.

He looked at me and simply said, "Only if you have to, Booker."

In the end, although there was no love lost, I released all animosity toward Dave. I had to for my own well-being. Harboring anger would only hurt me; it's just not healthy. Instead, I decided to respect him for having the courage to stand up when he felt he had to, win or lose.

There would be a time we'd have to work with each other and be professional performers under contract for Vince, the company, all the boys in the locker room, and the public. In the days and weeks to come, the story of our real-life fight was big news on the Internet. People got it wrong every time with their theories and assumptions.

All the boys who weren't there kept pulling me aside to

ask what happened, and I always told them the truth. Many of them heralded me as a backstage hero and a leader, but that's not how I felt about it. Respect is gained through time, performance, and behavior, not through swinging your way to infamy. Slowly but surely, a lot of the veteran agents, like Sgt Slaughter, Gerald Brisco, Jack Lanza, and Pat Patterson, approached me to let me know they respected what I did for the business—that I'd fought for everything they stood for.

Unfortunately, I think Dave wore our fight like a dark cloud over him for many years, feeling he had a lot to prove publicly. Maybe that was part of the reason he eventually retired from the WWE. He stepped into an MMA cage in 2012 and emerged victorious, and now he's established a successful career in Hollywood. I give him much respect for it.

At that *SD* in San Diego where I met with Vince, it was time to get on with the show. My match was with Kurt Angle, but Teddy declared he wasn't medically cleared after a story line injury from Mark Henry. I walked out, counted to ten, and declared myself the winner.

Now it was time to move on to Judgment Day 2006 in Phoenix on May 21 for the final match of the tournament against Lashley, whom I had some unfinished business with. I'd known Bobby since he first came into the company. As with The Boogeyman, I wanted to assist him in every way possible.

I approached the OVW graduate and former amateur

grappler to give him some advice. I let him know he was a mirror image of Brock Lesnar but he could work on his reactions in the ring. "Look at yourself," I said. "You're intimidating and have every asset to be a huge star in the company, but you've got to stop rolling around for the little guys. You gotta get in there and take charge. Come to my school in Houston, and let's work together, man."

To my surprise, he declined. "Look, I really appreciate the offer, but I've got to listen to what they tell me and not offend anyone."

Well, he just had. "Okay, I see. No problem." I didn't say another word.

After only a few months of being a WWE yes-man, Bobby was sinking fast. Fearing he'd be fired, he approached Sharmell. "Why doesn't Booker like me? What did I do?"

She said, "You must've said something to him he didn't like. Think about it."

Before I knew it, Bobby came to me saying it was time he apologized and came to Houston.

We started working hard at PWA, and right before my eyes he began applying his knowledge and rose to the very top as a bright star, making me a proud mentor and friend.

By that night in Phoenix at Judgment Day 2006 for the KOTR final, we got in there in front of fourteen thousand strong at the US Airways Center. I was ready to really test him. It was a strong match, and Bobby was using his size and power as any big man should, with pick-up-and-throw moves and belly-to-belly suplexes. I took it all to make him look like a believable freak of athletic ability, much like Brock. When it was time, I brought out the heel tactics to chop him down. Sharmell constantly distracted him, allowing me to get the upper hand, and after some more offensive exchanges, my new ally Finlay came down and hit Lashley with his heavy Irish shillelagh.

That was more than enough for me to claim the win and my rightful throne, thus beginning my proper reign in the *SD* Kingdom as King Booker, with Queen Sharmell by my side.

For that week's *SD* on May 26 in Bakersfield, I had my official coronation. William Regal, along with Finlay, joined King Booker's Court. Regal read from a giant scroll, "All hail His Royal Highness King Booker."

Sharmell and I came rolling out on a giant throne, enjoying the new character direction. We slowly nodded at Regal's every word as if we were about to weep from the joy of finally being recognized as royals. We demanded all the people bow as Sharmell crowned me, placed the cape upon my royal shoulders, and handed me a bejeweled scepter.

I loudly decreed Sharmell was my first royal queen, and we exited the ring.

Regal shouted, "Long live King Booker!"

It was the dawn of the most entertaining period of my

professional wrestling career.

Since childhood, I'd admired Bruce Lee and Blaxploitation films. I'd imagined entertaining people with unforgettable characters, and now I'd evolved from a thug rookie in WCW to the colorful King Booker. Growing up on the streets of Houston with my siblings after my mom died, just trying to scrape an existence from nothing, I never could've imagined this would have been my life. I couldn't get enough of it.

When creative first approached me with the concept of winning the reinstated KOTR tournament, neither they nor I had any over-the-top direction for how my reign would be handled. They simply trusted me to run with it.

It wasn't until after I became King Booker that certain ideas came to me. For example, some came while I watched Pope Benedict on the news. Others came while I watched James Bond films. More came while I studied Forest Whitaker in *The Last King of Scotland*. The more I absorbed their mannerisms, the more creative paths I could traverse.

In particular, I worked on developing my own version of the British accent. But I made a conscious decision to revert to my street speech whenever my character got flustered and upset during a segment. It was my wink to the viewers letting them in on the joke that I was still very much Booker T, only in disguise and denial. I started sticking my pinky finger out far and wide at all times like an aristocratic tea drinker from across the pond and attempted to make everyone kiss my feet, literally.

I think the greatest vignette I ever filmed as King Booker, or *King Bookah* as both Sharmell and I started saying, was when we went to downtown London in full character. I paraded around the streets with pomp and circumstance as if truly returning to my homeland of peasants, allowing them the privilege of basking in my superiority.

They loved my act, especially the accent. I kept looking for one of the royal guards to break their code and look at me with a smile. One of them quickly winked, and I lit up inside like a little kid. It was one thing to pull off the obnoxious British character in America, but to have won the British over, live on their very own streets, was overwhelming.

I wondered if Hollywood would catch wind of what King Booker was up to and come knocking on my royal door and whisk me away to the silver screen. I was that proud and confident of what I was doing, especially based on the reaction.

I was thoroughly enjoying my new role, but most importantly, Vince and the rest of the creative team really enjoyed watching the evolution of the persona as well. WWE started licensing various versions of King Booker and Queen Sharmell action figures, complete with the crown, cape, scepter, and even the throne. I knew, due to my royalty checks at the time, they were among the best sellers. It was gratifying to know I'd reinvented myself yet again, and there was still plenty of creative and physical fuel in the tank.

Along with the beauty of Queen Sharmell at my side and the brawn of King Booker's Court of Sir Regal and Sir Finlay steadfast in front of the throne, we moved straight ahead into every challenge sent our way.

Having Regal and Finlay with me was tremendous. The legitimate bruisers from the United Kingdom added credibility to the whole character. In the ring, those two put brutal beatings on anyone standing in front of them. If someone was fortunate enough to make it through the battery of my royal henchmen, then and only then I arose from the throne and took the melee back to 110th Street, medieval style, sucka.

I'm still amazed at how deeply the legacy of King Booker has ingrained itself in the minds of fans everywhere. Even today, no matter where I go, I'm still recognized for that persona. In Toronto, while promoting my book *From Prison to Promise,* I was walking down the darkened street on my way to dinner when, across the road, a homeless man sat up and yelled, "King Booker . . . Give me five bucks!"

I dig it every time.

26

ENTERING THE HALL OF FAME

The new United States Champion Bobby Lashley surfaced for a series of matches in June, but I had no desire for a title. The over-the-top King Booker character caught on with amazing heat from the crowd and became very professionally satisfying. I didn't need a championship; I was royalty.

If anything, I would've been looking for the World title to correspond with my golden crown and scepter. In early July in Philly, the Big Gold was in sight as I was entered into a No. 1 Contender's Battle Royal for a shot at the champ, Rey Mysterio, at The Great American Bash 2006. But before any of that could happen, someone committed another major crime against the royal Red Bull cooler.

By that point, the WWE had resurrected ECW as a third televised promotional brand with its own roster, and they taped their show before ours like a doubleheader.

That night I came into the dressing room and went for a can as usual, but alas, they were gone. I scanned the room, about to lose it. I saw Sabu, one of R.V.D.'s best friends and a cool guy, but then I saw a person next to him drinking a Red Bull.

"Where'd you get that Red Bull?"

"I got it out of the cooler," he responded.

Wrong answer.

I looked at him with anger and disbelief in my eyes. "Why are you in here?"

Sensing my growing temper, Sabu interjected, "He's cool, Book. He's a buddy of mine."

"No, he's not cool!" I snapped back.

And with that, I slapped the can right out of his hand to the ground. "You shouldn't be drinking *anything* in here! Not my Red Bull, not a Coke, not even water! You haven't earned it. Get your stuff. You're out of here!"

Everybody watched in stunned silence as I grabbed him and his gear bag and threw him out of the locker room. Then I said, "You know what? You ain't even allowed in the same building as me!" I marched him to the back door and kicked him right out of the Wachovia Center, never to be seen again. Done.

Not very kingly, I realize, but you don't mess with my Red Bull.

I settled for coffee—French roast with cream and sugar— and it all worked out. A couple of hours later, I entered and won the battle royal, earning a title shot at Rey Mysterio at The Great American Bash 2006 on July 23.

That night in front of almost ten thousand at the Conseco Fieldhouse in Indianapolis, the WWE Kingdom watched Queen Sharmell and me enter the arena, being driven in on a long platform with me seated on my throne. Fireworks lit up behind us as I sat there, humbly soaking in the jeers. Even though I was getting booed, I was sure to hold a posture of appreciation and humility. I milked my entrance for all it was worth, taking my sweet time stepping off the throne and basking in the royal adoration of my subjects, who packed the arena. I swear it must have taken me five minutes to enter the ring and thrill the fans with the sight of my red robe opening up like a giant umbrella as I spun in place in the middle of the squared circle, my arms outstretched. I love to entertain, and I was enjoying every single second of my regal entrance. Minutes ticked by as I slowly made my way around the ring, looking into the stands and saying, "Thank you . . . thank you." It was good to be king.

Rey and I put on a great match that I was proud of. Near the end, referee Nick Patrick was knocked out when Rey delivered his famous 619, followed up by a frog splash in homage to Eddie Guerrero. He covered me, hoping to secure his title victory, but there was no ref to be seen. With no official in sight, I gave Rey a low blow and a royal Book End to add insult to injury. While Rey was down, I rolled outside and grabbed a chair, bringing it back in the ring to finish him off. But Rey was too quick for me, and he dropkicked the chair into my face, knocking me down. As we both lay there in the ring, the crowd's energy built into a frenzy when Rey's longtime friend and Eddie's nephew, Chavo Guerrero, ran toward the ring and picked up the chair. Looking as if he would hit me while the ref was down, Chavo swung as hard as he could and directed the blow at Rey, smashing him in the head with a loud crash. I looked at each of them in disbelief and took the opportunity to cover Rey just as the ref was waking up. One, two, three . . .

I was now a six-time World Heavyweight Champion. And what a splendid champion I was!

By August, The Undertaker was next on my red carpet behind the velvet rope as we clashed in East Rutherford in a classic confrontation. After coming out on top, I knew the real clash was about to begin when Batista finally returned to the fold and wanted a shot at the King. Only this time it would be in a ring and not a rented mansion.

Since our fight, Dave hadn't shown his face backstage—or anywhere, for that matter. News of our meeting at SummerSlam 2006 in Boston was quickly spreading around as the spectacle of the show not to be missed. I work as stiff and snug as possible for the believability factor, which means cool heads have to prevail when we're in the ring doing our best

CHAMPIONSHIPS	
WCW World Tag Team Championship	11
WCW World Television Championship	6
WCW United States Championship	1
WCW World Heavyweight Championship	5
WWF World Tag Team Championship	1
WWF Hardcore Championship	2
WWE World Tag Team Championship	2
WWE Intercontinental Championship	1
WWE United States Championship	3
World Heavyweight Championship	1
Total	33

to entertain the fans. The question was whether or not Dave would respond professionally to my in-ring style or lose his cool.

The big summer event was finally here. Time to find out if it would all be water under the bridge or if things would escalate to the next level between us. My majestic music hit and Sharmell and I made our way out to the top of the ramp. "All hail King Booker!" she would say over and over again into her mic as I stood there basking in my own glory. This was SummerSlam, the second biggest PPV event of the year, and I was going to be sure to give the fans 110 percent from the time I walked out. On my way to the ring, a young man was proudly holding up a sign that said, If King Booker Wins, the Peasants Revolt. It was clear that I was at the height of my popularity. We entered the ring and humbly thanked the fans as I awaited my opponent.

The crowd erupted as soon as Batista's music hit, and he came down the ramp to a deafening pop. With his theme song blasting, the mood was perfectly set for the two of us to settle our differences and clash over the World Heavyweight Championship.

The bell rang to start the match, and we circled each other, building up the tension. When we locked up, Batista gave me a strong shove, backing me off him. He glared at me as I looked back with disbelief. Even though we were legitimately feeling each other out, we still had to perform, which meant that every look, every emotion, had to tell a story in that ring. We locked up again, and I reversed it into one of the corners. As I started to back off him, I moved my arm under his for a clench and gave him a really stiff right-handed smack across the face.

Dave's eyes filled with anger, and he shoved me off him and down onto my back. You could see he was ready to let loose, but then there was a moment he looked at me and looked down at Sharmell and froze. I just stood there, wondering how he'd proceed.

To his credit, he kept his cool, and we resumed a damn good match that had real personal heat blazing all over it. The match went back and forth between us, with me even taking an opportunity to smash my scepter over Batista's head while Sharmell distracted the ref. Batista would pay me back for it by crotching me on the top rope with an atomic drop and taking the advantage. Luckily for me, Batista couldn't capitalize on it, and we spilled out onto the floor, where I threw him headfirst into the steel ring steps.

JBL was on commentary, adding great emotion to the match by saying Batista was distracted by Sharmell's beauty, since she was like a "goddess on high." I was glad the commentator's focus stayed on our match and they worked as hard as we did to keep up the tension for the fans.

Building the story we were telling in the ring, I went to the top rope and delivered a missile dropkick, covering Batista for the two count. In frustration, I stood him up and hit him with a Book End for what I thought was surely my victory.

The ref counted, "One! Two! Thr—" and Batista kicked out.

JBL screamed, "This is what a World Championship is about!"

After the missile dropkick, and the Book End, I had one more trick up my sleeve. I yelled at Batista to get up and kicked him in the stomach, buckling him over. I bounced off the ropes and went for my scissor kick to ensure my win, but Batista dodged out of the way and took advantage with his own kick to my gut and then a powerful jackhammer, covering me for the pin. "One! Two—"

At the last moment I kicked out, bringing the fans to their feet in disbelief. Sharmell clutched her chest in a sign of anxiety as the camera panned to her. Everyone was playing their part to add as much intensity as possible to this match.

Near the end, Batista took advantage once more with a full-nelson slam. He looked to the crowd and motioned his gladiator-like double-thumbs-down, which signaled the setup for his finisher, the Batista Bomb.

Not wanting to see me succumb to defeat, Sharmell charged the ring, jumping over my back, and began slapping Batista over and over in an attempt to get him off of me.

Referee Nick Patrick had no choice but to ring the bell and stop the match, giving the DQ victory to Batista but allowing me to keep my title.

Any animosity Batista and I had between each other was

left in the ring. We put on a good match, told a good story, and left with much more respect for one another.

As was always the case when a performer held a belt for more than a couple of months, especially the WWE Championship or the Big Gold, it was up to creative to develop new angles to keep things interesting for the fans and talent alike. The idea they came up with was to book all three of the top company-branded champs—John Cena from *Raw* with the WWE title, Big Show with his ECW World title, and me with the *SD* World Heavyweight Championship—together in November at Cyber Sunday 2006 in Cincinnati to decide for the first and only time in history who the true WWE Champion of Champions was. The unique stipulation about this match, however, was that fans would vote and decide which title of the three would be defended that night. And none of us would know the answer until right before the match started.

On the night of the PPV, The Big Show, Cena, and I were all in the ring with three referees in a line holding each of our titles as the results were revealed. The graphic of all three of us appeared on the Titantron as the entire arena and fans at home waited. Out of over fourteen and a half million votes worldwide, 12 percent wanted Cena to defend his title, 21 percent wanted to see Big Show defend his title, and an over-whelming 67 percent wanted me to defend my World Heavy-weight Championship. I stood in the ring in disbelief as I looked around at the audience with a look of pure betrayal on my face. I had my work cut out for me.

Being in a triple-threat match meant it didn't matter who you pinned or submitted for the victory. So Cena and Big Show didn't have to defeat me, as long as they defeated someone. I had the most to lose that night, since I was the only one who could lose a title. They both had everything to gain. And since there was no count-out or DQ, I was in for the fight of my life.

It was an incredibly exciting experience mixing it up with Cena and Show on November 5. For the big boys, the night felt more like recess than work. The people were on their feet almost the entire match as we bounced and flew all over the ring with intensity, aggression, and passion for everything the WWE and our business stood for. Even Sharmell got in on the action as she took a strong Attitude Adjustment from Cena, adding to the drama.

Ultimately, when the time was right, celebrity guest of the night Kevin Federline, Britney Spears' husband at that time, interfered on my behalf by hitting Cena with the World Heavyweight title while he was trying to make me tap out to the STF. As John got up and turned his back to me to face K-Fed, as he was known, I grabbed the belt and hid it under me for the opportune moment. When John came back around to finish me off, I hit him square in the face with the title, securing my victory not only as king and World Heavyweight

Champion but now as the Champion of Champions.

I left the ring with my title and holding my queen in my arms. A personal sense of satisfaction and accomplishment washed over me as I caught my breath and reflected on one of the biggest nights of my career.

Like all great reigns, this one too finally came to an end. Fifteen days after the exhilaration of Cyber Sunday, at Survivor Series 2006 in Philly on November 26, I dropped the Big Gold to none other than Batista. It concluded my last and longest reign with the World Heavyweight Championship, clocking in at over four months, and I was grateful for every day of it. It was my turn to pass the torch.

Dave was the perfect choice. Not only was he still one of the most marketable faces for the company, but our real-life altercation added more realistic appeal to the product than advertising could have. What had transpired between Dave and me didn't merely blur the lines of disbelief; it obliterated them—something money can never buy.

In hindsight, I almost think the Champion of Champions win over Cena and Big Show was management's way of indicating their respect for me before going out and relinquishing the title. To be honest, after reaching the pinnacle, I wasn't sure where creative would go with my character. I thought maybe that particular incarnation of the heel version of King Booker had run its course and maybe I'd flip for a babyface run.

As always, not one to play politics, I trusted Vince and his team to guide me. Whatever they had in mind, I'd work hard to make it a success.

The remainder of 2006 saw my King's Court of Regal and Finlay dissolve as Fit threw his hat in the ring and ventured into the title picture himself against the likes of Cena and Batista.

At the beginning of the New Year, I was still riding the creative currents. I found land when I was entered into the Royal Rumble 2007 on January 28 as the twelfth entrant. Kane dumped me over the top for a ride home to Houston but not before I sneaked back in behind the referee amongst the chaos and eliminated the big monster for a quick, malicious payback.

Back in Houston, I kept my kingly duties on February 2, when the Ancient Order of Royal Houstonians, known to peasants as Houston's City Hall, gave me the key to the city. After having the key placed honorably around my neck, I proceeded to read from a speech I had prepared. In my best King Booker accent, I began to praise Queen Sharmell before turning my attention toward the fans. Breaking from my accent and tapping into the thug from 110th Street, I said with as much conviction as I could muster, "It's about damn time!" The whole thing was just a story line, but it was a blast to ham it up in front of my own hometown. I'd even brought in three guys from my wrestling school as the Ancient Order, and they were thrilled to be on a WWE stage that night.

Toward the end of my speech, I spotted Billy Gibbons from ZZ Top in the front row and ordered him to kiss my royal ring, which he refused. In a fit of anger, I shouted into the mic, "Kiss it, you sumbitch!" I then calmed down and told him that I knew his kind and that instead of kissing my ring, he wanted to kiss my royal foot. Again, he refused. My frustration grew as I directed my animosity toward the fans, calling them ungrateful and telling them they should all be bowing down to me.

As I was admonishing them, Kane's music and pyro hit, sending shivers down my spine. Kane wanted to gain revenge on me after I'd destroyed his chance at a WrestleMania XXIII title match during the Royal Rumble, and he made his presence known loud and clear. He stalked down to the ring and destroyed my guys before I tried to mount an offense against him. Overwhelmed by his monstrous power, I hightailed it out of there through the crowd, leaving Sharmell behind to catch up with me. With my key to the city gripped in my hand, I ran away to fight another day.

A week later in Omaha, I demanded an apology, but the only possible retribution that came my way was a match at No Way Out 2007 in Los Angeles. Unfortunately, after a hard-fought match, Kane would pin me cleanly in the middle of the ring with a chokeslam. My kingdom was crumbling.

In an effort to regain control of my empire, I wrestled and finally defeated Kane in a Falls Count Anywhere Match on *SD*. Although my victory was thanks to interference from the Great Khali, it still earned me a coveted spot in WrestleMania XXIII's Money in the Bank (MITB) Ladder Match.

On March 23 in front of eighty thousand rabid fans of the WWE Universe inside Detroit's Ford Field, I paraded into a minefield of ladders along with Edge, Jeff Hardy, Matt Hardy, Orton, Mr. Kennedy, Finlay, and CM Punk.

For the record, I hate ladders. I don't like cleaning my gutters with them, changing my lightbulbs with them, or even looking at them. But with a guaranteed title shot at any championship I'd want on the line, I was determined to bring my best.

At one point, I reached under the ring to grab a ladder to use, only to pull out a short stepladder. I stood there outside the ring in shock saying out loud, "Tell me I didn't just—" before getting pummeled by CM Punk.

Once I got my bearings and was able to roll back into the ring, I had a good run of offensive on each competitor, hitting them with scissor kicks and spinebusters. Once I cleared the ring, instead of grabbing the biggest ladder and climbing it to victory, I showboated and gave the fans a WrestleMania Spin-arooni, which allowed the Hardys the chance to knock me out of the ring with a ladder shot. Like I said, I love to entertain.

In the end, Mr. Kennedy would take the win and another

WrestleMania was in the books.

About this time, I was walking out of a hotel one morning when I felt my right knee lock out again. I shook it out and kept walking, thinking, *Not again.* Medical results proved it was in fact the exact same injury I'd faced several times before. I wasn't sure whether I had sustained the injury during my ladder match or from running as hard as I could as King Booker. Either way, it was another wake-up call as to how much I'd put my body through.

Once again, I had to be written off TV for surgery and rehab, which we did April 6 in Fort Wayne, Indiana. After I gave Matt Hardy a nice, clean win, Sharmell expressed her disappointment by giving me a big royal slap to the face.

Feeling dejected, I decided to win her back by attacking The Undertaker later that night, which was a grave mistake. Undertaker set me up for a Tombstone Piledriver on the announcers' table. However, what should have been a dramatic ending, with the entire table crumbling beneath our weight as he drove me down, turned out to be a stiff finisher on top of a table that didn't collapse. The move looked brutal as he drove me down headfirst, an abrupt end that left me lying there like a corpse.

The Undertaker stood over me, holding up the World Heavyweight Championship as *SD* faded to a close. It was a great and dramatic way for the character of King Booker to take his leave for the next few months.

With King Booker having exited the WWE for royal repairs, Queen Sharmell was excused from her duties as well. After I had arthroscopic surgery yet again, the two of us returned home to Houston and I began physical therapy while enjoying two other very important things. First, overseeing the amazing progress of the students at my school. And second, absolutely nothing. Other than hobbling around the PWA ring on crutches and instructing with Sharmell, I lay on the couch sleeping, eating, and watching TV.

Soon, I was approached by local Houston radio station KBME 790 and started hosting a WWE-themed show once a week called *Tea Time with King Booker*, which was really fun.

Before I knew it, a little over eight weeks had passed all too quickly and it was time to dust off the crown and report back to my loyal subjects of the *SD* Kingdom—or so I thought.

The week before I returned, Vince conducted another WWE Draft Lottery on *Raw* in Wilkes Barre, Pennsylvania, on June 11, and Sharmell and I were sent packing for Monday nights.

I was excited to head back to *Raw* because it was the flagship show and, more importantly, it was live. There's no feeling like the adrenaline rush you get from two cans of royal Red Bull *and* walking out to the live set of *Raw* every week.

However, just as I was amped up and readying myself to

hit the road with the company full-time, a devastating piece of news rocked my life.

On Friday, June 15, 2007, my dear friend Sherri Martel, Sister Sherri, died at her mother's house near Birmingham, Alabama. I was emotionally destroyed. I loved Sherri like a sister and had stayed in touch with her since she'd departed WCW permanently in 2000. There's not enough room in this book to properly articulate what Sherri did for my career when she came on board with Lash and me. Having her next to us as the ultimate heel manager of the ring had elevated Harlem Heat to a status of legitimacy we'd never thought possible.

Sherri knew how to play just as hard as she worked. I kept thinking of the times I'd put her to bed, fed her, and brought her hot cups of coffee, always looking over my shoulder to make sure she was still following me through airports and arenas. When she'd remarried shortly after the demise of WCW, I'd even been there to give her away in place of her father.

When she passed away, I jumped on the first plane headed for Alabama to say good-bye, and I took personal responsibility for the funeral expenses to ensure it was overseen properly.

Upon arriving at the service in Birmingham, I found it interesting and disheartening that, aside from Marty Jannetty, I was the only one there from the business. Here Sherri had given twenty-six years to the business as one of the most successful female professional wrestlers and managers of all time. She had worked with literally all the greats through the biggest booms in the industry during the eighties and nineties. It was a cold side of the business that met me as I looked around wishing for more familiar faces.

Fortunately, Sherri had lived long enough to walk onstage for her own WWE Hall of Fame induction in 2006, and I was glad I'd been there to give her a big hug. There will never be another one like my dear friend, the incomparable Sister Sherri Martel.

When I did my first *Raw* appearance on June 18 in Richmond, Virginia, still mourning Sherri, I found it overly macabre that the show revolved around Vince's staged limousine explosion death the week prior. I'd had enough death in reality to be written into a murderous story line. I desperately looked for the angle to be over so the gloom could clear.

But it was only going to get worse—far worse.

Seven days later, we were set for a full Vince McMahon Memorial *Raw* in Corpus Christi when the WWE was shaken to its foundation by an event that ignited television debates and newspaper editorials for months.

As Sharmell and I arrived at the American Bank Center that day, we were immediately informed that my friend Chris Benoit, his wife Nancy, and young son Daniel were found dead in their Georgia home the previous day, June 24. I went numb. I picked up my bag, turned around, and walked out. I couldn't participate in the interviews they'd started compiling with guys for that night's improvised tribute. It was too much.

Thoughts raced through my mind. *My God. First Eddie, then Sherri, and now Chris? What the hell's going on? Everything's out of control.*

It wasn't until the next day that we learned along with the nation that it was in fact Chris who'd killed his wife, son, and then himself.

That grisly information flipped me upside down. It was the absolute last thing I would've expected, and it was impossible to make sense of it. Chris had seemed down recently, but I'd thought the business was just wearing on him, as it does anyone who's been in the game a long time. But this wasn't the act of a sane individual. Suicides were not unfamiliar to our industry, but someone killing his family first? It was too heinous to comprehend. I've contemplated a thousand times what was going through Chris's mind, but that's an answer he took with him.

I just wished I would've reached out to him before it was too late. The tragedy will haunt me for the rest of my life.

Sharmell told me later that prior to my birthday, on March 1, Chris had approached her with a question. "I was thinking about buying Booker a replica of the WCW World Television Championship to commemorate our Best of Seven Series. Do you think he'd like it?"

She told him I absolutely would.

Although he never followed through with it, I was

thankful he'd valued our time together.

In the end, I'll never be able reconcile the memories of the friend I shared definitive moments of my career with and the stranger who ended his family's lives.

We returned to Corpus Christi on July 16, and although everyone was still reeling from the tragedy, we knew the show must go on.

Unfortunately, the combined losses of Eddie, Sherri, and Chris had taken my mind completely out of the business. It wasn't fun anymore, and I thought it would be better to walk away at the top of my game rather than be carried out.

With all this on my mind, I entered a brief but overdue feud with the other king, Jerry Lawler. It was a transitional setup to a program with Hunter, who was calling himself the King of Kings and was out with an injury for the time being. Since the day I'd won the KOTR, I'd wondered if they'd have Jerry and me square off in a royal showdown, and now it was finally going to happen.

That night Triple H's entrance song came on, driving the crowd into a frenzy. But when they saw Sharmell and me coming down the ramp instead, the cheers died. I told them there was only one king on *Raw*, and it wasn't Hunter. Then I went up to Lawler and told him to remove *King* from his name out of respect for my superiority in the role. Jerry told me he'd been a king for thirty years. I scoffed and told him to kiss my ring, but we brawled instead.

On July 23 in Sacramento, again I got in the ring and berated Lawler, calling him Jerome, which cracked me up, and he responded by calling me a royal pain in the arse before knocking me out of the ring.

Honestly, both of us were having so much fun with this angle. It was everything great about the art and entertainment of our business.

We wrestled two matches to settle our dispute over the king of the crown. The first time in Tucson, on July 30, Jerry took the victory by DQ and attacked me as I carelessly walked away.

But then on August 6 in Buffalo, I reigned supreme when it really counted in a Loser-Crowns-the-Winner Match with a clean pin fall.

My official coronation as the King of *Raw* was to happen at Madison Square Garden on August 13, but Lawler bitterly refused to crown me and instead told me I'd have to face Triple H at SummerSlam 2007 on August 26 in East Rutherford, New Jersey. For his insolence, I proceeded to pummel the former king and bash him over the head with a monitor.

However, Jerry's declaration of my match with Hunter was more anticlimactic than the people around the wrestling world could've ever imagined.

Even though I was having fun in the ring, overall I was still feeling overwhelmingly burned out. I knew it was time to take a step back and ask for my release from the WWE for the time being. To me, it was never going to be a permanent departure, just a breather to let things pass and return at a later date.

I sat down with Vince, and he said if that was the way I felt, then it was the right thing to do but the door to the WWE would always be open. It was my priority to leave on good terms, so I agreed to finish out the scheduled match with Hunter at SummerSlam. And it was just the right thing to do.

I headed straight to SummerSlam 2007 on August 26. It was to be Triple H against King Booker in Hunter's return match after several months off due to injury. At the same time, I was on my way out. It was an intense bout with both of us feeling something to prove that night in Continental Airlines Arena, and if there was one thing I could count on, it was for Hunter to dish it out as well as he took it. We tossed stiff shots and massive potatoes all night and gave it our all.

Nearing the finish, knowing it was potentially my last big event in front of the WWE Universe, I thought, *I'm going for the Hangover*, and climbed to the top. Hunter rolled out of the way, recovered, hit me with the Pedigree, and that was it.

There was no fanfare as I said good-bye to King Booker and laid down my crown, shook a few hands in the back, and walked out into the night, no longer a part of the world I'd worked my entire life to become a part of.

The next morning, I boarded my flight home to Houston. I stared out the window, watching the passing landscape, and wondered what would be next for me. Initially, I thought, *I'm just going home to focus on my family, my school, and anything in the world I feel like.* The future looked bright *and* relaxing for a change.

But it didn't take Total Nonstop Action (TNA), the fledgling wrestling company out of Orlando, long to give me a call to gauge my interest. Basically the deal they offered me was two years at a decent salary, only this required eighty dates a year rather than over two hundred with the WWE. I'd essentially get paid enough to take care of all my expenses just to go to Disney World once or twice a week with Sharmell, who was also offered a contract. Even though I was burned out, the idea of a much lighter schedule and the ability to still contribute to the business was enticing. We took the deal, and it was the easiest time in the business I'd had to date.

I didn't know what to expect from TNA, and when the time came in November of 2007, I arrived with a positive outlook and dressed to impress.

I made my debut on November 11, 2007, at their Genesis PPV as the mystery partner of Sting. My first match at TNA was actually a tag team match for the TNA World Heavyweight Championship, with Sting and I going up against Kevin Nash and defending Champion Kurt Angle. Kurt ended up retaining his title that night, and it felt good to be back in the ring with three guys I had so much history with.

Over time, I would become part of a stable known as The Main Event Mafia, along with Kurt Angle, Sting, Kevin Nash, and Scott Steiner. We were the veterans of the business, and all of us at one time were World Champions. We began a feud with a young group known as the TNA Frontline, and our goal was simple: we would teach these "originals" about respect.

In October of 2008, to be sure the Frontline understood just how much this business was built on our backs, I debuted a brand-new title belt, the TNA Legends Championship. It was a beautiful belt created by me in the story line to represent the most legendary in the business. I took it upon myself to declare me the first-ever TNA Legends Champion, and since it was my own belt, I said that I would defend the title when I so pleased.

That time was in March of 2009 at TNA's Destination X PPV, against their franchise player, AJ Styles. Styles would come away with the win that night, officially bringing the Legends belt under the sanctioning of TNA and

CHAMPIONSHIPS	
WCW World Tag Team Championship	11
WCW World Television Championship	6
WCW United States Championship	1
WCW World Heavyweight Championship	5
WWF World Tag Team Championship	1
WWF Hardcore Championship	2
WWE World Tag Team Championship	2
WWE Intercontinental Championship	1
WWE United States Championship	3
World Heavyweight Championship	1
TNA Legends Championship	1
Total	34

ending my reign.

Not long after that, at Victory Road on July 19, 2009, my longtime friend Scott Steiner and I teamed up against James Storm and Bobby Roode, Beer Money Inc., for the TNA World Tag Team Championship. It had been over ten years since I'd teamed up with my brother Lash in WCW, where we were used to wrestling against Scotty and his brother Rick. And now here we were, two guys from two of the most successful, legitimate brother teams in this business, taking our shot at tag team gold together. We'd come away the victors that night, bringing the TNA Tag Team Championships to the Main Event Mafia and making me a fifteen-time World Tag Team title holder.

Even though in front of the camera we put on good performances, the production behind the scenes was chaotic, and there was no united effort among the performers to raise the company to a higher level. Instead, a lot of people were there out of convenience and stability, with some crossing their fingers that the WWE would call them up. No matter how good my

CHAMPIONSHIPS	
WCW World Tag Team Championship	11
WCW World Television Championship	6
WCW United States Championship	1
WCW World Heavyweight Championship	5
WWF World Tag Team Championship	1
WWF Hardcore Championship	2
WWE World Tag Team Championship	2
WWE Intercontinental Championship	1
WWE United States Championship	3
World Heavyweight Championship	1
TNA Legends Championship	1
TNA World Tag Team Championship	1
Total	35

intentions were coming in, there was absolutely no direction in TNA.

Once I realized my employers at TNA were happy to simply have my name on the roster, along with other former WWE and WCW performers, I relaxed. They simply wanted to pay me to show up and work. *Okay, I'm content moonwalking right in here, hitting a toe spin, a split, cashing a check, and shuffling right out the door.*

And that's exactly what Sharmell and I did. In fact, we started thinking of our trips to TNA as a long series of Brazilian birthdays—because every time we went to Orlando, we went to the same Brazilian steakhouse, where amazing cuts of various meats were sliced and served to order at the table. When we first started going there, they recognized me and always gave me the 50 percent birthday discount, which made it even harder to resist. I swear, we went there so often that according to their computer registry, Sharmell and I are probably both three hundred years old. It still remains one of the highlights of our trips with TNA.

In spite of the lack of direction, I still had fun in TNA. However, when our two years were up in November of 2009, I walked away knowing there was no other company to complete my legacy with than the WWE. I felt well rested, and my desire to get back in the action was as strong as ever.

Soon after, I contacted John Laurinaitis and told him I wanted to come home. He said it was fantastic news but I'd have to go to Pittsburgh for the standard physical.

I started to get a little apprehensive. I'd injured my neck again, but I figured they didn't need to know about it. I packed my bags and traveled to Pittsburgh for a full battery of blood tests, MRIs, and CT scans and awaited a contract and start date.

Much to my chagrin, the scans revealed I had a bulging vertebra in my neck too close to a nerve for them to clear me to wrestle unless I had surgery. But before I even had time to consider it, the WWE let me know they felt surgery could be too much of a risk to my quality of life.

I honestly felt like I was being put out to pasture like a thoroughbred that had run too many races and was headed for the glue factory. I started to panic. *What am I going to do? Is my career really over on somebody else's terms?*

It was disappointing, but the most important thing about to happen in my life would surpass anything I could ever do in the ring.

After trying unsuccessfully for the better part of two years, Sharmell and I were finally told we were expecting—twins, in fact—the following August of 2010. We were overjoyed as husband and wife, best friends, and now parents-to-be. But now more than ever, because of my memories as a teenage orphan on the streets of Houston, the pressure of impending parenthood was immeasurable. I wanted to rise above the diagnosis of the WWE's physical and keep working to ensure the security of my family for years, even generations, to come if possible.

Suddenly, several bookings started coming my way from Puerto Rico and Mexico, and I felt they were a godsend. Those territories were the last true bastions of pure blood-and-guts professional wrestling I had yet to experience. I also thought if the WWE saw I was still working and my neck wasn't a factor, perhaps they'd call and take a chance on me.

On August 5, 2010, Sharmell delivered our beautiful babies, Kendrick James and Kennedy Rose. Man, did we have our hands full. Having these two blessings enter our lives was something neither of us could've fathomed when we first met in the business. Our son and daughter were the culmination of everything amazing our relationship represented and a bright beacon toward a future unlike my tumultuous past.

After almost a year of dates with several Mexican and Puerto Rican promotions, John Laurinaitis called me one day out of nowhere. He was the last person I ever expected to hear from.

"Booker, we want you to come back. We've got a couple of ideas already lined up for you. Let's bring you home where you belong."

I couldn't believe the timing. Soon after welcoming our twins, I was going back to my company of choice.

Many people blow it when leaving the WWE by bashing everything about it and everyone inside. When you leave a job—I don't care if it's McDonald's—you don't burn the bridge on the way out by saying things like, "Your fries suck, your Big Macs are terrible, and so is everything else about this place!" All too many guys have buried themselves with bitter departures and then found themselves down the road regretting it. I was thankful the WWE bridge was still open to me.

When I spoke to Vince personally about my return, he said, "Not only are you wanted back, Booker; you're needed back."

He offered me a behind-the-scenes role, a lighter schedule, chances to climb back into the ring if I chose, and most importantly the opportunity to remain relevant as my career came to a final curtain call.

It certainly felt as if I'd just been given the keys to the kingdom. Vince's graciousness and the warmth of my reception into the WWE humbled me.

I'd made it to the next level. Through the years, I'd wondered, *Can I make it? Do I have what it takes to maintain longevity in this business?* I finally had my answer.

I made my surprise second debut for the WWE at Royal Rumble 2011 in Boston on January 30. When "Can you dig it, sucka?" and my music piped over the PA, it was the single greatest pop of my career. Two Red Bulls raced through my system, but the instant those fifteen thousand people lost their voices for me, I was moved beyond belief. First John Laurinaitis called me up, then Vince made me an offer, and finally the WWE Universe welcomed me back once and for all.

After the overwhelming return at the Rumble, over the course of the following three years, I transitioned into several modes of operation.

First, I settled into a commentary spot with Michael Cole and Josh Matthews on *SD*. I had a good time while doing it, and it allowed me to enter a brief in-ring feud with Cody Rhodes, whom I requested to work with.

Not long after, I became Teddy Long's successor as the GM of *SD*. It was a great position that allowed me to still entertain but not have to test my physical limits in the ring.

The ultimate transition, though, was something I felt uneasy about and found myself almost attempting to avoid.

As WrestleMania XXIX approached on April 7, 2013, in East Rutherford, an agent approached me backstage at *SD*.

"Hey, Booker, we're going to put you in the Hall of Fame this year. What do you think?"

Shivers went up my spine. "Um, are you sure you want to do that now? Man, I don't know if I'm ready yet."

"Of course you are. It's your time. You deserve it, and everyone here wants you in."

Oh no, I thought. *If I accept the honor, will I ever be able to put my boots on and return to the game in the ring?*

After some time passed, the idea didn't seem so frightening, and I knew it wouldn't be the end of my career in the squared circle. I would accept the honor as a member of the performers, past and present, whom the WWE felt shaped the brand and communicated it to the world.

On Saturday, April 6, 2013, at the Continental Airlines Arena, my brother Lash and I formally reunited as Harlem Heat in public for the first time in over thirteen years. For me, it was a big step in helping to mend the tension that had kept us apart for the last eight years. Through it all, the good and the bad, my brother was the one responsible for my entry to professional wrestling when he'd invited me to Ivan Putski's WWA twenty-two years earlier. There was no one else I would've asked to be by my side that night, and I was thankful he'd agreed.

That night Lash called me out on stage, and I was overcome with emotion and gratitude for my family and countless friends and performers, still living and fallen. So many people had helped me get there through many obstacles along the way.

Stepping up to the microphone and taking a deep breath, I was just about to begin my speech when the entire arena erupted into a "Thank you, Booker!" chant that broke me even more. I was humbled. From my heart, I told the people I was the one who was thankful they'd allowed me to be a part of their lives for so many years.

I made it through the speech while looking down and seeing many peers, like Ron Simmons, Michael Hayes, and so many more. It was a surreal, timeless moment.

I glanced at Sharmell, who was holding our twins and had tears in her eyes, and told her, "My wife, my queen. I'd say, 'I do' a thousand times over. I love you more than anything in the world."

As I looked around at the arena, a huge sense of pride welled up in me. I had started at the bottom and made it all the way to the top. Bursting with gratitude and deeply humbled, I brought everything home the only way possible: "And, yes, I do take my place into immortality to the 2013 Hall of Fame. And it's like I always say: now can you dig that, sucka?"

I was overwhelmed as the people helped me finish the last line with a *sucka!* that rumbled the roof and my heart.

It was a rare moment when everyone watching got to see and hear from the man, Booker T. Huffman. Not G.I. Bro, not Booker T from Harlem Heat, and not even King Booker. It was 100 percent me, and I was grateful to be able to give my thanks to everyone who'd helped me along the way.

And just when I thought this Houston boy was ready to leave the stage, my brother stepped in my way and told me there was one last thing I had to do before it was over. He wanted it; the people started cheering for it; I knew I couldn't walk away until I did it.

I gave the WWE Universe a Hall of Fame 2013 Spina-rooni that no one will ever forget—especially me. I took off my tailored jacket and got down on one knee as the crowd cheered. As soon as I hit the ground for the backspin, I tore my right triceps right off the bone. The moment it happened, I felt the snap, pop, and pain and instantly knew.

I laughed to myself. *Shit. I'm gonna need surgery for this.*

It was just business as usual.

CHAMPIONSHIPS

WCW World Tag Team Championship	11
WCW World Television Championship	6
WCW United States Championship	1
WCW World Heavyweight Championship	5
WWF World Tag Team Championship	1
WWF Hardcore Championship	2
WWE World Tag Team Championship	2
WWE Intercontinental Championship	1
WWE United States Championship	3
World Heavyweight Championship	1
TNA Legends Championship	1
TNA World Tag Team Championship	1

35x
WRESTLIN
CHAMPIOI

ACKNOWLEDGMENTS

I would like to thank my wife, Sharmell Sullivan-Huffman, for her everlasting love and support and being an amazing mother to our babies; my brother Lash, who began the journey through professional wrestling with me over twenty-three years ago; my true friends in and out of the business Rob Van Dam and John Bradshaw Layfield for their contributions to my career and this book; Medallion Media Chief Operating Officer Adam Mock and his entire team for their creative vision in producing the second volume of my life; and lastly, Andrew William Wright, my two-time coauthor who dedicated himself to ensure a year's worth of interviews and research were crafted into the truthful and entertaining story within these pages.

—Booker T

As always, I have to thank my parents, John and Martha Wright, for their unwavering support and encouragement; Medallion Media and Adam Mock for more stake in the literary land of opportunity so I could pen this grand third publication; Medallion editor Emily Steele for always being a cheerful, guiding voice whenever called upon; and, of course, Booker T himself for allowing me to continue where we left off with *Booker T: From Prison to Promise* and complete the epic tale of his performance for all time.

—Andrew William Wright

BOOKER T
FROM PRISON TO PROMISE

BOOKER T. HUFFMAN
WITH ANDREW WILLIAM WRIGHT

As a six-time world champion, General Manager of *SmackDown*, a former TV commentator, holder of thirty-five major titles in WWE, WCW, and TNA, and a Hall of Fame Superstar, Booker T. Huffman knows what it means to fight. He learned long before he entered the ring, when daily survival was a fierce battle.

Booker T: From Prison to Promise details Huffman's struggles from his youngest years. Losing his father at only ten months and his mother at only thirteen years old, Booker was forced along with his seven siblings to navigate life alone. Wrestling with hunger, poverty, and criminal influences, he struggled to survive in urban Houston and soon spiraled out of control, gravitating toward gang life and ultimately landing in prison.

Finally confronting himself while incarcerated, Booker made a promise to rise above crime and hopelessness to accomplish greater things and become an agent of change in his community. From anonymity to stardom, from rags to riches, Booker T takes us on his journey *From Prison to Promise* . . . Now can you dig that, SUCKA?

ISBN: 9781605424682
Hardcover
US/CDN $19.99
Available Now